CLOSE ALLY OF U.S. PRESIDENTS AND MICHIGAN'S GOVERNORS, AS WELL AS PERSONAL FRIEND TO THE STATE'S BUSINESS AND POLITICAL ELITE, LOCKWOOD NEVER LOST THE COMMON TOUCH

"I am indebted to him because he set the standard for what a good Senate majority leader should be. . . . Emil won the respect of . . . both parties. He will be remembered as one of the finest in Michigan's political pantheon."

John Engler   Governor of Michigan, 1991-2002

"Lockwood is . . . a political prince who works best in an atmosphere of confusion. . . . He trades, deals, compromises on bills . . . and he gets what he wants. . . . He always seems to be a day or a week ahead of his opposition and characteristically carries his widest smile when deepest in trouble."

William Kulsea   Capitol Correspondent, *Booth Newspapers*

"Emil combined the brain of a theoretical mathematician with the heart of Mother Teresa."

Michael Pung   Life-long friend

"Emil reached out to Democrats, and . . . black legislators respected Emil too, because of his record of voting for minorities. Senators saw Emil Lockwood as a man of the world, not just a guy from St. Louis. . . . . He didn't choose sides ideologically, saying 'I just thought it was the right thing to do'."

Robert Vander Laan   Former GOP Senate Majority Leader

[Praising Lockwood's shepherding the first fiscal reform measure in decades through the Senate] "It was the most skillful leadership job I've seen in five years in the Capitol."

George Romney   Governor of Michigan, 1963-1969

"His wizardry lies in putting together endlessly different combinations of Republicans and Democratic votes to win."

Roger Lane   Capitol Correspondent, *Detroit Free Press*

"Emil . . . I can think of no other person among the political opposition to whom I would more readily pay tribute. . . . I have always found your word to be your bond."

Sen. Coleman A. Young (D-Detroit)   Later Mayor of Detroit

"Emil Lockwood was a moral giant in the Michigan Senate. He not only insisted—but he fought ferociously to assure that our laws treated all persons as equals."

Francis "Jerry" Coomes
Co-Founder and Partner: Public Affairs Associates

"Emil and Jerry created the model for lobbying. They set a standard that's as good as it gets."

Richard Whitmer   **CEO, Blue Cross Blue Shield of Michigan**

"Emil Lockwood [was] a legendary member of the Michigan State Senate . . . [who] served with honor and distinction . . . an individual of great integrity and professional accomplishment"

Richard M. Daley   **Mayor of Chicago**

"It was impossible to outwit Emil. . . . He had a unique style of lobbying, which he called the 'bank shot,' setting up a chain of events to achieve a desired goal. . . . He advised me, 'Never ask a public official to do something against his self-interest,' and 'Never do anything in this town that you don't want to tell a grand jury about'."

Richard T. Cole   **Senior VP Blue Cross Blue Shield of Michigan**
(Worked with Lockwood at Public Affairs Assoc.)

Emil Lockwood's characteristic smile captured in official portrait
as Senate Majority Leader.
Lansing (MI), 1967.

MAN IN MOTION

Michigan's Legendary Senate Majority Leader,
Emil Lockwood

by

Stanley C. Fedewa and Marilyn H. Fedewa

Llumina Press

Requests for permission to make copies of any part of this work should be mailed to Permissions Department, Llumina Press, PO Box 772246, Coral Springs, FL 33077-2246

ISBN: 1-932303-88-X
Also distributed by Michigan State University Press
Printed in the United States of America by Llumina Press

Library of Congress Cataloging-in-Publication Data

Fedewa, Stanley C.
  Man in motion : Michigan's legendary Senate majority leader, Emil Lockwood / by Stanley C. Fedewa and Marilyn H. Fedewa.
       p. cm.
Includes bibliographical references.
  ISBN 1-932303-37-5 (alk. paper) -- ISBN 1-932303-88-X (pbk. : alk. paper)
  1. Lockwood, Emil, 1919-2002. 2. Legislators--Michigan--Biography. 3. Michigan. Legislature. Senate--Biography. 4. Michigan--Politics and government--1951- I. Fedewa, Marilyn H. II. Title.
  F570.25.L63F43 2003
  328'.092--dc22

                                        2003020188

CONTENTS   Page

PREFACE

Emil Lockwood tried his hand at more ventures than most men – and excelled at nearly every one of them. His values, like those of so many of his generation, were forged during the Great Depression and World War II. He was a doer, and his record of achievement in numerous business, civic, and political endeavors are well documented in this biography. During a long life in public service, he never stopped trying to make a better life for himself, his family, and his fellow citizens.

It was politics that first brought me into contact with Emil. The year was 1970. I had just won my first primary for state representative while still a student at Michigan State University. I met Emil at a Republican candidates' strategy meeting in Mt. Pleasant. Emil was touring the state in his campaign bus, drumming up votes for his secretary of state candidacy. He was well known to us all as the recently retired Senate majority leader, the man who got things done in Lansing. I proudly pinned on a Lockwood campaign button and had my picture taken with him. He, in turn, put my campaign bumper sticker on his touring bus. Later, at the Republican state convention in Detroit, I supported Emil in his hotly contested—and successful—bid for the secretary of state nomination.

Our paths crossed numerous times over the ensuing years—most recently on June 17, 2002, not long before he died. At that meeting in my office, we reminisced about earlier times and the interesting people with whom we had worked. I am indebted to him because he set the standard for what a good Senate majority leader should be. For his decisive leadership, his total dedication, and his sense of fair play, Emil won the respect of men and women in both parties. He will be remembered as one of the finest in Michigan's political pantheon.

John Engler
Governor of Michigan
1991-2002

FOREWORD

Term limits, instituted by the voters of Michigan in 1992, today is everywhere under siege.

Lobbyists, journalists, government bureaucrats, and legislators themselves regularly excoriate the cap imposed on service in the state Senate and House of Representatives. The "institutional memory" gained through several decades of legislative seniority is a priceless commodity that the state can ill afford to lose, we are told. Government cannot be run by "amateurs" with no previous experience in the state capitol who aren't allowed to serve for more than six or eight years, so the argument runs.

Defenders of term limits have the perfect rebuttal, however. They have only to utter two words: "Emil Lockwood."

Elected to the state Senate in 1962 with no previous experience in state government, Lockwood served what would now be the constitutional limit of eight years before voluntarily quitting after the 1970 session.

During his tenure, he was seated with some of the most prominent names in Michigan government—Bill Milliken, Coleman Young, Stanley Thayer, Ray Dzendzel, Bob Vander Laan, Charlie Zollar, Sander Levin, Guy Vander Jagt, and Garry Brown. Yet he rose rapidly from raw rookiedom to become Minority Leader after a single two-year term, and then to Majority Leader for four years during several of the most significant legislative sessions of the 20th century.

But Lockwood wasn't just a "leader" in name only; he is generally credited with being the most accomplished power broker the Senate has produced since World War II. He was at the epicenter of frantic wheeling and dealing that led to Michigan's breakthrough state income tax in 1967, and to passage of "open housing" legislation a year later in the wake of the Detroit riots. He was instrumental in shepherding the agendas of two progressive Republican governors—Milliken and George Romney—through the legislative minefields when none thought it possible. He brokered the deal that gave Michigan its first and only Governor's residence.

Then he walked away from it. After a brief, unsuccessful campaign for the office of Secretary of State, Emil Lockwood launched an entirely new career built on the skills and contacts he had developed in the previous decade. Back in the private sector from whence he came, Lockwood co-founded a new concept in lobbying—the multi-client firm, which has become the model by which success as a legislative agent is judged today·

Once he got Public Affairs Associates off the ground, Lockwood again voluntarily took his leave—disappearing into the Florida Keys, never to return to wield power in Michigan again.

Isn't that the way term limits is supposed to work?

Emil Lockwood was an extraordinary figure, yes, but most importantly, his brief, meteoric career in the state capitol teaches us that it is possible—and better for us as a society—to be Cincinnatus rather than Methuselah.

William S. Ballenger, Editor
Inside Michigan Politics

INTRODUCTION

The sum total and shape of a man's life often eludes the writers who face the task of portraying his unique contribution to the people with whom he has shared the planet. This can be true for many reasons, not the least of which is the fact that so many people wear distinctly different public and private faces. In fact, it is not unusual to discover that one's private demeanor stands in marked contrast to that of the more widely known public persona.

This assuredly was not true in the case of Emil Lockwood. Without exception, family, friends, former colleagues, as well as journalists, testify that Emil Lockwood confidently wore the same face in both public and private. His trademark gregariousness, quick wit, can do attitude, and sense of humor were never absent from any scene for very long. Except for the quality of being comfortable in his own skin, the only other sweeping generalization we—his biographers—can rightfully put forth in this anecdotal retrospective of his life is this: The most predictable trait of Emil Lockwood was surely his unpredictability.

From his early manhood on, Emil came across as the guys' guy, the Alpha Male, a self-confident leader, but one who didn't lord it over others. He treated everyone on the square, and was loyal to a fault to his friends. He hailed from Ottawa, Illinois—a picture postcard of Norman Rockwell's "Small Town U.S.A."—but in later years tackled the sinister specter of urban racism as he led a divided Michigan Senate to adopt the state's first Open Housing law, a measure which gave black citizens the right to live where they wanted to live.

Born in 1919 at the dawn of the Roaring Twenties, and coming of age in the Great Depression, Emil became equally as interested in his grandmother's poker hand as he was in her books, learning to count by instinct and keep running mental tallies at an early age. And he learned early how to carry his own economic weight. Throughout the years of his schooling in Ottawa, at Kemper Military School and the University of Michigan, Emil perfected the art of multi-tasking long before the chattering class gave it a fancy name.

Emil somehow managed to keep his head above water academically while juggling such jobs as soda jerk, janitor and grass mower. These work habits undoubtedly served him well in later life as he forayed into such diverse roles as World War II Naval officer, wrestling coach, certified public accountant, accounting teacher, farmer/sheep raiser, owner of multiple businesses, school board member, State Senator, and big time lobbyist. To borrow from the German philosopher, Friedrich Nietzche, Emil became walking proof that "what doesn't kill you, makes you stronger." Even Emil's so-called retirement demonstrated that his early work habits stuck with him throughout his life.

Most Michiganians remember Emil for his high-profile public career, which unfolded mainly in the 1960s and 70s in and around the State Capitol in Lansing—especially his successful tenure in the State Senate. According to Michigan Governor John Engler, a former Majority Leader of the same State Senate himself, Emil "set the standard for what a good Senate Majority Leader should be." Yet it was a post that Emil gladly left at the peak of his political power. He went on to master yet another role, for which the news media dubbed him "the pre-eminent lobbyist in the state." Then, after several successful years, he contentedly walked away from the hard-won cash cow and political clout to retire in the Florida Keys.

At this juncture, and by now predictably, Emil developed a new definition of retirement just for himself. The "Man in Motion," it seems, found it impossible to sit still, and cozy up to retirement. His wife, Anna, remembered that "Emil didn't bring home the bacon anymore—he brought home entire businesses." To name but two, Emil bought and resuscitated an ailing radio station, and joined other investors to buy a bank, which he dutifully oversaw. These projects intertwined with other energetic pursuits, such as mentoring candidates for local public office and raising money for them; championing the creation of a new tax district as a board member of the property owners' association; hosting a nonstop parade of visitors from the mainland; and traveling the world with Anna and their many friends.

So, Emil and Anna handily survived the Twentieth Century, still presiding over their idyllic abode in Duck Key, Florida each winter, and their home near Ann Arbor, Michigan during the summer and fall. There they hatched new projects and plots, sharing their lives with family and friends almost right up to Emil's unexpected death on August 2, 2002 at St. Joseph Mercy Hospital in Ann Arbor. It was a life filled to the brim and often times nearly overflowing, but always adventurous, goal-driven, and generous.

As long-time good friend Mike Pung spontaneously eulogized at Emil's memorial service in Michigan's State Capitol in Lansing, "Emil combined the brain of a theoretical mathematician with the heart of Mother Teresa."

We will all miss him dearly.

Stan and Marilyn Fedewa
September 15, 2002

PART ONE

From the King's Court to Starved Rock Park

pre 1919 – 1943

1

GENE POOL WATERS FAMILY TREE

"My great great *great* grandfather made a hat out of sugar and gave it to a king," Emil had teased his own grandchildren occasionally with this and other alluringly sparse morsels of information about their family tree.[1] The incredulous youngsters listened over the years to various fragments of their family heritage as they might to a voiceover in a sci-fi film. When in 2001 Emil's son Eric produced a handwritten 32-page illustrated summary of their family history and Emil's political career—as a Father's Day present to Emil—it almost had the feel of fiction, comedy, or both, because of its larger-than-life elements.

Closer scrutiny of Emil's life, however, reveals an even greater treasure trove of family lore, as recorded in historical archives and Emil's own albums. Buttressed by Emil's humorous and often self-deprecating tell-all approach, the story that emerges weaves an intriguing tale from beginning to end.

On both sides, Emil's ancestors were builders, leaders, and earnest community participants. Entrepreneurial instincts also pulse in both branches of the family tree, as revealed on street and building names in Saginaw, Michigan and business ledgers throughout Michigan's "thumb" region. Though substantial, such historical facts do not reveal the dramas behind them, nor the depth of roots supporting the charismatic, hard-driving but likable, character who fell from the Lockwood-Achard family tree on September 23, 1919 in Ottawa, Illinois. Or the fact that the roots of the tree intertwined with others—*beet* roots, for example.

At first glance, the 18th century ruffle-shirted, long-haired Prussian philosopher and chemist, Franz Carl Achard, seems startlingly opposite the square-jawed, brush cut American, Senate Majority Leader Emil Lockwood of the 1960s.

The ancestor's flyaway curly hair alone would quickly divert most family tree detectives to another branch. Yet Achard's penetrating glance says otherwise. It shows a watchful curiosity for elements beneath the surface, and the sparkle of desire to create something new from them.

Achard's mentor, Andreas Marggraf, after all, had isolated sugar from beetroot in 1747,[2] but had not developed any practical applications for it before Marggraf's death in 1782. Achard changed that in 1799 when he submitted a ground-breaking treatise to Prussian King Frederick III on how to extract sugar from the roots previously relegated to cattle fodder. As director of the Royal Prussian Academy of Science, he commanded the King's attention immediately.

Philosopher chemist, **Franz Carl Achard** (1753-1821), director of Royal Prussian Academy of Science, noted for pioneering discovery of isolating sugar from beetroot. *Etching circa 1801*

When Frederick III replied four days later by asking Achard to develop a process to make the sugar sap into powdered form, Achard went back to work and soon personally presented Frederick with a foot-high sculptured crown composed entirely of sugar. By developing the process, he made sugar affordable to the masses, instead of a rare worldwide luxury available at that time only from sugar cane. His crown of sugar also put Achard humor on the map, as wryly presented by Emil, generations later.

"You can check the history books," Emil said, "but they don't tell the half of it."

Accolades followed. Even 100 years down the road, Emil's great aunt Clara Achard made sure that the family knew about the plaque honoring Franz Carl Achard and Andreas Marggraf still standing on Dorotheen Street in Berlin. Meanwhile Frederick III gave Franz Carl a farm in Silesia (in contemporary southwest Poland) where, along with another scientist, Achard perfected the process all the way from growing the beets to manufacturing the sugar. When Britain blockaded incoming supplies of cane sugar from much of continental Europe in the early 19th century, Achard temporarily returned to his father's homeland of France, having been commissioned by Napoleon to develop the process there. As a result, in 1811 the first beet sugar processing plant was erected in France.

By the time Franz Carl's grandson, Anton William Waldemar Achard, emigrated to America in 1849, beet sugar manufacturing had already preceded him to the New World. Primitive factories operated as early as 1830 in Philadelphia,[3] 1838 in White Pigeon, Michigan, and 1840 in Connecticut. All these initial enterprises had failed, however—including the southern Michigan effort in White Pigeon, which closed in 1840—due to lack of a thorough understanding of the manufacturing and production process.[4]

"But sugar was in his blood, you might say," Emil said, recalling his great grandfather's participation in the American arm of the industry. Though an architect and builder by trade, regional historians credit Anton for his support of beet sugar manufacturing in Michigan's thumb region, both financially and by promoting the fledgling industry for many years.[5] Indeed, by the latter half of the 19th century, it had reappeared in Bay City, Michigan as a thriving concern.[6]

Achard übcrreicht König Friedrich Wilhelm III. den erſten aus Rüben hergeſtellten Zuckerhut.

Achard ingenuity cooks up crown of sugar. Franz Carl Achard (2nd right) presents King Frederick William III (far left) crown of crystallized sugar (held by associate, far right). 1799. *Published in Michigan Through the Centuries (W.F. Dunbar), Vol. IV, p. 605.*

Like many American pioneers enamored of owning their own back-forty in a new country that far outsized the land of their birth, Anton also tried his hand at farming. After two years, however, the yen to create an architectural legacy won out. By 1864 he had built the first brick block structure in Saginaw—the Burrows Bank Building[7] on Bauer Block[8]—as well as Wayne County Saltworks[9] and many other landmark buildings and private dwellings. At the same time he served on school, bank, cemetery and water boards.

What won him kudos in present Lockwood lore, however, was the massive Saginaw Hardware Company, which he founded in 1864 and which endured through 1960, when it was sold to other interests.[10] In 1887 the future source of Emil Lockwood's wagons, bicycles and sleds comprised 20,000 square feet of floor space.[11] By 1918, the year before Emil was born, its three stories and basement covered a vast city block, and it was listed in James Mills' *History of Saginaw County* as the "largest and most modernized Hardware Store in Michigan".[12] By then, Anton's son and Emil's maternal grand-father—Emil Felix Achard—had long since wooed and wed Augusta Ritter, a woman of commendable traits, one of which was a penchant for playing poker.

"My grandfather and I had the same birthday," Emil said. "That's how I got my name. But," he added, "I got the poker from her."

Following in his father's footsteps, Emil Achard secured his own place as a city father, serving in 1889 as a founding alderman on the council of the newly consolidated Saginaws.[13] Ten years later, in 1899, he served as treas-urer and a founding incorporator of Saginaw Plate Glass Company,[14] exclusive supplier to Ford Motor Company in subsequent years.[15] The exper-tise Achard gained in this new endeavor later drew him to Ottawa, Illinois for a superior source of the silica sand used in glass manufacturing. There he and Augusta rented an apartment, and he co-founded the National Plate Glass Company that was later bought out by Owens Bottle Company, a precursor of Libbey-Owens Ford.[16] More importantly, he had acceded to ownership of Saginaw Hardware Company, and with Augusta's assistance, had fathered Emil's mother, Mabel Pauline Achard.

ACHARDS LOCK STEP WITH LOCKWOODS

Lockwood members of Emil's gene pool team hailed from English ances-tors who first appeared in American records in 1638 in Watertown, Massachusetts. From there, Joseph Lockwood's descendants forged farther inland every two or three generations,[17] following the scent of new potential in a land not yet fully settled or civilized.

By 1854 a racial and political pot boiled throughout the American pioneer states, foreshadowing an important aspect of Emil's political life. The Free Soil Party in Michigan derived its name in part from its adamant anti-slavery stand. But when the Kansas-Nebraska congressional bill opened a large terri-tory in the west to slavery, protests erupted everywhere, ultimately resulting in the formation of the Republican Party.[18]

There still exists some disagreement among political junkies today, about whether the actual founding of the party occurred in Jackson, Michigan or Ripon, Wisconsin, in 1854. Those heralding from Ottawa, Illinois also claim some ownership in nurturing the new party there, at the historic site of the first Lincoln-Douglas debate on slavery in 1858. In any event, future G.O.P. standout Emil Lockwood claimed two out of three states as part of his per-sonal heritage. For the truly authoritative version, Emil suggested listening in on the version heard late at night around campfires in Starved Rock Park near Ottawa.

When the Michigan branch of the United States Land Office moved from Flint to Saginaw in 1857,[19] Cincinnati's Nathan and Permeley Lockwood had just given birth to Emil's paternal grandfather, George Sevy Lockwood. The agricultural potential in the thumb area of Michigan pulsed with possibilities, and Nathan Sevy Lockwood responded. He was not alone. Within ten years the influx of immigrants into Michigan nearly tripled the state's headcount from 450,000 to 1.2 million.[20] The average farm size was 112 acres,[21] and the majority of those who owned them were Republican.[22]

"The land is pure and genuine virgin forest," a fellow Saginaw pioneer wrote in 1867. "There is not even a small place the size of a room without trees. [But] my ax is sharp enough and wherever the wood is dry enough, fire will show its might."[23]

Trees that were not burned had uses beyond cabins, wagons and cradles. Many were cut into planks to line the surfaces of roads.[24] Over these end-to-end boards, Nathan Lockwood drove his wagon to countless county meetings after being named a vice president of the newly formed Saginaw Central Agricultural Society in 1873.[25] Long after he moved his family into a more auspicious home in the increasingly gentrified Saginaw, he would regularly retrace his tracks back to the tiny log cabin to farm the land.

As his children sprouted their own families, more Lockwoods in Fremont and Saginaw bore titles such as town treasurer, highway commissioner, and board of review president.[26] Nathan's son George was as much a civic participant as his father, and is noted in historical records at the Public Libraries of Saginaw, as the developer of Adams Boulevard.[27] Perhaps that is when the family tree's roots squirmed with anticipation at the germination of the Achard-Lockwood seedling twinkling in his granddads' eyes.

"I suppose my grandfathers got to know each other pretty well during all this," Emil said.

New construction and expansion of the Hamilton and Adams location of the Saginaw Hardware Company in 1884 and 1887, served as quiet testimony to the likely frequency of encounters between company treasurer Emil Felix Achard and developer George Sevy Lockwood. No one was surprised, therefore, when Emil's daughter and George's son started keeping company just after the turn of the century.

Following their 1907 wedding, Henry Clare Lockwood and Mabel Pauline Achard frequently vacationed at the Achard family cottage at the popular Point Lookout Beach on the shores of Michigan's Lake Huron. Just west of Saginaw, "Clare"—as Emil's father came to be called—found a small inland lake, and named the property around it Lockwood Beach. In a burst of entrepreneurial fever, he built log cabins along the beach, outfitting each one with its own slot machine.[28] It was one of many ill-conceived entrepreneurial ventures, and in a restless hunt for greener pastures, Clare and Mabel struck out for Ottawa, Illinois, so he could try his hand at the glass business.[29]

Emil's grandfathers revisit old homestead—George Sevy Lockwood (far left) and Emil Felix Achard (center)—visit tenant farmer at original 1857 Lockwood farm. Saginaw (MI), 1920.

Several years later George Sevy Lockwood revisited his father's original homestead farm with his friend and now-familial compatriot, Emil Felix Achard. During the visit, they posed for a snapshot, initially standing stiffly by Lockwood's modernized flatbed truck, straightening their suits and hats while a tenant farmer faced forward, pail in hand. But, as the photo shows, while the photographer must have fidgeted and delayed, they took off their hats and hiked up the pantlegs of their suits, to sit on the sideboard and commiserate, perhaps about their kids. Clare had already failed at several business ventures, and Mabel had her hands full with two rambunctious boys, a new baby, and a lean household income growing leaner by the year. It was 1920 and the two worried fathers schemed about how to help their children or entice them back home.

2

THREE BROTHERS IN THE "TOWN OF TWO RIVERS"

Emil Lockwood, the third son of Mabel Pauline Achard and Henry Clare Lockwood, sprang into the world on September 23, 1919 in Ottawa Illinois, an area saturated with national character and historic values. Site of the first Lincoln-Douglas debate on abolition in 1858, and the founding on U.S.A. soil of the Boy Scouts of America, Ottawa's rivers and canal pulsed with "golden veins of commerce" that were rooted in her Native American heritage "to trade"—*ad-a-we*.[30] Ironically, Ottawa's waters also connected to the nearby Kaiser production site for the Landing Ship Tanks (LSTs) aboard which Emil would later serve in the kamikaze-riddled Pacific Theater of World War II.

When Emil was just three months old, his mother's hemlines were on the rise with the onset of the Roaring Twenties, while the Prohibition lowered the boom on his father's robust drinking habits. Several months later—in presidential election year 1920—his mother gained the right to vote with the passage of the 19th amendment to the U.S. Constitution. By November, newspapers reported the first American radio station's broadcast of Harding's landslide win of the U.S. presidency, a public radio program heard live by a scant 100 families throughout the country.[31]

"We couldn't afford one right away," Emil said of the newfangled wireless music boxes.

The 1925 broadcast of the Scopes Monkey Trial changed that, when fascinated Illinois listeners throughout the state leaned into their radios straining for 12 days straight to hear celebrated attorneys Clarence Darrow and William Jennings Bryant duke it out over Darwin's theory of evolution, on Chicago's WGN.[32] In the following year, the stream of financial subsidies flowing from grandfather Emil Achard's Saginaw Hardware Company provided, among other things, a radio for Clare and Mabel's family. While Emil's 14 year-old brother George was beyond such childishness, 9 year-old Jim and 7 year-old Emil were similar enough in age and disposition to thoroughly enjoy vaudeville favorites such as *The Happiness Boys* and *Amos 'n Andy.*[33]

"There was a good fight on the radio every now and then, too," Emil said, recalling his and Jim's eager boyhood relish for the radio transmission of the 1926 World Heavyweight Boxing Championship match between Jack Dempsy and Gene Tunney.

On Sundays preceding their weekly march to Ottawa's Episcopal church, Mabel Achard Lockwood dictated at least two of her sons' attires: George in his "man pants," and Jim in his ten dollar knickerbocker suit. Emil, characteristically, had already dashed out of the house to serve as an altar boy at the same high service. Whether from devotion, or from the opportunity to cover up his scuffed knickers with the long flowing cassocks of altar service, he will not tell, even now.

"At first," he said, "I just lit and put out the candles, or carried the cross for processions. But when I got a little older I had to recite a lot of long Latin prayers." Not one to settle for rote repetition, Emil engaged a Latin tutor to hurry the process along, despite the fact that Latin was later offered at every grade level at the Ottawa Township High School. Recalling that by then he had already financed his Latin tutor's fees through playing cards, and seeing no conflict with the religious connection behind it, he chuckled. "It was worth it," he said. "There was a good looking girl at the church."[34]

As a young boy, Emil listened to stories of his Achard ancestors, and noted strange etchings of ruffle-shirted Prussians and sugar beet crowns among his mother's prized possessions. During the same period, he frequently accompanied his father to speakeasies near and far, sitting watchfully by on a stool, while Henry Clare Lockwood drowned his demons in bootlegged gin and told stories of his failed businesses.

"My father went back and forth to Michigan a lot," Emil said, "once to drill for oil."

With all the Achard and Lockwood contacts around Saginaw, Clare Lockwood was able to put together a substantial group of investors for his early financial ventures. Dwindling returns, however, soon reflected in a shrinking pool of participants—errors Emil noted, and resolved never to make himself. "If you put all the oil from my father's wells into a pail," Emil said, "it would be empty."[35]

"Every time he came back from Michigan to Ottawa, he'd give me a bicycle or BB gun or something," Emil said. "I used to think he bought them from the Saginaw Hardware Company. Later I learned that they came from there, but he never paid anything for them. After a while we got used to reading the notices in the Chicago paper in Ottawa saying, 'Henry Clare Lockwood went into bankruptcy today'."[36] Even the Lockwood Glass Company, outfitted and funded by Emil Felix Achard for his son-in-law,[37] would have fallen to the same fate, had Clare stuck with it. As a key retail supplier of National Plate Glass's superior product, the Lockwood Company came complete with prestigious flagship clients—auto manufacturing plants throughout the country.[38]

Whether he was counting his dad's business ventures, or counting the pages in Grandmother Augusta's books as she read to her young grandsons, Emil Lockwood was always counting, wondering, computing. Mesmerized by his grandmother's poker hands from the age of four on, Emil was Augusta's willing pupil, learning to count by instinct and to keep running tallies in his head—skills that would provide the basis for both complex poker and political moves lasting throughout his lifetime.

The watchful Lockwood mind also counted failures and wins in his ever-widening circle of comprehension. Emil observed his parents' struggle during the Great Depression, his father's drinking, his mother's forbearance, each of his grandparents' wealth, and his own brothers' divergent approaches. Young George Lockwood seemed to follow the rocky path forged by his father, while Jim—Emil's idol and a lifelong friend—stormed the world with his hard-hitting, often brilliant, approach to life and business. Emil did surmount these childhood hurdles, but not without significant turning points.

THE LOCKWOOD CHARACTER EMERGES

Even as a youngster at the still standing Lincoln Grade School, Emil made his own choices and his own money, catching and selling perch during summer vacations at his grandparents' cottage at Point Lookout, Michigan. "I had quite a business going with the Roman Catholics," he recalled of the Depression Era. "I'd take their orders—whether they wanted the perch gutted or filleted—then I delivered the fish for $2 a dozen, in time for Friday dinners."[39]

Emil was quick to learn math in his early years, yet he bested his excellent academic scores in all subjects by even higher grades for effort.[40]

"My mother didn't want me to do what George did," Emil said. He recalled a trip he took with her in the spring of 1934 at the end of his freshman year in high school, to attend George's graduation from Knox College in Tennessee.

"George wasn't there," Emil remembered. "What's more, we found out he had left several months earlier, without completing his studies." Mabel Achard's eldest son, it turns out, had taken the money she had scraped together herself and from her father, and spent it on nefarious items other than tuition, then traipsed off to the Chicago World's Fair for a job.[41]

"She was steamed," Emil recalled, "and she tagged me and Jim like a hawk after that."

As a result, when Emil turned a high school junior, Jim—who wasn't wild about the thought of a military life—went off to Annapolis at his mother's insistence. Emil was left to fend for himself with friends Harry Cook, Sam Parr, Harry Eichelkraut, and Tom Haeberle, while his mother struggled to keep the family together.

Saginaw city father inspires namesake: Emil Felix Achard (1856-1944), Saginaw Hardware Co. owner, co-founder National Plate Glass Co., (later sold to Libby-Owens Ford precursor). Saginaw (MI). 1910.

Emil (center) ushers in Roaring Twenties with mother Mabel (Achard) Lockwood (1882-1959), brother George (left) (1912-1963), and brother Jim (1917-1992). Ottawa (IL), 1920.

Poker aficionado, grandmother Augusta Ritter (1860-1943) reads to grandsons Emil (left), George (top), and Jim. Ottawa (IL), circa 1923.

Beach boys and company: Emil (left) and brother Jim (right) with friends near the Achard family cottage. Point Lookout (MI), circa 1924.

Ready for heavy sledding. Emil at 1260 Ottawa Ave. home Ottawa (IL), circa 1925.

Clare had already left Ottawa, informally, to headquarter at the roughhewn cabins along Lockwood Beach just northwest of Saginaw. He returned to see his family at Christmas and other holidays throughout the year, occasionally bringing a badger or other catches to add his meager offerings to the family larder, on view for all to see in the public locker housed at the local grocery store.[42] The family also reunited for a few weeks in the summer, either at their Point Lookout cottage, or for a canoe adventure along one of the many rivers in Michigan's thumb region.

Adjusting to the shifting sands of his home life was not always easy, although Emil seldom speaks of hardship. In his third year at Ottawa Township High, however, his grades dipped, along with his "deportment." In the second half of his junior year, his monthly reports were dotted with marginal Bs and Cs, along with deep scratches crossing out "good" and "satisfactory," next to the options describing a student's deportment. The resulting evaluation of his conduct—"unsatisfactory"—would rarely, if ever, be ascribed to him for anything in his life again.

In June of 1936, Emil struggled to think of challenging subjects for his senior year in high school. "Bookkeeping," he wrote in pencil on the back of the final report card for his junior year, followed by "U.S. History, Commercial Law, English IV, Physics, and Biology." "Typing" was also scrawled in a slant at the end of the list, a thought probably prompted by a desire to see the good-looking girl from church, who also attended the high school.

In October 1936 Emil failed Physics, but by November he was back on the Honor Roll. Then he saw that course offerings for his final semester included something new for his high school and a depression-ridden country: "Salesmanship." It was not a tough sell for Emil, and it proved a handy substitute for the unlikely typing class that he could never quite bring himself to take, despite the girl. Regardless of the course, by graduation time his grades were all the same, A+s and A's.[43]

Confronting racial prejudice at his high school graduation, Emil recalled that not everyone subscribed to his homespun philosophy of fairness. Raised with the best of Ottawa's small town values, where everyone is a neighbor, Emil described the only black family in town as "real nice people." "They owned a flower shop," he said, "the only one in town as I recall. It didn't seem like any big deal to me."

Of the family's two sons, Emil explained, one was in his class. "I got fairly well acquainted with him," Emil said. "Then just before the graduation ceremony, a white parent came over to me and asked if I would sit between his daughter and my black friend." The man explained to Emil that if he couldn't rearrange the seating, he would be compelled to defend his daughter from the indignity of having a black student sitting in close proximity to her.

"I said I'd be more than glad to," Emil recounted. "Then I realized that there were a lot of people in town like that, but I hadn't faced up to one until then."[44]

One of the few times Emil wore a three-piece suit with pocket square. Brother Jim (left). Ottawa (IL), circa 1930.

Ready to roll—Emil sports new two-wheeler from Saginaw Hardware Store. Ottawa (IL), circa 1931.

Emil foreshadows 'Casual Fridays' at Ottawa Township High School. Ottawa (IL), 1936.

Altar boy's holiday—Emil (right) in black, at Episcopal Confirmation ceremony. Ottawa (IL), circa 1930.

Youthful shenanigans—Jim Lockwood capers in ladies swimwear at beachfront cottage, to mother's chagrin. Pt. Lookout (MI), 1941.

After graduation, Emil's mother organized a canoe trip near some of her father's property along the Au Sable, a river running east from Grayling into Lake Huron, on Michigan's northeastern coast. "We canoed a lot in the summer," Emil said. "It was hard work lifting the canoes up and dragging them across the portage, but I always loved the water."[45] Sometimes—he refrained from saying—it was even harder to adjust to family difficulties.

"The summer before I went to Kemper Military School," Emil continued, "my dad and I were supposed to meet my mother and the others at this one spot on the Au Sable River."

"It was going to be a longer trip," Emil said, "ten days or so. My dad put a canoe from Lockwood Beach on top of the car and then picked me up in Saginaw. It should have been a short drive; we could have been there in a couple of hours at most. Instead, he stopped at every bar to get a drink."[46] Clare was fortifying himself, Emil thought, for another reunion with his immediate and extended family.

By the fall, Emil was more than ready to strike out on his own.

3
LOCKING HORNS
WITH LOCKWOOD

At his mother's urging to acquire more discipline, and with financial help reluctantly accepted from both grandfathers, Emil began college studies and wrestling practice at Kemper Military School in Boonville, Missouri. Through his studies at Kemper, and his wrestling practice, Emil escalated his abilities to set goals and keep score, important lifelong skills. Wrestling matches also yielded gains in Emil's mental agility and physical endurance. All these were qualities that would appear time and again in his maneuvers on Michigan's Senate floor as one of the state's most prominent and effective "moderate Republicans."

At Kemper, Emil quickly earned the nickname Moose.

"I wasn't that big," he said, "but I liked my opponents up close. Guess I sort of locked horns with them. Still, I never really won that much myself," Emil recalled with a wry smile, in direct contradiction to the testimony of his classmates. He did admit, however, that his individual maneuvers helped his team to win, despite the fact that he was often down on the mat, pinned by a stronger opponent. How? "One way," Emil explained, "is by losing the least number of points."

The wiry moves in college wrestling took place, then and now, in matches lasting no more than two to three minutes. To get pinned down meant points for the attacker, but if he kept the hold for five seconds, his points could double. Too, if the attacker held both shoulders of his opponent on the mat, the match was over on the spot. Once pinned, Emil rarely let either happen. He also developed a facility for reversing his opponent's hold by flipping him and pinning the attacker beneath him, or at other times just escaping again to face the rival. The latter move is seldom accomplished, and therefore rarely generated points.[47] Except in Moose's case, that is.

"The coach mapped it all out for the best score," Emil said. "Sometimes I knew I'd get pinned, and my coach knew, too. Where I was good, though, was in getting out of the hold. When he saw that I was flexible, he taught me the moves. So I'd be down, but we'd hardly lose any points because I was out of it so fast."[48]

Emil's knack for flexibility—adapting to the challenge at hand—got another unusual boost through wrestling.

"I wasn't that good of a wrestler," Emil continued in his typical self-deprecating fashion, "and we played some pretty tough teams, like Penn State, and Navy. But my coach figured out that I could be a swing player. I was right in the middle, you see—between middleweight and heavyweight."[49]

Kemper Military School '37-'38 wrestling team and coach. Emil (top center).   Boonville (MO), 1938.

Each season, Emil recalled, his coach would size up the Kemper team by skills and shortcomings in each of the nine weight classes.   A college wrestler's competitive class was the weight level just above his own weight. At his usual weight of 170 lbs., Emil qualified for the 180.5 lb. class, but he was only a 7.5-lb. loss away from the 163 lb. group. He could also put on 11 lbs., and at 181 lbs. he'd be in the 198 lb. weight class.[50] "Whatever we needed most at the time," Emil said, "I would either bulk up, or lose weight, and that would be my weight class for the semester."[51]

Before the end of his second year at Kemper, despite the fact that it was a four-year school, Emil set his sites on a Bachelor's Degree from the University of Michigan. His grandparents, he was told again, would help, although he was determined not to accept their money, and to work to earn as much as he could himself. Emil's brother George had already moved back to Michigan and married, and now one more Lockwood-Achard would return. It seems that the scheming grandfathers were making progress.

"Colonel Lockwood," wrote one of Kemper's few black students next to his yearbook picture, "I wish I could have known you longer." "Don't forget me—remember me, Moose," exhorted many others, with reminders of Emil's great "run in the kickoff," and references to his being "the company's A-star football, basketball and tennis player," and a great wrestler and debater to boot. "You're always going around with a smile," wrote another, "and you're a swell fellow even though you were in love with Mary." "It's meeting guys like you," one of his friends summarized, "that makes me glad I came to this hole."[52]

Nevertheless, Emil's mind was set, and he was ready to go. "My mother was behind it," Emil said, "but she didn't think I could get accepted at U of M as a junior. She said U of M was a tough school and that I should play it safe, start out as a freshman."[53] These were fighting words, for a talented young man whose attributes did not include patience and repetition.

Emil received his Associates Degree from Kemper Military School in June 1939. From June through September he worked as a soda jerk, waiter, and cashier at Bianchi's Restaurant and Confectionary in Ottawa, Illinois. Then in the fall he set out for Ann Arbor. While he did not win any scholarships in the admission process, he did meet his goal, and entered the University of Michigan as a full-fledged third year student.

In full dress uniform, Emil receives Associates Degree at Kemper Military School. Boonville (MO), 1939.

WRESTLING WITH WPA JOBS
AND THE FOOTBALL TEAM

"My only 'scholarship' at U of M was from Eleanor Roosevelt," Emil said, remembering the First Lady's depression era Works Projects Administration (WPA), and all the jobs he worked at to avoid his grandparents' subsidy.[54]

"After my first semester at the dorm," he said, "I rented a room over a store for $15 a month. It didn't have any hot water, but I figured I didn't need it, because I was on the wrestling team, and I could shower at the gym."

Emil waited on tables at the Sigma Alpha Epsilon fraternity and supervised three other waiters. One of the few perks that augmented their meager wages was chowing down on the meals themselves. "I don't recall ever seeing the inside of the library," he said while looking over a pictorial history of the University of Michigan, "but I was a member of Phi Delta

Wrestlers used "for practice," Emil hears of U of M football team. Ann Arbor (MI), 1939.

"Rout the wrestlers!" football coach Fritz Crisler (left) charges U of M backfield team, including Emil's friend Tom Harmon (2nd right). Ann Arbor (MI), 1939. *Photo #2514 courtesy of Bentley Historical Library, University of Michigan.*

Theta, and I did make it to most of my classes."[55]

Emil remembered the U of M wrestling program, and training with noted football legend and friend Tom Harmon. "The football team used the wrestling team in their practice sessions," he said. "It was an important experience for me in becoming a team player. We all felt that if we were going to win, we were going to do it by sticking together."[56]

Emil did not limit his loyalty to the football field or gym. "Once my dad came to see me in my cold water flat," he recounted. "He told me he had 'forgotten' to get his check cashed, and asked me to loan him 30 bucks. Sure, I gave it to him," Emil said, "and I knew I'd never see it again. It was okay, though," he said without rancor, "I had more ways to make money than he did."[57]

Through Tom Harmon, by now a good friend and fellow entrepreneur, Emil put to good practice the principles he learned at the salesmanship course at Ottawa Township High School. Harmon had contacts with sales firms, and when he saw that his friend needed money, he found ways for Emil to participate. Emil, of course, was a natural. "I sold jewelry for him some times, ran a cigarette concession other times, you name it."[58]

Luckily, by the time he ran the cigarette concessions in the fall of 1940, Emil had already turned twenty-one. Otherwise, it would have been much more difficult to fulfill a pact he had made years earlier with his poker idol, Grandmother Augusta Ritter. Knowing exactly how to motivate her grandson, Grandmother Augusta made Emil an offer he couldn't refuse.

"She promised to give me my first car, if I didn't smoke until I was 21," Emil said, recalling the shiny Model T he received as his end of the bargain. It wasn't easy, he admitted, and shortly after his September birthday, Emil initiated what became a lifelong brand-loyalty to Salem Light Menthol 100s. Thereafter, press clips and family photo albums alike often captured Emil with a cigarette in his mouth or hand, whether negotiating on the Senate Floor or giving his opponents high-fives on tennis and shuffleboard courts across the country and the decades.

WINDS OF WAR

Throughout Emil's undergraduate years at Kemper and U of M, newspapers abounded with accounts of international conflict and combat. The University of Michigan was involved from the beginning, and developed nationally renowned training programs for experts in cryptography and the Japanese language, both of which would be key in the American war effort.[59] As on every other campus throughout the land, U of M also hosted the U.S. Military Reserves, offering patriotic students the opportunity to take officer training during the course of their studies. Kemper graduate Emil Lockwood was a natural for this, too, easily incorporating naval reserve training into his already jam-packed schedule.

When asked why he selected the Navy over the Army or Marines, Emil chuckled. "I don't like to walk," he said, "and I don't like to be in the mud all the time." He also tilted his head and shrugged that his idol and friend, older brother Jim, had done similarly, having enrolled at Annapolis a few years earlier.[60]

Emil wore dress whites more on Ferry Field, shown here, than during actual Navy tour. Ann Arbor (MI), 1940. *Photo #2452 courtesy of Bentley Historical Library, University of Michigan.*

Two days before Emil's birthday in 1939, Soviet troops were reported marching into Poland while Nazis threatened to shell Warsaw.[61] Along with the rest of the country in early 1940, Emil warily watched from afar, as Japan and China warred, Great Britain and France battled Nazi threats in Europe, and Hitler waged blitzkrieg assaults in Russia.

Emil, now an economics major, heard news reports of Japan's offensive moves throughout Southeast Asia, and he cheered at the U.S.'s response: halting steel and fuel sales to Japan, and persuading the British and the Dutch to do the same.[62]

By Emil's birthday in September 1940, Germany had occupied Denmark, invaded Holland, and taken over Paris. Italy sided with Germany against France, and bombed Allied naval bases in Egypt. Within two hours of the event, the U.S. House of Representatives adopted the "two ocean" navy bill, expanding U.S. Navy forces throughout the Atlantic and the Pacific, into what they called "the most powerful navy in the world."[63]

As he often did throughout his life, Emil effectively combined his own needs with the needs of the times, sometimes through calculation, and sometimes through instinct. He learned during his senior year at U of M that employee earnings throughout the country averaged $1,299 per year. He also noted that by 1940, while the unemployment rate had dropped to 14.6 percent from 25 percent after the stock market crash of 1929, it was still far afield of the 4 percent rate the country enjoyed the year he was born.[64] He rightly concluded that he needed to increase his chances for success, and that further educational credentials in business were his ticket.

Emil set his sights on a summer job at the General Motors Machine Gun Plant in Saginaw, in order to finance his upcoming graduate studies at the University of Michigan. His work experience there, when combined with his naval reserves training, would determine his entry level position in the U.S. Navy the following year.

Two of his grandparents did not live to see him graduate in the spring of 1941. George Sevy Lockwood had died the previous December, two weeks short of his 84th birthday, his wife Julia having preceded him several years earlier. But Augusta and Emil Achard looked on with the rest of the family as their grandson Emil, ever a student of numbers and people both, earned his Bachelors Degree in Economics and Sociology from U of M's College of Literature, Science and the Arts.[65]

Prior to graduation Emil had commuted to Saginaw on weekends, to complete a 90-hour training program at the GM plant, but he could not start to work there until July 1. Shrugging off the opportunity for a perfectly justifiable month of vacation, Emil trekked back to Ottawa for a month of manual labor at Starved Rock State Park. There, in his typical egalitarian fashion, he befriended Carter Hale, a subordinate co-worker, a deaf mute who the following year would fleetingly surmount the limits of his handicap in order to save Emil's life.[66]

Starting in July, Emil's wrestling muscles got sufficient workout—if not more—operating a milling machine and drill press at the GM Machine Gun Plant.

"We made machine guns for the Brits," he recalled of his daily 4 p.m. to midnight shift, and the extra hours he also worked. "They gave good pay," Emil said, but his enthusiasm and stamina did not win him points with his co-workers.

"The other guys working there didn't get along with me all that well," he said. "Some of them said I'd better slow down, or I'd get in trouble when the union came in."[67]

Knowing that the union would negotiate production rates relative to compensation, but that the program was not entirely in place, Emil found a way to placate his fellow workers. "I can't sit around," he told them. "I'll do my stuff, and you do yours. At the end of the summer, I'll be gone. If I'm lucky the union won't come in until after that." And that was just what happened.

"It felt good," he said of the vigorous labor and the opportunity to help the war effort. "Besides that, sometimes I got to the beach during the day."[68]

In these welcome though rare respites from a loaded work schedule calculated to maximize income, Emil visited familiar haunts in the Saginaw area and parts north. Along with many other Michiganians, as well as vacationers from other states, he was partial to the beaches of Point Lookout along the upper reaches of Saginaw Bay.

There, an important acquaintance was soon to be made.

4

POINT LOOKOUT AND STARVED ROCK PARK

No one was a stranger for very long at Point Lookout. This was certainly the case for the handsome, red-blooded, steely-eyed entrepreneur from the University of Michigan. Too, the high cheekbones and dancing dark eyes of a Chicago area brunette, Jane Martin Durand, were guaranteed to catch his eye, especially in swimsuits in which she was often photographed at pool openings for the *Chicago Sunday Tribune* society pages.[69]

"She was pretty smart," Emil said sparingly of his first wife, recalling her undergraduate degree from Northwestern University. "Her uncle had a jewelry store in Saginaw—that's how she wound up spending summers in Michigan. But she was born in Illinois, like me," he added.

Emil went back to Ann Arbor in the fall, with plans to see Jane over the holidays. He recalled standing on a downtown street months later, where campus buildings intertwined with galleries, shops, and restaurants. There with spellbound others he watched military parades thunder through the quaint civilian town. It was December 1941, and in a single blow Japan had just crippled the American Navy at Pearl Harbor.

Chicago Sunday Tribune

Chicago area society pages featured Emil's vivacious wife-to-be Jane Martin Durand at summer openings of Glen View pool. Evanston area, Chicago (IL), 1937.

The university's ROTC units conducted military maneuvers in the campus arboretum early in 1942, and Emil remembered marching to U of M's Ferry Field in Navy dress whites, as U.S. armed forces prepared to take a more active role in the war.[70] At the same time, the campus was buzzing with the news that Charles Lindbergh had just arrived in Willow Run, Michigan in April 1942, to help Henry Ford make B-24 bombers.[71] News of the war was everywhere.

"It was hard to stick with my studies," Emil said, "when what I really wanted was active duty in the Navy."

Emil did manage to meet up once or twice with Jane, then finished out the first year of his two-year M.B.A. program in the spring. Following the 1941-1942 academic year, he returned to summer employment at Starved Rock Park, through the Illinois Division of Parks and Waterways. There he cleaned toilets, operated power mowers and tractors, and again met up with Carter Hale, his hearing and voice-impaired friend.

Operating some noisy equipment one day by the side of an unpaved park road, Emil did not see or hear the car that careened out of control as it sped directly at him. Carter was working nearby. He felt a tremor in the ground, and—conditioned from childhood to vigilant alertness in compensation for his handicap—he looked up to see a funnel of dust following a car about to mow Emil down to certain death.

Carter had never spoken in his life, unable to generate sounds through his dormant vocal chords, except for an occasional guttural murmur. Desperate to alert his friend, and seeing nothing in reach to swiftly make a ruckus that might alert Emil in time, Carter did something he had never done before and would never do again. He yelled and yelled again, scrambling toward Emil and waving his arms at the car. The startled Emil looked up,

Emil's "graduate work" at Starved Rock State Park, following '41-'42 graduate studies at U of M. Outside Ottawa (IL), 1942.

wheeled around to see the car, and leapt to safety.

There were a few leveled bushes and mangled pieces of equipment that day, but the maintenance staff of Starved Rock State Park stood tall and intact.

Prior to this, the gregarious Emil had picked up some of Carter's sign language in the simple spirit of camaraderie and communication on the job. Afterwards, he determined to learn the language fully, in an act of gratitude and solidarity with his friend, also picking up some lip-reading in the process. They were skills he would use after the war, as athletic director at Missouri School for the Deaf, where he also coached football with visual signs.

Reporters and political opponents in later years speculated that he used sign language and read lips on the Senate floor as part of the maverick magic he worked on the playing fields of politics and the press.[72]

THE "90-DAY WONDERS"

Unable any longer to hold himself back from participating in the war effort, Emil signed up for full-time officer training. By August 2nd he had completed brief indoctrination classes at Notre Dame University in South Bend, Indiana,[73] and was looking for more. He opted immediately for a rigorous program available to university and college graduates: special training in all areas of a ship's function and staffing needs. Its purpose: to prepare officers for the unpredictable yet inevitable need for flexibility under fire. Approximately three months in duration, its graduates were often labeled "90-Day Wonders" by sardonic enlisted men under their charge.

"They needed men with degrees," Emil said, "people who could figure out how to do anything on a ship and keep it going no matter what, from engineering to cooking."[74]

Volunteer Reserve Midshipman Lockwood, therefore, reported in on August 7th at Abbott Hall on the Northwestern University campus in Chicago.[75] Ironically, he was on Jane's turf now, but there was no time for socializing until after the program's end. Besides classes, Emil recalled frequent exercises held on the shore of Lake Michigan. "We went down by the water and we did exercises all the time, all the time, all the time—once for thirty days straight."[76]

"Proceed to San Diego, California," he was finally instructed on October 30, 1942, "and report to the Commander, Amphibious Force, Pacific Fleet, for active duty in amphibious operations." His orders included a delay until November 9, "such delay to count as leave."[77] Emil did make it count, and was a frequent caller at the Bennett residence in Elgin, Illinois just outside Evanston in the greater Chicago area. There he visited the dark-haired beauty, Jane Martin Durand, stepdaughter and daughter respectively, of Mr. and Mrs. Sidney Bennet.[78]

When Emil arrived by train in San Diego on Sunday, November 8, 1942, the Navy shipyard echoed with reports from the Pacific. Sailors and officers alike cheered the Army's success on Guadalcanal in the Solomon Islands[79] as they readied their ships to join them. Next on the docket for Ensign Emil Lockwood: intensive three-month training in the weaponry, ships, and techniques of amphibious warfare, forecasting dangerous duties he would willingly embrace.

In anticipation of the inevitable fatalities, all personnel completed papers, naming a widow, children, or dependent relative as beneficiary to receive six months pay, providing death was inflicted from "wounds or disease not the result of his or her own misconduct." Emil's form clearly stated "Not Married," a status he had not spent much time thinking about. He named his mother first, and in the event that Mabel predeceased him, he listed his next dependent as his brother George, who had been stricken with polio a few years earlier.[80]

Throughout his training, Emil's head for figures easily absorbed the construction specifications and operation of battleships, submarines and LSTs (Landing Ship Tanks), the latter having been hailed by their crews as "King of the Amphibs."[81] It was aboard the LST that Emil was ultimately directed to serve. "Three hundred and twenty-seven feet and nine inches long," he recalled the LST's dimensions in an interview 59 years later, "with 50 feet across the beam."

Amphibious warfare training complete, Emil reported in San Francisco to the Commanding Officer of the Twelfth Naval District aboard U.S.S. Landing Ship Tank #478.[82] Although the 478 was built in Richmond, California, Emil recognized the ship's builder, Kaiser, Inc., from one of the five sites where LSTs were made—off the shores of the "Town of Two Rivers" just outside Ottawa, Illinois. It was like a call from home. He settled into the Waterfront Service Unit on San Francisco Bay, and debated how best to take a break.

In San Diego he had watched young officers and sailors kick up their heels in edgy wartime revelry and carouse with all too many willing patriots of the feminine persuasion. Emil quickly saw that San Francisco would be more so. He didn't object, necessarily, but with the reminder of home he put in for a 10-day leave, listing a contact address at his brother George's in Saginaw.[83]

Wide-eyed family and friends—already familiar with Navy terminology from Jim Lockwood's service as a Navy pilot aboard the U.S.S. Saratoga—pulled from Emil detailed accounts of the stanchions, booby hatches, engines, and elevators aboard the LSTs. Hoping for distraction from the war, he heard the familiar crack of someone cutting a deck of cards, and joined Grandmother Augusta in a welcome round of poker. It was the last time he would see either of his Achard grandparents alive.

As before, Emil returned to the West Coast via Chicago where he saw a certain young lady, before returning to the base.[84] Back in San Francisco, he met many of the men with whom he would serve aboard the LST 478. Several names listed on the ship's first roster, and others added later, would also appear on Emil's calendar over the ensuing decades, at reunions dating into the new millennium. Ray Custer, Engineering Officer. Russell Lake, Commissary Officer. Bob Keefe, Navigation Officer. Andy Caffrey, fellow water-skiing adventurer. Friends all, survivors all—poker players, too.

With his new comrades-in-arms, Emil worked to equip the docked LST 478 for departure, memorizing every groove and corner of its 327 foot 9 inch length and every quirk of its 400-ton hulk and equipment. It was time well spent, as its welded steel construction would be their home and haven under fire for the next three years.

The 478 and its companion ships were armed to defend themselves with topside artillery and machine guns, but their primary function was to transport fighting tanks and weaponry, complete with fuel, ammunition, and a full complement of troops to operate them. Some LSTs were even outfitted with internal railroad tracks, and transported entire trains across the channel between England and Cherbourg, France.[85] LSTs were propelled by pumps powered by twin diesel engines comprised of over 100 motors, which in turn were powered by three diesel generators.[86] Emil's penciled notes on a document dated later that year, read "72,140 gallons of fuel oil [pumped] to YOG 31," signifying the amount of fuel used aboard LST 478 during its coded routes between March and December.[87]

At noon on March 11, 1943 the ship was pronounced "in full commission" with all officers and enlisted men on board. Within two days all operations checked out, and the engines revved under the watchful eyes of two admirals standing alongside. At 13:05 p.m. LST 478 was underway at 8 knots and climbing. It entered the Mare Island Navy Yard Channel at 15:26 p.m., having successfully completed its first shakedown cruise. Upon arrival and docking, there was one person that Gunnery Officer Emil Lockwood could not wait to call.[88]

"Jane was a very straightforward, nice, good-looking gal," Emil said. "When I saw the number of women around the ship and shore—and they all seemed to want to hook up with Navy men—I called Jane and asked her if she'd like to get married."[89]

Two weeks later Emil and his shipmates were commandeering and loading tanks destined for the Aleutian Islands, Jane was situated in an apartment in San Francisco, and the following announcement had already run in Chicago area newspapers:

"MRS. ENSIGN"—Jane Martin Durand, who went to the west coast last week to visit her fiancé, changed her plans upon arrival to include a wedding and is now Mrs. Emil Lockwood. Ensign Lockwood, USN, is stationed at the Naval base in San Francisco, and the marriage took place in the base chapel on Thursday....

The couple, now honeymooning at Palo Alto, Calif., plans to live on the west coast where Ensign Lockwood is stationed. Friends of the bridegroom were present at the ceremony read last Thursday in the chapel at the Naval base in San Francisco, and attended a reception and dinner which followed.

PART TWO

Emil's New Stage: the Pacific Theater

1943 – 1961

5

LARGE STATIONARY TARGETS

When Ensign Emil Lockwood set foot on LST 478, he joined forces with millions of officers and "GIs" from across America—"Government Issue" enlisted men and women, all outfitted with government issue togs and equipment, and all determined to defend their country. With the bombing of Pearl Harbor, the U.S. Navy had swiftly mobilized multiple strategies throughout the Atlantic and Pacific oceans. At home, manufacturing plants operated around the clock to produce tried-and-true artillery, as well as innovative weaponry adapted to unprecedented military conditions emerging across the globe. The U.S. soon earned a reputation as the "Arsenal of Democracy," amply supplying her own and Allied forces throughout the war.[90]

LSTs delivered these arsenals by sea, complete with operating troops, as fast as they could be produced and loaded. Often their highly charged cargo more than quadrupled their own ship's tonnage to well over 2,000 tons.[91] Emil's new stage, therefore, was a moving enemy target, hustling to unload its incendiary goods and at the same time assist in occupying the Aleutian Islands, supplying the Ellice Islands, and capturing the Gilbert Islands. And that's just in 1943.

By the war's end, Emil and his fellow 478ers had distinguished themselves in landmark battles resulting in five Battle Stars each, and Emil was individually singled out for three more stars on his Victory Medal for outstanding service in the Philippines and Okinawa. He had fleetingly trod the same path as General Douglas MacArthur, 20 year-old Lt. George H. W. Bush, and even another Lockwood besides Jim—Rear Admiral Charles A. Lockwood, Jr., (distantly related) commander of U.S. Submarine Forces in the Southwest Pacific.[92]

"We were always in the thick of it," Emil said, "because it was our job on the LSTs to carry personnel-operated tanks, artillery, supplies—anything, you name it—into the heart of a war zone."[93]

Because of the unique nature of their work fueling the American war machine, this unceremonious, can-do group of seamen quickly earned the moniker "Dungaree Navy."[94] "We really couldn't maintain a dress code when we were on the job," Emil said, "it just wasn't practical." Nor, as acknowledged by many, were their delivery orders practical, often requiring breakneck speeds into Pacific Theater combat zones, on ships with manufacturing specs of cruising and maximum speeds between 8-12 knots, equivalent to 10-14 mph.[95] At times like that, the crew of the "king of the amphibs" had little time to worry about life and death implications of their craft's other nicknames as "floating bathtubs" or "Large Stationary Targets."

There was never any doubt, however, that their missions were vital to the Navy's success. "The destinies of two great empires seemed to be tied up by some God-damned things called LSTs," wrote William Brinkley in a 1966 retrospective entitled *The Ninety and Nine*.[96]

The LST 478 had achieved near battle status by late June 1943, but one important step remained—final inspection. On June 30, the 478 pulled out of Monterey Bay and headed south to Port Hueneme, for just that purpose. That same day, Navy forces had finally launched an offensive in the Pacific, at Rendova in the Solomon Islands east of New Guineau. The 478 arrived in Port Hueneme just north of Los Angeles on July 1, just as Secretary of the Navy, Frank Knox, arrived in L.A. to inspect Pacific Coast installations. There Knox met with reporters, and confidently declared that the attack at Rendova was just the beginning.[97]

Knox passed the 478 and others in her fleet with flying colors, and Emil was off to battle, but not before some poignant news from home. The previous week, he learned, 83 year-old Grandmother Augusta had died in Saginaw, Michigan. Dedicating his first mission to the feisty woman who had initiated him in the arts of poker and numeric wizardry, 23 year-old Emil Lockwood prepared to go to sea.

As a card-carrying 90-Day Wonder, Emil wore many hats in a relatively short period. By the time he and his shipmates aimed for the Aleutian Islands in early July, he had already served as Gunnery Officer, Navigator, Censor, Ship's Service Officer, and Assistant Engineering Officer. Before they left port, he had also trained in fire fighting as well as ship and aircraft recognition.[98]

As Gunnery Officer aboard LST 478, Emil trained crew members in the use of battle guns. He also supervised their operation and supply. These ranged from handguns such as .45 pistols and submachine guns, to the 40 mm anti-aircraft machines located strategically at the bow and stern of the ships. The 40 mm guns rotated vertically and horizontally, and fired 120 rounds of shells per minute, for a range of up to 5,100 yards. Emil—in coordinated moves reminiscent of his wrestling matches at Kemper—taught operators how to aim the guns by swiveling them with two-handed cranks, and simultaneously pushing foot pedals to fire them.[99]

"At first we only had 20 mm guns on deck," Emil recalled warily, "and they weren't worth a damn. When we got into trouble," he said, "I had to station shooters out there with Browning automatic rifles until we could upgrade the mounts back at the base. It was a tough way to learn," he said, "but it's what happened."[100]

PUMPING ADRENALINE AND WATER

Propelling an LST, complete with its diesel engines, generators, and 100-plus motors, did not only call for propellers. In addition, pumps and anchors were used in intricate combinations to effect the ship's movement.

"Each ship had three anchors and some complicated pump systems," Emil explained. "In order to move forward or backward, engineers pumped water in and out in various quantities and directions, depending on how fast or far we needed to go." Dropping an anchor on one side pivoted the ship in that direction, to turn. Likewise, drawing water in at the bow caused a reverse direction, and pumping it out at the stern propelled the ship forward. "When we were out to sea, it was simple," Emil said. But maneuvering in and out of narrow twisted channels, and actually beaching the LST, was another story. "Then," he said, "we were dropping and raising anchors all the time. Pumping in and out, depending on what we needed." Low tide, he recalled with a grimace, presented a "particular challenge".[101]

While much of Emil's service in the Pacific was undertaken in equatorial zones riddled with danger, the LST 478 quietly launched its impressive military record in the North Pacific, off the coast of Alaska. There, the Aleutian Islands had suffered Japanese seizure and occupation the year prior. By January 1943, American forces had reclaimed part of the islands, yet in May they still battled the enemy in snowdrifts up to 10 feet deep. It was time for reinforcement from sea.[102]

That summer the 478 pumped toward the Aleutians as part of a joint American and Canadian amphibious assault on Kiska Island. The fleet all but surrounded the island, carefully maneuvering its way in through a thick blanket of fog. Anchoring in Bamboo Bay on August 15 without incident, along miles of shore line, the ships threw open their 20 foot high doors, and lowered wide planked stairs to the beach, disgorging armed troops and tanks at a run. Emil and others of the 478 charged along.

"It turned out to be a good training session, nothing more," Emil said. "There was nobody home, because the Japanese had already left two days earlier. They'd cut their losses," he explained, "knowing there would be more American attacks."[103]

For three weeks, Emil's crew and others outfitted the U.S. occupation forces of the Aleutians, then headed back to San Francisco for the last time before the war's end. After spending his 24th birthday there with Jane over three whirlwind days, he and the crew of the 478 headed for Pearl Harbor. It would serve as their naval headquarters between battles, for the duration.[104] From this point forward, Emil's assignments aboard LST 478 would not be so simple, safe, or northern as the islands off the Alaskan coast.

90 Day Wonder, Ensign Lockwood completes three-month intensive at Notre Dame and Northwestern universities; learns amphibious warfare and fire-fighting at Naval Training Station. San Diego (CA), 1943.

A long way from Pt. Lookout—LST officers (left to right) Bob Keefe, Emil, John Ralph, at naval home base. Pearl Harbor (HI), 1943.

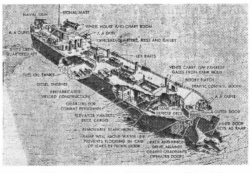

Emil enjoys rare moment of reflection after trouble-free occupation of Kiska Island in Aleutians. Pearl Harbor (HI), 1943.

LSTs—400-ton "Large Stationary Targets"— aboard which Emil served in WW II's Pacific Theater, carried cargo up to four times their weight, including troops, tanks, artillery and supplies. *Diagram from C.J. Adams, Jr. collection, LST 281, as preserved in Emil's papers.*

Home away from home base—when he didn't make curfew, Emil was guested at Utaka and Jean Morowaki's, friends who later visited him in Michigan. Honolulu (HI), 1944.

On October 31, 1943 the 478 set course as flagship, leading multiple units toward Funafuti Island,[105] north of Fiji in the South Pacific Melanesian Sea. There, Allied troops battled without food or medical supplies, to hold off the onslaught of the Japanese. Throughout repeated high level Japanese bombing attacks from November 11th to the 16th, Emil and crew delivered the goods, then with the remaining cargo intact, led the fleet south to join a major offensive in the equatorial Gilbert Islands. As it turns out, everything until then was warm-up.

6

"OTHER TYPES TOO NUMEROUS TO MENTION"

O f the many strategic breakthroughs ascribed to World War II, the most frequently touted one in Navy circles was the aircraft carrier. Such was the U.S.S. Saratoga, aboard which Emil's brother Jim Lockwood served. The seafaring carriers offered not only safe passage for planes and their pilots, but runways for launchings and landings as well. Other less heralded newcomers were the landing ships such as the LSTs, uniquely equipped for beach and coral landings, even carrying portable bridges when needed. It was a new brand of naval warfare and by the fall of 1943, it paid off for the Allies big time.[106]

This was immediately apparent to the Japanese pilot scouting over the Gilbert Islands on the morning of November 19, 1943. Shocked at the sight of a vast American "armada" approaching from the east, he radioed back to his base: "Enemy contact report . . . fleet sighted . . . several carriers and other types too numerous to mention . . . ."[107]

If size and volume were the only determining factors, the Navy could have written its triumphant report right then. Nature, however, intervened, as shore watch patrols from nearby New Zealanders soon revealed. The tide, it seems, was way down. Conflicted Navy and Marine commanders arranged an impromptu meeting at sea. A New Zealand officer warned them of the dangers of landing in low tide, and advised them to delay the assault until late December. The commanders disagreed, fearing a loss of momentum.[108]

"You won't have three feet," New Zealand Major Frank Holland argued even as they overrode his advice.[109]

Faced with the impossible order to land in such shallow water, the 478 and others launched LCVPs, smaller landing crafts of which each LST carried four. Even the LCVPs, however, needed a minimum of four feet of water to float when fully loaded with armed personnel.[110]

"It was a case of admirals trying to overrule nature, or common sense, or both," Emil recalled of the November 20 onslaught at Tarawa in the Gilbert Islands. "The fighters had to wade ashore under heavy fire. We lost a lot of 'em."[111]

Low tide and bad timing at Tarawa forced GIs to file ashore on foot as LSTs unload far offshore at key battle site. Gilbert Islands, 1943. *National Archive Photo (#1168).*

LSTs open at bow doubling as doors, lower gangplank onto beach, transport up to 250 armed troops, 20 Sherman tanks, even railroad cars (as at Cherbourg, France). Pacific Islands, 1944. *National Archive Photo (#59509).*

LSTs were often first ashore, unloading under heavy bombing. Kamikaze attack-planes 1st appeared in WW II off Leyte Island in Philippines (shown here), 1944. *National Archive Photo (#1209).*

The entire Gilbert operation covered a series of islands of which Tarawa was the principal objective. Eighteen thousand Marines landed on Tarawa, a two-mile long island "honeycombed with [Japanese] blockhouses, pillboxes, and artillery emplacements covered with concrete." Japanese aircraft repeatedly bombed the LSTs and other U.S. ships as they tried to unload from offshore, while underwater mines and ground fire blasted the emerging men on foot. U.S. ships retaliated, bombarding the island with 300 tons of high explosives. The entire attack lasted 76 hours, killing 1,009 GIs and wounding another 2,100.[112] Emil, mercifully, was not one of them, though the 478 was the first to actually beach during the invasion.[113]

The Allies ultimately prevailed, gaining valuable territory on the path to the next objective, the Marshall Islands. But it was a bitter victory heaped upon great losses. Days later, in the wake of death and destruction, Thanksgiving Day dawned on Tarawa over thousands of wounded and exhausted men, medics and nurses. The LST crews continued to unload their vast store-houses, and delivered food and medical supplies as well as weapons and ammunition, throughout the many encampments working to occupy the island. Often the cargo they delivered exceeded some of their own depleted wares.

Emil spotted a large shipment of turkeys on the 478 that had yet to be distributed to U.S. personnel on the island. As the battle-weary crew indiscriminately shouldered crates of other foodstuffs to take them ashore, Emil quickly computed the number of turkeys. Then he got the crew to carry them instead, to give the traumatized boys a taste of home. Not, however, before he had also finagled 150 of the birds for his and other nearby ships.[114] It wasn't the only time he watched out for his shipmates.

"I had a real good crew," Emil said with a nod. "If my ship-fitter caught KP when there was a shore leave, I'd tell him to go and I'd take care of it. I knew he needed the break."[115]

In the shock and aftermath of the Tarawa battle, crew members concocted a token of appreciation for Ensign Lockwood. They presented Emil with a certificate of honor from the mythical King Neptune, Lord of the Sea himself, embossed with the official 478 seal which had been temporarily "borrowed" from the CO's desk. The certificate was signed by His Majesty's Scribe, Lt. Davey Jones, as well as Lt. Comdr. Neptunus Rex, Ruler of the Raging Main. It came complete with typed honorifics as well as artistic renderings of Neptune and his mermaid brigade.

Sixty years later, it remains in chronological order among Emil's officially bound Navy papers:

Imperium Neptuni Regis

"To all sailors wherever ye may be, and to all mermaids, whales, sea serpents, porpoises, sharks, dolphins, eels, skates, suckers, crabs, lobsters and all other living things of the sea. Know ye that Ensign Emil Lockwood, having been found worthy to be numbered as one of our trusty Shellbacks has been duly initiated into SOLEMN MYSTERIES OF THE ANCIENT ORDER OF THE DEEP. Be it further understood: that by virtue of the power invested in me I do hereby command all my subjects to show due honor and respect to him wherever he may be. Disobey this order under penalty of our royal displeasure."[116]

UNEXPECTED DANGERS AND DUTIES

By Christmas, LST 478 left the Gilberts and set course for its home base at Pearl Harbor for long-needed repairs and refurbishing. Emil, having acquired even more titles in the line of duty—Damage Control Officer and Division Officer—was nominated in January 1944 for promotion to Lieutenant. His adrenaline still pumped from the heat of battle, however, and the prospect of rising through the ranks, away from the action, was not a palatable one.[117]

Remembering that the headquarters for the Pacific Submarine Fleet had arrived in the Hawaiian Islands about eight months prior, Emil requested transfer to submarine service. "They were headquartered at Midway to work on the torpedo system for a while," he said. "I heard all about it when we got back to Pearl Harbor," Emil recalled, "and I wanted in."[118]

The Pacific Fleet subs were run by the newly promoted Vice Admiral Charles A. Lockwood, Jr. "I never met him," Emil said, "although many years later someone looked up his family tree, and I guess we do go back to the same Lockwoods who landed in Massachusetts from England.[119] His troops called him 'Uncle Charlie,'[120] he was so popular, but he wasn't my uncle—I just liked the sound of the submarine work."

Emil qualified on January 31, after successfully withstanding endurance tests at 50 lbs. of pressure underwater. "DEFECTS NOTED: None," the

Senior Medical Officer wrote.[121] Emil occasionally liked to quote that singular qualification to Jane long after his return.

While awaiting transfer approval, Emil diverted himself one day by inviting others to take out a smaller LCP boat recreationally. "I thought we might as well have some fun, and I liked to ride behind the boat on a makeshift water ski. They opened a six-pack and didn't notice, when all of a sudden I fell back and flipped. My legs were kicking above the water, and the rest of me was underwater. Every time I came up for air, I yelled, but the engine was pretty loud and they were busy drinking the beer. I thought my time was up," he added laughing, "but they finally got me out."[122]

Despite his underwater endurance recreationally and officially, Emil's request for transfer was denied. The LST 478, apparently, needed him more.

After two and a half months of considerable repairs, the 478 was again on its way delivering much-needed weapons, ammunition and medical supplies to the troops, this time in Guadalcanal and Milne Bay in the Solomon Islands. Just when Emil had all but forgotten his restless search for a new challenge, the Commanding Officer of the 478 received two requests for Lieutenant Lockwood's services, "provided you feel that subject officer can be spared."[123]

The first request, involved sister ship LST 26's mission into Dutch New Guineau's Tanah Merah Bay, and then further inland into the foothills of Tanahmerah. Its extraordinary cargo?—Christian ministers. "Supplying men of the cloth to a hostile island? What will they think of next?" Emil remembered wondering.

"It was a combination search and supply party," Emil said. "There was an area held by the Japanese, and we needed to deliver troops and supplies to our fighters. The ministers were part of it, we figured later, because of the confidential reports about the awful things that were going on there."[124]

Emil recalled riding inland in a caravan of jeeps transported aboard the LST 26. Along with several guards and combat personnel, he rode with the ministers northwesterly over the rough terrain along the Digul River. At some point, the jeeps and supplies were parked and camouflaged, and the cautious party proceeded into the foothills on foot. The nature of what they would find was not subject matter that fit into the terse form of transmittal orders, and when they arrived at the first village, they understood why.[125]

"The New Guineau women were nursing pigs," Emil said. "Initially it was forced on them by the Japanese, in order to fatten their food supply." Then somewhere along the line, he explained, after being pillaged and abandoned, the native people continued the practice. Looking around their impoverished half-demolished surroundings, he and the others understood that it was a choice they had to make between starving and surviving. "Then the women were impregnated on purpose," Emil said shaking his head, "so their people could continue eating."

The ministers were apparently sent in to the natives who had become

Christianized, to help them deal with their experiences and reconstruct their lives. "It's something I'll never forget," Emil said.[126]

While Emil was temporarily assigned to LST 26's amphibious operations in the New Guineau area,[127] Navy officers again traded for his services. On April 14, 1944 Emil received an interim order superseding his original temporary order. "That was the type of stuff you had to get used to in the Navy," Emil said, "par for the course." Emil was "hereby directed to report to the Commander LST Group Twenty-One in the LST 18 to take part in coming operations."[128]

For two critical weeks aboard the LST 18, Emil served as Liaison Officer between the Army and the Coast Guard, uncovering new abilities in compromise and negotiation under fire, to help coordinate Navy supply mechanisms between those two branches of the military.[129]

When he returned to the 478 on May 10, Emil learned of the death of his namesake, grandfather Emil Felix Achard. Pressing orders, however, left no time for mourning. Emil and his shipmates were directed immediately to their next assignment—deliveries to the Russell Islands near Guadalcanal in the Solomons, followed in quick succession with much-needed supplies for Kwajalein in the Marshall Islands.[130]

Pushing off to Pearl Harbor to refuel in early June, they watched Lockheed Lightning P-30's flying overhead. Radio scuttlebutt had it that Charles Lindbergh flew amidst the formation, stretching the rules of his assignment as a civilian test pilot, to include combat missions.[131] At the same time, the LST 478's crew rallied at even more fortifying news.

It was D-Day—June 6, 1944—and Allied forces had just successfully landed in the Atlantic, along the coast of Cherbourg, France.

7

DIVEBOMBERS OVER THE MARIANAS

The LST 478 had just left the Marshall Islands on June 9, 1944, when orders came in for Guam and Saipan. "In raw miles," Emil said, "this was as close to Japan as you could get, other than the Philippines. And they were next."

Over air and sea, Allied forces in the Pacific amassed for the next assault, as 127,500 troops, 775 ships, and 956 planes converged off the eastern coast of the Mariana Islands due south of Japan. With them came all their high-powered Army, Navy and Marine commanders, many of whom disagreed on strategy, still reeling from the heavy losses at Tarawa and other locations. During one planning session, it took the commander in chief of the U.S. Pacific Fleet, Chester W. Nimitz, to quiet the rising interservice rivalries.[132]

Lieutenant Lockwood was not at the meeting, of course, but the word he heard from the grapevine was borne out years later in historic accounts of the preparatory meetings for the Mariana assault.

"This all reminds me of the first amphibious operation—conducted by Noah," Nimitz told commanders of the three branches of service. "When they were unloading from the Ark, Noah saw a pair of cats come out, followed by six kittens. 'What's this?' he asked. 'Ha, ha,' said the tabby cat, 'and all the time you thought we were fighting.' "[133]

They didn't have kittens, Emil opined, but the disparate strategies did come together, and what's more, the weather cooperated, too. Tides were not a factor, he recalled, and Saipan—though it was mountainous inland—offered four miles of level beachfront for the landing LSTs. The 478 and others approached Saipan in the Marianas on June 15, as chaplains throughout the fleets blared prayers over loudspeakers. Six hundred amphibious tractor tanks spilled from the opening jaws of the LSTs, as nearby destroyers fired rockets and rounds, to give them cover. The Japanese responded with heavy mortar and artillery fire, but within 20 minutes 8,000 Marines had landed. By nightfall, their numbers rose to 12,000.[134]

Through the night, thousands of Japanese troops and tanks charged down from the hills, in a vain attempt to drive the Americans back into the sea.[135] For days, the battles raged on land and sea, and the 478 battened its hatches under continual bombardment as its crew fired back.[136]

"After maybe two days of fighting," Emil recalled, "we were still trying to penetrate the island, when a Marine hobbled up to the 478."[137]

"Everybody in my platoon is dead," the shell-shocked Marine told Emil's crew, asking to come aboard to clean up and rest up. He was quickly invited in, carrying a Japanese rifle he had acquired in battle. Setting it down on a chair, he went inside to shower, and one of the sailors picked up the rifle out of curiosity.

"It wasn't disarmed," Emil said, "although nobody knew that then."

When the sailor set the rifle back down it fired accidentally, sending a rifle shot through the bulkhead and into the shower stall where the survivor washed, unawares.

"We lost him on the spot," Emil said. "Everybody was numb."[138]

The sudden approach of enemy aircraft gave little time to ponder the strange ways of fate, however, as low flying Japanese dive-bombers zoomed down to bombard the Americans onshore and inland, among them, the LST 478. Emil and others ran for their guns, simultaneously siting the Japanese fleet trying to breach their lines under the protective fire of the dive-bombers. Although the Japanese were outnumbered on all fronts, their resistance did not subside until July 9, and it took another month to fully secure Saipan. In the end, almost 3,500 Americans lay dead, while Japanese fatalities in the Marianas were closer to 24,000.[139]

According to Emil, there were many chilling incidents beyond the obvious, often resulting in mass fatalities. One such event occurred during the Saipan campaign when his ship was going back and forth between the Marianas and the Marshall Islands, transporting troops and weapons. Japan's officials had for the first time admitted the possibility of their ultimate defeat, causing panic among Saipan's residents. Soon the LST 478 GIs and others witnessed mass suicide plunges, when thousands of fearful Japanese civilians leapt from Saipan's cliffs to their deaths, further adding to the tragic fatalities.

As the carnage ebbed, the war machine moved on. American Seabee engineers landed on Saipan and other islands to expand and improve the airfields left by the Japanese, which would then provide a launching pad for B-29s to assault Japan's mainland.[140] Among the Seabees was an old friend of Emil's from Ottawa, Illinois—Harry Cook.

HARRY FROM THE DAIRY

Harry Cook's family business back in Ottawa, Illinois was a full scale dairy, with products ranging from manure to bottled eggnog. While Emil would not claim endowing Harry with his nickname, he was certainly responsible for propagating its use long after their school days together.

"Harry wasn't an engineer to begin with," Emil said, "but in the service you can become anything—look at me. That's how Harry came to be a Seabee. But to me, he was still 'Harry from the Dairy'."

"Harry tracked me down through some kind of radio network," Emil said. "Turns out, he was doing some work on Goodenough Island, off the coast of New Guineau. [141] Well, I knew they had watched some movies over in the Marshall Islands before all the bombing started,"[142] Emil said, "and that gave me an idea. I thought Harry could probably use some cheering up. I couldn't get a movie projector, though, so I got a camera and thought we could take some pictures."

The trick was getting there. There were always people going back and forth, he reasoned, and he did have a couple days of leave coming. But he'd have to go by seaplane in order to get back in time for his next watch. In that his own rank and officer stripes were pretty recognizable, and he didn't want to manufacture any false paperwork, Emil settled upon a disguise. He would dress as an enlisted man, borrowing some clothes from an accomplice under his charge. Then he would slip in among a small flight group he had pinpointed.[143] Weary of the bloodshed and the ever-present specter of death, he realized it might be his last time to see his friend.

It was more than a thousand-mile journey by air, skipping from one secured airfield to another through the islands between the Marianas and New Guineau. As the sound of shells receded behind the engine's drone, Emil alternately dozed and kibitzed, occasionally patting the deck of cards he had put in his pocket.

On Goodenough Island, the war machine operated in a different gear. Emil and his companions saw rows of Quonset huts as they approached a narrow landing strip. Harry was there to greet him, and gave a quick tour of the round low metal buildings he and his men had been building to house the occupation forces there. Soon the two friends were under a palm tree with a beer and a deck of cards. The horrors of the war were momentarily forgotten. And, somehow, even though their visit took place in a flicker of time, it stood out for decades in Emil's memory of those blood-stained years.

"Harry from the Dairy" (Harry Cook, right) under banana palm; shows Emil Quonset huts he and other Seabees built on Goodenough Island. New Guineau, 1944.

Initial officers of "Dungaree Navy's" LST 478. Ensign Lockwood (front left) with H. F. Holmshaw (C.O.), Lt. Leon Alderhold, Lt. Joseph Harrison, Lt. J. C. McCormick; and Ensigns: Robert Keefe, Russel Lake, Scott Tennyson, Andrew Caffrey, C. I. Ingve. Pearl Harbor (HI), 1943-44.

Key Pacific Theater locations, where officers of LST 478 received five battle stars for service under kamikaze and bombing attack: (1) Tarawa in Gilberts, 1943; (2) Saipan in Marianas, 1944; (3) Leyte in Phillipines, 1944; (4) Luzon in Phillipines, 1945; and (5) Okinawa, 1945. *Lockwood archives.*

Thinly disguised as enlisted man, Emil (top right) finagles leave and flies 1,000 miles to see Ottawa (IL) Seabee friend Harry Cook (top center). Goodenough Island, Papua New Guineau, 1944.

When the 478 returned to Pearl Harbor in mid-August 1944, Emil and his ship-mates learned that they had just missed Franklin D. Roosevelt, who made a presidential visit to the base in July with General Douglas MacArthur and Admiral Chester Nimitz.[144] Everyone anxiously devoured war news from all directions, quickly getting up to speed on Allied wins and losses in the Atlantic.

"Some new friends on Honolulu—Utaka and Jean Morowaki—helped us to celebrate our wins," Emil recalled. "They were real nice people despite the fact that they ate uncooked fish," Emil said of his rare encounters with sushi.[145] With these friends and other officers, Emil speculated on the progress in France, and soon his men were making bets on when the tide would turn against Germans forces there. Emil predicted it would happen before September, while others were not as optimistic.

After some welcome R and R, the 478ers had dry-docked the ship and were busily patching up its holes on August 25,[146] when word flew through the islands of important breaking news. Free Paris Radio had just announced the surrender of the German commander in Paris, even as American, French and British forces continued to drive the Germans back.[147] Emil was on shore leave at a steamy airport dive on a nearby island.

"The crap games were going nonstop," he recalled, and the celebratory revelry went on and on, at the announcement of the news. There was no thought for the approaching mandatory curfew.

"Finally, we only had about an hour left to get back across the channel by midnight, " Emil said. "Another guy was supposed to pick us up an hour earlier, but he never did. My friends were going to wait for another boat," he said, "but there was still a little daylight and I decided to swim for it."[148]

"All of a sudden," he said, "I looked up and there was a huge aircraft coming right for me, lights flashing and all. You've never seen a guy swim so fast!" he said, chuckling. "But it was just one of ours, coming in for a landing at the airport near the bar. I wound up swimming through some oil slicks, but I finally made it back, grease and all."[149]

Unbeknownst to Emil, however, he was soon destined to encounter a more diabolical approach from the air than ever before imagined.

HELLCATS MEET THEIR MATCH

At MacArthur's meeting with President Roosevelt at Pearl Harbor in July 1944, the general pushed to proceed with his offensive in the Philippines. It was a plan that had been in place awhile, and MacArthur had promised the Filipino people that he would return to recapture their islands, after they had fallen to the Japanese. Many people objected, including Admiral Nimitz. It was strategically unnecessary, they said, because of the considerable conquest in the Marianas. They argued instead that the B-29 Hellcat bombers were now ready to directly assault Formosa and the Japanese mainland.[150]

So what happened? "It's simple," Emil said. "MacArthur said he would return, and he did. I was there."

The LST 478 arrived at Leyte Island in the Philippines in October, even as General MacArthur waded ashore for the newsreel cameras. Everything looked good at first, Emil recalled. The tide was up but the surf was down, and there hadn't been any mines or explosives to greet them. Overhead fire was light, and it looked to be an easy take. American torpedoes crippled the Japanese ships, while the smoke billowed and U.S. troops forged ahead on land.

"Nobody guessed what would happen next," Emil recalled. "The Japanese knew they couldn't win, but they wanted to hurt us—bad."

And they did, firing on the U.S.S. Princeton, and igniting its torpedoes in fierce explosions. American Hellcats flew over in protective fire, but it was too late and the Princeton went down. The battle raged for three days. Allies ultimately pushed back the Japanese fleet, but not before a new and more terrifying tactic was revealed.

Kamikazes.

"It was at Leyte, toward the end of the war," Emil said, "when the Japanese started using their planes to crash into our ships and kill us. In a way, it made it easier for LST guns to hit them, because usually they were too high for our range. But that's pretty thin for good news."[151]

"Three planes attacked us, perhaps four," Commanding Officer G. K. Bradford recorded in the 478 ship's log. "Fighters and dive bombers . . . came in intermediate and fast. During the attack," he noted, "every gun on the ship fired—eighteen 20MMs, one 3"50", and five 40MMs," expending over 1,530 rounds of ammunition in two minutes. "The first plane was approximately 1000 yards distant when the first shot was fired," he recorded, adding that they hit their first plane just four seconds later.[152]

Emil and crew didn't suffer any kamikaze hits—this time at least—although seven personnel were noted in Bradford's report as receiving "superficial shrapnel wounds from a bomb burst close aboard to port."[153]

After a decisive victory at Leyte, the crew of the 478 spent the next three days unloading supplies before heading for their next location along the New Guineau coast. After that, Emil once again followed General MacArthur's path, this time to Australia.

"One of my friends was a captain of the LST 482," Emil said, "and he wanted me to go on shore leave with him to Australia. I was all for it, but by then I was Assistant Executive Officer, and my own captain wasn't too happy about my leaving for awhile."[154]

How did Emil solve this conundrum? "I wanted to do it fair and square," he said. "So I talked him into a hand of poker," he recalled with a laugh.

Needless to say, Emil went to Australia, a trip his CO described in official paperwork as "rehabilitation to be considered as temporary duty." When he and his friend arrived in Sydney, they once again lucked out. "Somehow we got ushered into a penthouse. It was a real zinger," Emil recalled of the luxurious suite General MacArthur had just vacated.[155]

8

"MILK RUN TO MINDORO" AND
EXECUTIVE OFFICER LOCKWOOD

The LST 478 made it back from New Guineau to Leyte Island on the tailwind of a typhoon, just in time to deliver a shipment of new equipment there for Christmas 1944. En route, Emil and his shipmates learned that kamikaze attacks had become a more frequent hazard in the Philippine Sea, even downing two LSTs less than ten days earlier.[156] Replacement Japanese pilots were young and inexperienced, and generally unable to hit targets effectively. They could, however, dive the planes into their targets, at the sacrifice of their own lives as well as the enemy's.

Mindoro Island, MacArthur and others knew, was not an important strategic acquisition, but its airfields would prove useful to the next invasion, and troops and supplies were needed there in order to launch the next offensive. When they observed increased traffic in the seas neighboring Mindoro, the Japanese responded by attacking and damaging many American ships.[157]

"By the time we got back to Leyte, though, we thought it had settled down," Emil said. Then he and his shipmates were scheduled for a routine operation to supply a temporary base at Mindoro, on the other side of the Philippines from Leyte.

"We called it a 'milk run'," Emil said, "because supposedly we had captured the Philippines, and by then ships had been going back and forth for a while. Still," he recalled, "the admirals didn't take any chances, and secret dispatches were flying left and right.[158] They needed a lot of soldiers and food supplies at Mindoro, so we loaded supplies and over 220 enlisted men into the hull, and made room in our quarters for 20-some of their officers. Then we were in a big flotilla with some other LSTs, and all of us were flanked by a couple of battleships. It seemed safe enough."[159]

Suddenly, Emil's LST and dozens more were shaken by deep sea mines exploding beneath their ships. "Well," he said, "I wasn't too worried," explaining that LSTs did carry defensive explosives beneath their hulls, but that the mines were planted too deep to either damage the ship directly, or ignite their own explosives. So, what does any self-respecting senior officer do at a time like this?

"I looked behind me," Emil said, "and I saw one of my men acting kind of worried. 'Why don't you get me some hot chocolate?' " Emil suggested to the somewhat bewildered seaman, instantly earning a reputation as a chocaholic with nerves of steel.[160]

So cheered at his boss's show of confidence, the subordinate—a petty officer in charge of rigging—lurched across the heaving deck to the galley, in a move that likely saved his life. As he returned with the hot chocolate, the quiet sky overhead thundered with enemy aircraft out of nowhere, and the LST 478 was riddled with rapid-fire shells. Suddenly a kamikaze plane spiraled in a roar onto the 478, splitting apart its deck where the petty officer had been standing.

"The force of it blew the bosun into me," Emil said, "and we were both knocked out of range. He was hurt, but not too bad, and we were on the guns in a flash," he said, "shooting every which way."[161]

"It was bad," Emil said, "explosions kept coming up from underneath. We found out later the Japanese had deployed mini-submarines, too. They let off bombs from about 40 to 80 feet below, but LSTs ride high when they're closer to shore, and we weren't hit. Then a kamikaze cartwheeled on a nearby ship and exploded," he recalled sadly of the escort carrier *Ommaney*. "We watched it go down."[162]

There were more, too. The final count in the Sulu Sea off Luzon Island in mid-January was 24 sunken ships, and 67 damaged, including LST 478.[163] "It went on and on," Emil said, "we threw barrel mines overboard, and we made it through, but barely."[164]

"We set up a smoke screen so the enemy couldn't see us," he said of the surviving ships, explaining that as a result the U.S. ships were also blinded. They crept out in single file, he explained, describing how each ship followed the ship immediately in front, due to the barely visible sight of the spray of water in its wake. "We called the sprays 'rooster tails'," Emil said. "A lot of us got out that way."[165]

Throughout his life, Emil's comments on most events—fortunate and unfortunate ones alike—were generally nonjudgmental. In this case, he broke his own unspoken rule.

"It was terrible," he said. End of conversation.

The Commanding Officer's description of Emil's performance at Mindoro was equally as brief. "His performance of duty under fire and air attacks was commendable," wrote CO Bradford, simultaneously recommending Emil for promotion to Executive Officer of LST 478.[166] How did a 25 year-old Lieutenant Junior Grade get promoted to the equivalent of Chief Operating Officer of a naval vessel? Even when asked if it might be attributed to skill and bravery, Emil had already retreated to his laconic brevity.

"I was the only officer left besides the CO," he said. "The others were either killed or had nervous breakdowns."[167]

Survivors notwithstanding, Emil and his shipmates still had a lot of work left between the Solomon and the Philippine islands, outfitting occupation troops while dodging deep-sea mines and low flying planes. Mercifully, they were somewhat off the beaten track in the West Melanesian Trench on Manus Island, when U.S. Marines stormed Iwo Jima. And they were loading cargo in the Florida Islands in the Solomons when American planes bombed Tokyo on the mainland of Japan. But when battle plans came for the early April assault on Okinawa, the LST 478 was once again in the thick of it.[168]

"L" FOR "LOVE" OF LIBERTY

Due south of Japan, the tonnage and manpower called in for the Okinawa campaign exceeded by far the amount used in the Normandy invasion. Allies called it the most ambitious amphibious operation yet undertaken by the Americans.[169]

The LST 478 left the Solomon Islands on March 15, setting course for the Ulithi Atoll southeast of Okinawa, where it would await the call to battle. Kamikaze attacks threatened from the north, south and west. Combined Army-Navy fighting forces totaled 180,000 troops, with three more divisions in reserve and another 115,000 supporting troops aboard Landing Craft Infantry Ships (LCIs), sister ships to the LSTs and other amphibious innovations designed by the Americans. The total fleet of aircraft carriers, battleships, destroyers, transports and landing ships, of which the LST 478 was part, numbered about thirteen hundred. Easter Sunday—April 1, 1945—was designated as "L-Day," the Pacific Fleet's counterpoint to D-Day in the Atlantic.[170]

"L," for "LOVE" of liberty, Emil liked to recall.

Resistance on land was minimal. The LST 478 beached on April 6 at Green Beach #2 to disembark the 71st Naval Construction Battalion.[171] Then over 700 Japanese planes unleashed their fire on the American fleet still out to sea. Of these, 355 were kamikazes, each determined to sink a Yankee ship. Other LSTs and transport and cargo vessels stationed themselves offshore, to release a continual flow of men and supplies onto the beach. American battleships roamed the shoreline firing to protect the landing forces. Instead of immediately targeting the battleships, however, Japanese subs and planes attacked the outer rim of the circle, and worked inward. Bombs, torpedoes and exploding suicide planes demolished five American destroyers and three other ships.[172]

"An LST went down that day,"[173] Emil said. "We took a lot of fire, too, but we gave as good as we got."

Pacific Fleet headquartered at Pearl Harbor and surrounding islands, where Landing Ship Tanks were repaired between assignments. Hawaiian Islands, 1945.

Elaborate LST pump system pulled in water when out to sea (for stability and depth), and pumped it out for shallow beachfront landings. Pearl Harbor (HI), 1945.

As the carnage raged, the 478 was badly damaged. But not before Emil was deemed "mentally, morally and professionally qualified" for another promotion. He was nominated on April 8 to serve as a commanding officer of a new LST.[174] The next day depth charges hit the LST 478 off the starboard bow, and on the 17th it was sent back to Pearl Harbor for considerable repairs.[175] The welcome news, that Okinawa had been secured on June 21, reached Emil and others while they were en route back to base. They knew that Okinawa would serve as a final springboard for the invasion of Japan,[176] fully expecting they would be patched up enough by then to participate.

"We had less than two weeks for repairs," Emil said, "before we were loading amphibious trailers and transporting them to the Mariana Islands. So some things didn't get fixed. When we got to Saipan, we had to repair the bow anchor chain while we were unloading. Then we brought Navy and Army troops on board, to take them to the Marshall Islands. In between every run," he recalled, "we repaired what we could, and we held drills and emergency exercises while we were underway, thinking our next assignment would be Okinawa. By the time we got back to Pearl Harbor again to reload, though, things had changed."[177]

On August 6 and 9 the U.S. exploded atomic bombs over Hiroshima and Nagasaki. In the sudden wake of the bombing's horrific results, shocked and traumatized troops everywhere suddenly realized that the Pacific war had ended. The Pacific Theater, it seemed, would not be needing another LST.

9

SEMI-CIVILIAN AND SEMI-SENIOR-ACCOUNTANT LOCKWOOD

In late August 1945, Emil saw a heavily marked map taped to the kitchen wall in Jane's San Francisco apartment. He immediately recognized all the locations of the Pacific Fleet's campaign that he had written to her about after each battle's end. "I wrote after we left an area," he said of the war's protocol of confidentiality, "and then she wrote back that she prayed for me every inch of the way." Emil believed it, seeing the map, and knowing Jane's strong-willed character and her Christian Science faith.

But the war had tried Jane's faith in ways previously unimagined. She grappled with painful images of the wounded and dying, including— potentially—her dashing young officer husband. Frightening outcomes not-withstanding, she confirmed her commitment to the noninterventionist medical approach of her religion. When dating and first married, it wasn't a problem for Emil, who didn't cotton much to doctors anyway. Later, how-ever, as a surviving veteran and young father, it would become an unanticipated and unwelcome controlling factor. A factor that would eventu-ally cost Jane her life.[178]

Oblivious to the future and euphorically reunited, however, the Lock-woods started their new life together. Emil's post-war orders sent him to the Navy V-12 Unit at Westminister College in Fulton, Missouri. There he taught amphibious warfare and seamanship, augmenting the syllabus with dynamic real-life examples from his own experiences in signature battles of World War II. Ironically, the paperwork for his next promotion just caught up with him as Emil was released to inactive duty in November 1945.

Jane was still teaching in a public school nearby. Resourceful as ever, the newly promoted Lieutenant Senior Grade uncovered an opportunity to put into practice an unusual skill he had learned at Starved Rock Park. He signed on through the end of the academic year as athletic director at Missouri School for the Deaf, where he coached football with the visual signs he had learned years earlier from his friend Carter Hale.

"We didn't win any games," Emil recalled, "but we had a lot of fun."

By now the Lockwoods were pregnant, and Emil knew it was time to complete his M.B.A. studies at U of M and get on with his career. He and Jane settled in Brooklyn, Michigan within reasonable reach of U of M in Ann Arbor, and an accounting job Emil had targeted in Adrian. Their son, Eric Achard Lockwood, was born in July 1946.

Emil completes MBA classes in U of M's first skyscraper, then dashes to accounting night job at university hospital. Ann Arbor (MI), 1947. *Photo #2298 courtesy of Bentley Historical Library, University of Michigan.*

Emil joined Root and Nocolai Accounting Firm in Adrian, signing on in November for a job that dubbed him a "semi-senior accountant." He worked for $45 a week for three years, completing the necessary apprenticeship to comply with requirements to earn his C.P.A. license. At the same time, Emil completed course work at the University of Michigan. He commuted between his day job at Root and Nocolai, and his night job in accounting at the university hospital, somehow keeping his head above water.

Unbeknownst to Emil, however, he was not really a civilian yet. An accounting fluke in his records revealed that he was indentured to something else besides his demanding schedule and his new family. He owed 90 days of military service, the Navy informed him, before he could collect his Mustering Out Pay and effectively revert to reserve status. What was a young enterprising father to do? Why, coordinate his military requirements so he could satisfy them locally, of course.

Emil quickly devised a plan with his brother Jim, a Navy pilot also home from the war. His brother's Beachcraft Bonanza plane would provide the vehicle, and his brother the instruction, for Emil's newest credential. His pilot's license, he explained to Navy officials, would further enhance the skills he offered to the service, and he would complete the necessary training hours as part of his 90 day obligation. They bit, of course, and Emil got his pilot's license over the next three months, in his "spare time."[179]

"I didn't see much of the library that time either," said Emil of his 1947 Masters Degree in Business Administration. "I did my studying and assignments in short breaks whenever I could."[180] Within three years he rose to senior accountant and partner at Root, Nicolai and Lockwood, co-founded

Bradley-Lockwood Builders, set himself up in farming at his new home in nearby Cambridge Junction on Washington Lake, and managed all three businesses without missing a beat.

NEW BRANCHES ON THE FAMILY TREE, AND NEW VISTAS

Emil attended the Builders and Traders Exchange in Detroit, to gain some insight into his construction business, the Bradley-Lockwood Builders, which he had set up with a friend in Adrian, Michigan. "Bradley knew the building end of things," Emil said, recalling his days as vice president of the general contracting firm, "and I was good at the numbers." Together, in moves reminiscent of both of Emil's grandfathers, the two built a school in South Lyons, a church in Monroe, and many other buildings in the area. When, however, his partner wanted to bid $2.5 million for a job that Emil knew would take $4 million to do, Emil signed over his share of the business without rancor or hesitation.

"I knew he'd fizzle," Emil said, "and he did, but I got out in plenty of time."[181]

Emil stayed in just long enough, he recalled, to complete the construction of his new home in Cambridge Junction just outside Brooklyn, Michigan.

"It was a great place designed by an architect at U of M," his son Eric recalled, "a unique tri-story with floor-to-ceilings windows overlooking a deck and a small lake."[182]

While maintaining his partnership at Root, Nocolai & Lockwood C.P.A. Firm, and raising Shropshire and Hampshire sheep on his back-forty, Emil picked up a job teaching accounting for a semester at Adrian College to take up any slack in the family budget. He also maintained his position as Secretary to the Southern Michigan Contractors Association and Secretary-Treasurer for the Angle Engineering Sales Corporation, a business affiliated with Bradley-Lockwood. He still remembered making time for his son, however. When Eric was 6-7 years old, Emil recalled, "I bought a jeep and we used to drive around our 80 acres together, 'surveying the kingdom'."[183]

At the same time, Emil and Jane were both very sociable, and frequently hosted family and friends at their Cambridge Junction showplace. Emil's father, Clare, visited on occasion, and Eric recalled one of his frequent assignments as a child, to carry "grandpa's water"[184] to the aging Lockwood who never seemed able to quench his thirst. Local society pages on July 20, 1952 reported the idyllic annual Optimist Club picnic held for its 75 members by "Mr. and Mrs. Lockwood at their country home on Washington Lake."[185]

Emil (top center) spends Christmas with family. Left to right: mother Mabel, sister-in- law Ruth (Jim's first wife), niece Lynn, son Eric, wife Jane, and father Clare. Adrian (MI), 1950.

WW II veteran turned father— Emil, now "Semi-Senior Accountant" at Root & Nicolai Accounting, holds infant son Eric after Tour of Active Duty. Adrian (MI), 1946.

CPA multiplies more than numbers—daughters Lori (left) and Lorette after romp in snow with Dad, now a volunteer on local school board and a Gratiot County Board of Supervisor. St. Louis (MI), 1957.

All fingers and toes accounted for by owner of Yeo & Yeo CPA firm, Emil holds daughter Lori, in second marriage (Mariella Coffey Lockwood). St. Louis (MI), 1954.

Herd of 70 Shropshire and Hampshire sheep kept Emil busy at his Cambridge Junction farm, between CPA job and teaching at Adrian College. Brooklyn (MI), 1946.

All was not idyllic or optimistic, however, behind closed doors.

"I came home from work one day," Emil recalled, "and I saw our dog lying in a pool of blood on the road by the house." Concerned that his son would see the horrific sight, Emil called for Jane and learned how the dog was killed by a truck. "I wanted to move it, of course," he said, "but she said not to, that if we prayed the dog might rise again. I realized then, that things had gone too far." Recalling other incidents, and confronting Jane, Emil saw the handwriting on the wall. "She wouldn't change, and even brought the church fathers out to the house to defend her. Healthy living and praying is one thing," Emil said, shaking his head, "but not attending to the bleeding and the dead—." With painful flashbacks of the many fast-firing traumas of his wartime experience, he finally gave Jane an ultimatum. Either she would change her approach within four months, or they would separate.

It was a tough year for the Emil Lockwood family. Jane did not relent, and Emil saw no recourse but to separate. He was deeply conflicted about divorcing her and leaving his son, hoping that she might yet come around, after some time alone. He resigned from the Naval Reserves and his board positions, because of time and geographic constraints, and moved alone to Alma, Michigan. There he set up the Emil Lockwood C.P.A. Firm, and worked for a few clients alongside his brother Jim—an arrangement that he hoped might be temporary.

Jane stood firm, however, and a reconciliation was not in the cards. In the mores of the time, Emil knew Jane would maintain custody of their son, and after their divorce he reconciled himself to the single life once again. He took on some partners in Alma, renamed his company to Yeo and Yeo C.P.A. Firm, and relocated it to nearby St. Louis, Michigan.

St. Louis may have been in the exact center of Michigan's Lower Peninsula, according to its city fathers, but Emil did not delude himself that it was the center of the universe. In typical Lockwood fashion, he threw himself into putting his business on the map, with time left over to spare. Late in 1953, Emil began seeing Mariella Coffey, and by 1954, they had married and given birth in September to his second child, their daughter Lori, followed in 1955 by the birth of their daughter Lorette. During this time he made sure to find time for his son Eric, who remembered going on excursions with his dad and new stepsisters and their dog named Sputnik.[186]

Inevitably, in a dapper salute to his ancestral family tree, Emil's boundless energy spilled into the public service arena, as he was elected to volunteer positions on the local school board, the Gratiot County Board of Supervisors, and served as the President of the St. Louis Rotary Club. He managed the Gratiot County campaigns for G.O.P. gubernatorial candidates Albert Cobo and Paul Bagwell, and Jim Harvey's U.S. congressional campaign in Michigan's 25th district. Filled with conviction at the need to revise the Michigan Constitution, he ran for the Republican party nomination for "Con-Con," the Michigan Constitutional Convention. Defeated but not daunted, Emil decided to kick back awhile.

It was the summer of 1961, and the President of the Rotary was expecting a foreign exchange student.

THE BELGIAN CONNECTION

"We arrived in New York," the now president and CEO of VG Airlines recalled many years later, "and were given our location assignments for the summer. I was happy to see on my Greyhound Bus ticket that I was going to St. Louis, as we had studied American geography carefully. We had been up all night, and I didn't notice," Freddy Van Gaever added, "that it said St. Louis, *Michigan*."

As his bus pulled out of the station early in the day, and headed for points west, several other of the teenaged exchange students chattered on excitedly, as it appeared that Freddy was going to the biggest city among their group. They watched road signs eagerly, noting city names on their maps as they followed the progress of the bus.

"At some point my friends transferred to other busses, and my own bus turned north," Van Gaever said laughing. "It passed cities named Lansing and St. Johns, and I wondered if there could be another St. Louis," but he checked his map printed in Belgium and found nothing. "Here's your stop," the bus driver told him, as they pulled up to an outpost in Alma.[187]

"There must be a mistake," Freddy told the driver, who shook his head and pointed to the group awaiting him.

He saw three men outside—Tom Cavanaugh, Larry Zoppa, and Emil Lockwood. "They all spoke very quickly, in a new kind of English from what I had heard in Belgium," said Freddy, who ultimately went home with Emil. It was midnight, and Freddy had been traveling for 36 hours, but when "Emil pushed on a little box and a huge garage door opened itself on Emil's instructions from his car," Freddy went inside and wrote to his family immediately about it. By the time he mailed the letter the next morning, he had added other marvels about a beautiful heated swimming pool, and a "garbage disposer in the kitchen whereby leftovers, peels, egg shells, and more, disappeared in seconds via the sewer."

"I loved their house from day one," Freddy said, "and Emil was so friendly and exuberant."[188]

Emil took Freddy to client meetings and social events alike, over the course of the summer. He also brought him to local and area Rotary meetings, Freddy recalled, getting him on the program as a speaker about "Belgium: My Country." In the evenings, the two would talk up a storm about world problems—poverty, war, bureaucracy, religion—and still have time for a game of cards. "We played Little Casino," Freddy recalled. "It was a pleasant enough game if you knew which cards had already been played, which Emil always did."

It was during one of these evenings that Freddy became party to some insider knowledge on Emil Lockwood's thoughts about his future.[189] Coincidental—or no accident?—that Emil chose to confide in a young man who would soon be whisked out of the country, leaving it to Emil's own compatriots to come to him and press the issue.

PART THREE

Emil Makes His Mark on the State Capitol

1962 – 1971

10

EMIL DRAFTED FOR STATE SENATE

From a bird's eye view of Emil's adult life so far, at 42 years old, he had paid his dues. He had survived seven invasions in the Pacific Theater as a naval officer. He had married Jane, then Mariella, and fathered three children. He had taken successful turns as athletic director, insurance business owner, real estate developer, owner of his own C.P.A. firm, and attracted favorable attention as a member of the Gratiot County Board of Supervisors, the St. Louis School Board, and several civic and fraternal organizations.[190] You might assume that Emil would, as in many career profiles of successful entrepreneurs, seize the opportunity to reap the rewards of his hard work, and make serious money. Anyone who assumes this about Emil is seriously mistaken.

Emil whet his whistle in local politics by chairing county campaigns for two G.O.P. gubernatorial hopefuls. He also served on the elected County Board of Supervisors, and took a shot at running for local delegate to the Michigan Constitutional Convention. But he had to be persuaded by a group of Gratiot County power-brokers to run for the State Senate.

In early 1962, a group of eight prominent men met several times to map out a strategy to elect a State Senator from Gratiot County, which had not fostered one in over 20 years. During that period, each of the three other counties comprising the 25th Senate District—Ionia, Mecosta, and Montcalm—had all been represented by a Senator who lived in that county. Since two-term incumbent, Senator John Stahlin (R-Belding), had announced his bid for Lieutenant Governor, and the district remained safely Republican, now was the time for Gratiot County voters to elect a replacement from their own county.[191]

Over the course of these meetings, one by one the participants found excuses for not running for Senator themselves. One day they put Emil in their crosshairs. "Why don't you run, Emil ?" they asked. "You're a decorated veteran, you're an M.B.A., and a C.P.A. You've held local offices, and you know practically everybody."

Timing is everything, Emil thought, recalling his musings with Freddy the previous summer. After spending 11 years building his C.P.A. firm and dabbling in insurance and real estate, Emil sensed a unique opportunity. So, he shrewdly answered: "I'll run for the Senate on one condition—that all of you pledge your full support to me, and only me, in this race. That means in fund-raising as well as endorsements." They agreed, and Emil's career in state politics was born.

"It's not like I had planned all this out—I mean, to purposely play hard to get, and end up getting drafted to run for state office," Emil remembered. "It was just the right time. And, I didn't run for the Senate because I had some overwhelming selfish desire to make my mark on the State Capitol. The truth be known, I had gotten a bit tired of the C.P.A. business. So when I saw all these guys—mind you, there was the head of the big refinery, a bank president, a mayor, and other big shots there—when they all promised to go full bore for me, I couldn't turn them down."[192]

EMIL'S FIRST SENATE PRIMARY

Emil knew what faced him. His home county of Gratiot was his only political base of support, and it couldn't even boast the 25th District's largest population. In fact, it barely qualified for second place. Ionia County actually held the largest number of people: 43,132. Gratiot came next at 37,012. Montcalm placed third with 35,795, while Mecosta brought up the rear with 21,051.[193] This meant that Emil would be competing against fellow Republicans from these other counties, with each of them trying to corral votes in their own home counties. At the same time, his own home county comprised only 27% of the district's population.

Moreover, as he formally announced his candidacy on March 8, 1962, he was acutely aware of his strong opponents in the August 7 primary. He would face the secretary-manager of the perennially popular Ionia Free Fair, a prominent citizen of the 25th District by the name of Allan M. Williams. Also on deck were William G. Gover of Sheridan (Montcalm County), and Carl Geiger, a well-construction contractor from Belding, also located in Ionia County.[194]

Emil knew he had to win big in his home county, hope that the two candidates from Ionia County split the vote there, and place a strong second or third in Montcalm and Mecosta. There was only one sure way to gain visibility with voters in those other counties—he had to take the "Lockwood for Senate" show on the road.

Newspapers throughout the four counties carried the announcement of Emil's candidacy for the 25th Senate district. The accompanying photographs showed a serious, congenial 42 year-old businessman who surely appeared up to the job of representing the district. The articles, no doubt gleaned mainly from the formal written announcement, stressed his strong financial education, his successful business ventures, and his wide-ranging community leadership in such activities as the County Board of Supervisors, St. Louis School Board, St. Louis Rotary Club, Elks Lodge, VFW, and the Episcopal Church.

Emil began making the pitch to Gratiot County voters that they had not elected a State Senator from that county in over twenty years. This became a rallying cry he would use in his home county loudly and often, because he knew he couldn't win without a runaway majority vote in his own backyard.[195]

CPA/Contractor/builder Emil (2nd left) inaugurates Westgate Park Subdivision, along Pine River. In *Clarksville Record* with others, including Al Fortino (far right). St. Louis (MI), 1962.

Emil wouldn't own up to any such moniker as "political natural," but it is just that label that comes to mind when the story unfolds of his first campaign for state office, and his adroit entrance as a greenhorn into the august ranks of the Michigan Senate. He used all the conventional campaign tools, of course, such as lawn signs, brochures, bumper stickers, receptions, debates, local community appearances, neighborhood get-togethers, and prominent endorsements. His family assisted where possible, too, as evidenced by the newspaper photograph with his towheaded daughter, Lori, unloading posters from the family pickup, to distribute in schools before PTA meetings. But he knew he had to do more to stand out from the crowd.

So, Emil came up with an original idea. How about gathering copies of all his opponents' nominating petitions, sending a letter to each of the citizens who signed them, noting his opponents' constructive participation in the political process, and asking anyway for the signators' votes? It was controversial, and it was legal. Emil remarked, in retrospect, that "anybody in his right mind could have thought of that."

But, of course, no one else did. His opponents, as one might expect, made a beeline to the newspapers crying, "Foul." The press prominently mentioned the dust-up, noting that the technique was legal, and defending Emil's right to do so. First round to Emil.[196]

Since the key to winning the primary lay in capturing a huge majority in Gratiot County, it was time to start picking up chits from his original backers. Emil rightly treated the primary as a general election, amassing a formidable war chest, galvanizing volunteer campaign workers, and appearing at every gathering (it seems, at least) of four or more people in his county, and carefully targeting larger events in the other three.

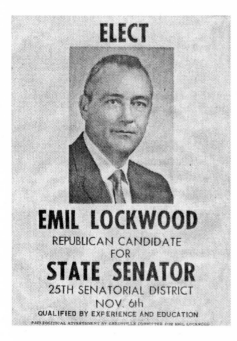

ELECT

EMIL LOCKWOOD

REPUBLICAN CANDIDATE
FOR

STATE SENATOR

25TH SENATORIAL DISTRICT
NOV. 6th
QUALIFIED BY EXPERIENCE AND EDUCATION

PAID POLITICAL ADVERTISEMENT BY GREENVILLE COMMITTEE FOR EMIL LOCKWOOD

Campaign poster for 25th district Republican senatorial candidate Lockwood. St. Louis (MI), 1962.

"Campaigning is 90% common sense," Emil noted with characteristic self-deprecation when asked where he learned how to campaign so effectively.[197] Altogether, Emil made a lot of waves, and the results of the August 7 election, buoyed by numerous contested Republican primaries in Gratiot County, amply demonstrated the effectiveness of the newly-minted candidate's campaign strategy.

Emil's hometown newspaper headlined the victory: "Lockwood Scored An Easy Victory," and noted that "the home folks did it for Emil Lockwood." Emil's vote from Gratiot County totaled nearly three times that of the other three candidates combined, while he placed second in Mecosta, and third in Ionia and Montcalm. The strategy had worked like a charm. His local newspaper described the winning nominee as "a warm type of man who has built a large accounting firm . . . [and] speaks with earnest conviction."[198]

Emil's Democratic opponent in the general election would be William H. Noud, of Morley. Since past election results virtually assured a Republican victory in November, Emil realized that the purpose of the next 90 days would be to consolidate his support among Republicans throughout the four counties. After all, the next election for Senate rolled around in just two years, since the new state Constitution didn't mandate four-year Senate terms until 1966.

Her father's daughter—7 year-old Lori Lockwood helps Republican senatorial candidate Dad mail campaign posters. *Daily Record Leader*, July 26, 1962.

GENERAL ELECTION CAMPAIGN, LOCKWOOD STYLE

Now came the fun. Emil attacked the general election like a shrewd general planning a battle. He set out to become the legitimate legislative representative of all four counties of the 25th District, not just his own. He knew all too well that the momentum he had just gained in the primary came from Gratiot County citizens who recruited and supported him, based on the premise that their county had lacked true representation in the state Senate for over 20 years. Future opponents from other counties were likely to pull off a similar tactic in future elections. To blunt such criticisms in neighboring counties in the future, he knew that he must position himself early as their go-to-guy.

But first Emil had to follow ritual and tradition, a maxim that he soon learned is very often the case in state politics. It meant going off to the annual Governor's Day at the Ionia Free Fair just one day after the primary to hobnob with newly nominated candidates for statewide office, other nominees from Ionia and surrounding areas, as well as a Who's Who of local business and agriculture.

The 1962 Ionia Free Fair ranked as more exciting than usual, because George Romney, the charismatic leader behind the recent successful Constitutional Convention, had just won the G.O.P. nomination for Governor. In the process, Romney had dramatically thrown down the gauntlet to incumbent John Swainson, attempting to end a seven-term hold on the Governor's office by Democrats. Emil was introduced to the large luncheon crowd along with the other candidates, and later met the impressive, square-jawed, gray-haired man who would soon become his party leader, and friend, George Romney.

The editor of the *St. Louis Leader-Press*, who attended Governor's Day for the first time, had some choice observations about the event that only a seasoned small town editor would likely make public. His first observation: "If all the energy in shaking hands was harnessed, the mountain could move not only to Mohammed but almost any place." He went on to opine that "America has in my opinion about 10 good speakers. I can tell where all ten weren't Wednesday afternoon."

Nevertheless, the crusty editor did have some good things to say about Emil: "In our home area there should be joy over nomination of Emil Lockwood to the State Senate. He has the traits and qualifications to do a good job and with his accounting background he can contribute knowledge in the field of taxation. The smashing support he got in his home county of Gratiot was a sign of the rating he has with his neighbors."[199] A brand new entrant into state politics couldn't hope for a better endorsement than that from a skeptical local editor.

Next came the real action. Emil obtained a list of all state institutions in

Michigan, and set out to visit as many as he could. During the coming weeks of the campaign, he would visit more than a dozen, noting later to the *Kalamazoo Gazette* that, all told, he logged 25,000 miles over the course of the long campaign.[200]

His first stop was the State Reformatory in Ionia. He told the St. Louis Lions Club later that he discovered there are six guard towers, but only one guard, because the Michigan Legislature had not appropriated enough funds. Will he, as Senator, help the institution get more state money? Not necessarily, he told the crowd. First off, he will find out whether they need those five other towers, instead of five more guards.

Emil's next stop, he continued telling the Lions Club, was the Southern Michigan Prison located in Jackson. There, an old-time guard commented on the state of affairs from his viewpoint: "These head shrinkers [psychiatrists] cost the state a lot of money and they don't do anything that someone with plain good sense couldn't do, and [they] make a lot of mistakes that someone with good sense wouldn't make." Emil vowed to look into that one too.[201] He was on a roll. The crowd loved him.

Emil was fond of telling campaign crowds that the funniest thing that happened to him early in his campaign came one day when he was handing out plastic bottle caps inscribed with "Vote for Lockwood." The caps were designed to keep the fizz in a bottle of pop once it was opened. He offered one to a lady on the street in Ionia one day. She shrank away with abhorrence. "But lady," he said, "they are only to save [the] part of the bottle you can't drink right now." She knew, however, the insidious ways of sin. "Today a bottle of pop," she said, "tomorrow a bottle of beer, the next day a bottle of whiskey——oh no!" Emil said that the lady's leveling guilt by association at him "is worse than being called a communist because once you knew a Russian."[202]

The new Senatorial candidate hatched another novel idea to gain attention and forge new friendships throughout the 25th District's four counties. Instead of merely manning a star-spangled booth at each of their County fairs and shaking a lot of hands like all the other political hopefuls, why not make a splash by showing up at the highly popular animal judging and auctions? Oh yes, and buying the prize animal to boot?

Emil remembered that he did get a lot of attention from the proud farmers, and a lot of good will too. He ended up with a few prize steers, but especially recalled the near perfect pig he bid for and won at the Mecosta County Fair. "The Lockwood family ate prime pork and beef to their heart's content for a long time after that," he said.[203]

When Emil appeared at special rallies in some of the towns, he brought guaranteed excitement with him. "I had four or five guys with me who could kick up a storm," according to Emil's recollection. "They all played different musical instruments. The piano player—he was always near the stage where I gave my speeches. And he was surrounded by the sax player and the other guys who were tootin' and bangin' away. I guess when we left, almost everybody knew we had been there."[204] For a beginner, as he surely was in 1962, Emil showed he had the right touch.

The hottest issue on the campaign trail in 1962 was state fiscal reform, a subject that had long dominated the Capitol's news from Lansing. Six-term Governor "Soapy" Williams and his successor, Governor John Swainson, both Democrats, had been fighting over state finances with the Republican-controlled legislature for years. The nationwide publicity received by Michigan over its infamous "payless paydays" for state employees in 1959 still left a bad taste in voters' mouths. Because of the fiscal stand-off, and the dreary nature of the state's finances, prospects for a state income tax had become a lightning rod for prospective legislators on the campaign trail.

Emil's extensive business and accounting background, of course, made him the perfect candidate for the times. While he called repeatedly for fiscal reform throughout his travels during the fall campaign, he carefully avoided an outright endorsement of any particular scheme, including a state income tax. He only went as far as telling audiences that "the need for tax reform and revenue sources are inevitable," and, therefore, "the state income tax would appear to be the most logical solution."[205]

He learned firsthand on the campaign trail the explosive nature of the tax reform issue, a lesson that would serve him well as he rose to leadership in the Senate.

EMIL WINS HIS FIRST SENATE SEAT

As predicted, Emil trounced his Democratic opponent, William Noud, almost two to one in the November general election.[206] The headline grabber of the fall election statewide, however, was political newcomer George Romney's defeat of Democratic incumbent John Swainson, in an election in which Democrats swept all the other statewide offices. Romney's vote plurality only totaled 80,573, but that was enough. Along with his recent championing of Michigan's new Constitution, it propelled him into the national limelight of potential presidential candidates.[207]

The fact that this well-regarded former savior of American Motors—a moderate, practical Republican—occupied the Governor's bully pulpit at the time of looming fiscal disaster, accomplished something else, too. It set the stage for the new moderate Senator from St. Louis, a man with a business background himself, to rise quickly in the Senate ranks. During the next six years, Emil would become an indispensable ally, and more often than not, the popular Governor's legislative "field marshal," as Michigan faced such

widely diverse issues as tax policies, civil rights, race riots, auto-safety legislation, teachers' salary disputes, and labor problems.[208] But first the neophyte
Senator had to, as they used to say at the State Capitol, "find his way to the
men's room."

KALAMAZOO GAZETTE, MONDAY, DECEMBER 3, 1962.

**New Sen. Lockwood Working Now
On Duties He'll Assume January 1**

By CHARLES BARMON
Gazette Lansing Bureau

FRESHMAN SENATOR EMIL LOCKWOOD ALREADY BUSY
He'll Take Office on Jan. 1

**Freshmen Senator Lockwood anticipates start
date,** touring dozen-plus state facilities after driving
25,000 miles in his district's five counties during campaign. *Kalamazoo Gazette*, December 3, 1962.

Prior to setting up base in
Lansing, Emil took care of
business at home. His C.P.A.
firm had flourished over the
past many years, but he clearly
could not own the firm and do
justice to his new Senate post
at the same time. So, he sold
it, with one important provision: He would take payments
of one tenth of the firm's revenue for five years. This would
help support his family while
he pursued public service.[209] It
was an arrangement that Emil
would renew in 1967, due
mainly to the fact that the
firm's principals wanted to
keep Emil from ginning up a
new firm of his own.

Just as he had not taken anything for granted in the general election, Emil
took seriously the need to learn the ropes as a new Senator serving under the
Capitol dome in Lansing. "I have a lot to learn," he told the *Kalamazoo Gazette* in December after the election. That's
why he had burned the rubber visiting a
dozen state institutions, attended a major
highway study report conference, participated
in the orientation for new legislators, set up
an office in his district, and met with William
Seidman, interim financial advisor to the
Governor, to help prepare the state budget for
the following fiscal year.[210] And that was
only just the beginning.

Emil had already made up his mind about
which committees he wanted to serve on.

Mr. Lockwood goes to Lansing—newly elected Senator poses at Capitol by Gov. Austin Blair (1861-1864)
statue. Lansing (MI), 1963. *Family album, newspaper
unknown.*

Republicans still controlled the Senate, so even though he could not expect a chairmanship as a freshman, he realized that placement on powerful committees would allow him to contribute more, serve his district better, and give him more clout with fellow Senators. What could such plum committees be? Where the money is, of course: the Appropriations, and Taxation Committees. Had any other first-term Senator ever been named to either of these committees, let alone both of them? No. But that fact did not deter Emil.

Emil entered the Senate as one of eight new members, out of 34 total, representing a significant turnover. Party-wise, Republicans controlled the chamber by a whopping 23-11. Of the freshmen, five were Republican and mostly moderates to boot. These mavericks, as some of the old guard called them, were studiously advised by veteran moderates. Adding to their influence in the Senate was the fact that Romney, himself a moderate Republican, had chided the old guard during his campaign. This resulted in some of them losing their bid for re-election.

Mr. Lockwood goes to Washington—Sen. and Mrs. (Mariella) Lockwood with 8th District Congressman Jim Harvey, for whom Emil managed Gratiot County campaign. Washington DC, 1963.

Emil sensed this power shift early on, but shrewdly initiated dialogue with both sides. He made a genuine attempt to see the ramifications of both old guard and maverick arguments, and that's why "both sides trusted him," according to former Senator (and former Majority Leader) Robert Vander Laan, who also entered the Senate that year. Decades later Vander Laan still recalled Emil's ability to establish rapport with Senators of all philosophical persuasions, and noted that "he didn't choose sides ideologically." This, of course, helped Emil get named to the powerful committees he desired, and allowed him—also remarkably for a first-termer—to help engineer Senator Stanley Thayer's election as Majority Leader.[211]

Emil didn't much like labels, at least for his own political philosophy. In later times he just remarked that he "only wanted to get things done." He remembered that the G.O.P. freshmen Senators that year were called "newbies" by some. Emil asked them to get together for a meeting, so they could agree among themselves which committee assignments each wanted. If they could pull this off, he prompted them, they wouldn't have to compete against each other, and could therefore represent a united front to the Senate leadership. Emil kept his own choices pretty close to the vest at first.

With a little discussion about the pros and cons of each committee, one by one the new members decided. It seemed only natural in the end that with his M.B.A. degree, his C.P.A. and business background, Emil should try for Appropriations and Taxation. He did, of course, gladly.[212] After all, he had been the man with a plan.

EMIL GOES TO WORK IN THE SENATE

Ferris Institute becomes college—Gov. Romney signs bill Emil (right) introduced; college president Victor F. Spathelf (left) and fellow legislator. Cover photo, *Ferris Expositor*, May 17, 1963.

Somewhere in the midst of the holiday season, the official swearing in ceremony, and politicking for key committee assignments, Emil had three bills readied for introduction. His first, of no great significance in itself, tipped his hand that he believed ordinary constituents back home always deserved a front row seat. The bill proposed that backgrounds on all highway signs be the same color. Its aim?

"Some road signs were stacked up like old grocery store ads," Emil recalled. "I thought it should be easier for drivers to figure out where they're going, especially at confusing intersections."

The second bill Emil introduced was aimed at a more elite but no less important constituency—the president, faculty, students and parents of an important institution of higher learning, Ferris Institute, located in Big Rapids. The measure intended to broaden the Institute's appeal by renaming it Ferris State College. For his third bill, the new Senator exhibited his C.P.A. background by proposing a uniform pro-ration of taxes on the sale of real estate.[213] Throughout the next eight years of his Senate career, Emil would champion scores of bills, many of historical import. But for the first few months, at least, he knew it was most important to focus on his district's needs first.

The ensuing months saw a very busy, productively engaged freshman, learning the ropes and trying to make an impact. His assignments to the Taxation and Liquor Control Committees, as well as Appropriations (and its penal institution sub-committee), kept him jumping. And, frequent trips back to his four-county district kept him driving to attend events. In addition, legislative general sessions and committee meetings most weekdays, as well as innumerable Lansing-based events, required his presence. All of this hubbub, however, didn't prevent Emil from getting the jump on the new Governor.

11

EMIL UPSTAGES NEW GOVERNOR

Romney's principal issue during his recent election campaign had been the urgent need for fiscal reform. He had been meeting since June 1963 with business men, labor leaders, educators and citizens' groups in an effort to gain ideas about what kind of an income tax could best help the state regain its fiscal footing. He convened a meeting of 20 G.O.P. legislative leaders at the Governor's mansion on Mackinac Island on August 8, after the Legislature had adjourned for the year. His aim was to find out first hand from them what kind of a package could garner enough votes to pass a new income tax into law.[214]

Bud Vestal, a veteran Capitol correspondent representing Booth Newspapers, described the meeting as resembling a "summit conference about nuclear weapons . . . [where] nobody wanted to mention anything specific for fear the whole thing might blow up." Romney was telling the press that while he planned that very day to tell the attending legislators what in general he wanted to propose, he would not go into detail until he delivered his opening address to the special session of the legislature he had called for September 11. But Emil, combining the brashness of a freshman lawmaker with the eagerness of a man who likes to get things done "yesterday," had cooked up his own tax reform proposal with fellow G.O.P. freshman Garry Brown. They announced to the press the same day that they intended to introduce a two-bill package on their own.[215]

This stunt surely got the discussion going fast and furiously at an event that was designed to show a harmonious front of Republican support for tax reform. Romney expressed some surprise when asked by the news media about the Lockwood-Brown proposal, answering rather coolly that they had not discussed their plan with him. Senator Clyde Geerlings of Holland was also upstaged by the maneuver, and told Vestal (erroneously) that "they are talking about a 5% income tax, and that's too high."

Emil did cover his political backside, however, by showing the plan beforehand to Senator Stanley Thayer, the Senate Majority Leader, who told the press that he not only was familiar with the Lockwood-Brown program, but that "it certainly merits our consideration—I think it has possibilities."[216] The new Senator had learned early that one important role of the caucus leader is to

Seasoned Senators reminisce on rookie days—Emil (left) with Garry Brown (R-Schoolcraft), years after they designed and championed multi-year statewide tax reform effort, upstaging Gov. Romney. Lansing (MI), 1968.

make sure the train never jumps the track.

It was Emil's first big bill and, understandably, it didn't make it into law. Despite his somewhat naïve upstaging of the new Governor, however, he had established himself as a lawmaker committed to tax reform, and decidedly one who wasn't afraid to take chances.

During Emil's first term, he was absent from legislative sessions only six times in 1963, one of which marked the untimely death of his brother George of polio. He missed only nine days in 1964. He was responsible for passing 6.16 bills (includes bills that he was partially responsible for passing). This statistic stands in marked contrast to the fact that 45 legislators (including the House of Representatives) passed less than one bill each during the same period.[217] Emil's hard work as a legislator during this seminal first term guaranteed that the Governor, fellow legislators, and constituents alike would take him seriously during the coming election and ensuing term of office.

EMIL MEETS HIS FUTURE

Encounters with two more individuals during this period are particularly worth noting. The first is Francis J. Coomes, known to all as Jerry, then Executive Director of the newly formed Michigan Catholic Conference, an agency founded by the five Catholic bishops of Michigan to act as its voice in political and social action matters. Jerry Coomes was trying to enact a landmark piece of legislation in 1963 that would be dubbed The Fair Bus Law. The measure would allow public school buses to transport school district kids to non-public schools. Even though the Catholic population in Emil's Senate district amounted to a distinct minority, Emil agreed to back it.

"I wondered what we were doing, keeping some of our kids off the buses," he remembered, "and I thought it was a fair proposal."

The bill was enacted that same year, and the two men began a professional and personal relationship that would later develop into a prominent business centered around legislative advocacy.[218]

The other individual Emil met early in his freshman term was fellow

G.O.P. Senator William G. Milliken, who had just been elected Majority Floor Leader, usually considered the second highest leadership post in the Senate. Milliken, serving his second term, would run for Lieutenant Governor in 1964, winning his party's nomination, and then, as the new Constitution allowed for the first time, he would run on a joint ticket as George Romney's running mate. Milliken would serve as Lieutenant Governor for several years, and in that capacity perform the largely ceremonial duties as presiding officer of the Senate. When Romney was tapped later on by the newly installed President Nixon for a cabinet position, Milliken would rise to the governorship, commencing an unprecedented 14 years in that post. It was foreordained that Emil would cross paths, and sometimes swords, with Bill Milliken.

"I've learned more about politics seated between these two legislators in 30 minutes than I have learned in my lifetime," says William Seidman, special financial advisor to Gov. Romney, later chairman of FDIC. Emil (right) and Rep. Lloyd Gibbs (R-Portland, left). *Ionia Standard*, April 29, 1963.

Other concurrent developments also greatly impacted Emil's political future. An historic U.S. Supreme Court decision in 1963 mandated a "one-man, one-vote" rule for all federal and state legislative districts. The resulting redistricting in 1964 drastically affected, among other things, the geographic boundaries of Emil's district—as well as the entire make-up of both the Michigan Senate and House of Representatives.[219]

"The deck really got shuffled that year," Emil recalled with relish. "It was almost as good as poker."[220]

Too, the enactment of the new Michigan Constitution in 1964 meant sweeping changes in the organization and execution of the state's responsibilities. The provisions affecting Emil most directly were the ones aimed at the make-up of the Senate. Henceforth, there would be 38 State Senators, instead of the present 34, and beginning with the election of 1966, Senate terms would last four years, while House members' terms remained at two-years. The new provision, allowing the Governor and Lt. Governor to run as a team, also affected the Senate make-up in the coming 1965-1966 legislative session.[221] Since the new Lt. Governor Milliken, a former G.O.P. Senator, had vacated his Senate seat, it meant that: (a) even more new blood would be elected to the upper chamber; and (b) the serving G.O.P. Senate Majority Floor Leader had thus removed himself from leadership consideration, clearing the way for Emil's rise to a higher role.

In addition, Senator Stan Thayer (R-Ann Arbor), with whom Emil had become good friends, and who had served as Majority Leader during Emil's first term, decided to run for Congress in a newly redistricted 2nd District.

"Of course, he couldn't run for the Senate and Congress at the same time," Emil noted later, acutely aware that as a result another seat had opened for a freshman—G.O.P. Senator (Gilbert E. Bursley)—leaving Emil's own pathway open to the top Republican leadership post.[222]

There can be no doubt that, taken altogether, these interconnecting developments caused a whole new set of opportunities, or—depending on one's point of view—problems. By January 1965, Michigan had witnessed, in a very short time, the election of the first Republican Governor in seven terms, the enactment of a new, and badly-needed Constitution, the implementation of the ground-breaking "one-man, one-vote" redistricting rule, and the reshaping of the state's legislative bodies. As a result of the political forces unleashed by these events, Governor Romney won his re-election in 1964 by almost 400,000 votes in the face of an otherwise Democratic landslide, and was thus given a clear mandate to lead the state out of its fiscal woes.

In contrast, Emil recounted, both the Senate and the House went overwhelmingly Democratic for the first time in decades. The important posts of Secretary of State and Attorney General were also won by veteran Democrats James Hare and Frank Kelley, respectively.[223] There was mostly a new government, and many new faces. The old legislative leadership had suddenly evaporated. A new political balance of power reigned in the Capitol.

Soon it would be time for Emil to make his move, but he had to get re-elected first.

EMIL WINS RE-ELECTION TO THE SENATE

This time it was easier. Emil enjoyed the advantage of running his second campaign for Senator as an incumbent with a good record. He had received favorable press attention throughout his term. He knew the issues. His membership on the powerful Appropriations and Taxation Committees gave him high visibility among his Senate colleagues. Interest groups that tracked public policy in the Capitol had begun to take note of the affable, hard-working 45 year-old lawmaker from St. Louis. He knew the ropes, and didn't have any trouble raising money for his re-election.

Under the 1964 mandated reapportionment, Emil's former 25th district had changed to the 30th district, and altered the geographical boundaries considerably.

"There was bad news and good news in that," Emil recalled.

The bad news was that all of Ionia and Mecosta Counties, and part of Montcalm County, were spun off to other districts, significantly eroding his recently acquired political base. The good news was that the map drafters left his home county, Gratiot, undivided in the new district. But, further muddying the waters, all of Clinton and Shiawassee counties were added to his new district, along with parts of Eaton and Ingham. Once again, since Republicans had usually prevailed in general elections in these new areas in the past, Emil's only real opposition would come in the August primary.[224]

After waging the typical energetic and colorful Lockwood-style campaign, Emil beat his three Republican opponents quite easily, outdistancing his nearest opponent by nearly 2,500 votes. It helped him, of course, to gain a huge margin of victory in Gratiot County, just as in 1962, this time outpolling his closest opponent there by 7-1. Too, voters were probably confused that two G.O.P. candidates in the primary bore the same last name— Meier. Between the two of them, they split over 8,000 votes, though still not enough to beat Emil's total of 8,709. Again, Emil had used the same strategy for campaigning this time—concentrating heavily on his home base.[225] Again, it worked like a charm.

The fall of 1964 also echoed his earlier campaign for Senate. In a few short months, Emil wanted to gain visibility in the areas that had been added to his new district, develop political liaisons, and find out what was on his constituents' minds. His Democratic opponent, Joseph H. Kurka, Jr., came from populous Shiawassee County where voting sentiments in the general election turned out to be pretty evenly divided between the two political parties.

"I knew I needed to come close to matching Kurka's vote in Shiawassee," Emil reminisced, "and then beat him in the other five." And, that's just what he did: Emil came within 339 votes of matching Kurka in Shiawassee County, making it impossible for Kurka to win in the other, more Republican areas. The final overall tally registered Lockwood: 42,340, Kurka: 35,360.[226] Emil had been victorious again, this time in a new district, the one that he would represent until he left the Senate for good.

❖

12
A SEISMIC SHIFT IN THE LEGISLATURE

Not only had the political balance of power shifted in the Michigan Legislature from Republican to Democrat as the 1965-1966 session approached, the Senate and House chambers also underwent a make-over. Starting shortly after adjournment of the Legislature in the Spring of 1964, a six month remodeling of both the Senate and House chambers commenced with a legislative appropriation of $160,000. The nearly threadbare carpet was ripped out and replaced, the worn furniture upgraded, and the walls repainted. In the 110 member House, the voting system was re-engineered. The new system more efficiently allowed members to vote from their desks on each measure under consideration by the chamber, and simultaneously view the results on a huge lighted board at the front. (The 38 member Senate chose to vote by voice roll call until late in the 1970s.)[227]

Claude Sampson, chief architect of the project, said, "Michigan should have the most modern legislative floor in the nation." The United Press International (UPI), commenting wryly on this somewhat questionable status symbol, noted that perhaps it was "befitting a Legislature that will be paid as high as any in the nation," pointing out the fact that "only New York equals Michigan's new $10,000 salary and $2,500 expense account."[228]

Senators also had the option to buy—for fifteen dollars—the large, leather chair that they had been occupying on the floor of the Senate during legislative sessions. Emil, like most of his colleagues, purchased his for his Senate office, and used it for his remaining years in office. The UPI memorialized Emil's purchase for posterity, snapping a picture of the well dressed, slightly amused Senator carrying it off the near empty Senate floor.[229]

The Michigan Legislature may have enjoyed overly generous salaries and perks in the eyes of the press, but it was not a point of view shared by Emil. He recalled how most of the legislators at the time had to work at other jobs or have other sources of income, because of the low legislative salaries and expense money.

"Take the farmers, for instance," he said. "They wanted to adjourn the legislative session as early as possible, so they could get back to their farms, and save their crops. As for me, my sheep were worth more than I earned from being a Senator the first few years."[230]

Renovation of their work space hardly qualified for a concern of the first order of magnitude, as the newly elected legislators met after the November 3 election to choose their leaders for the upcoming session. For the first time since 1938, Democrats had won both houses by huge majorities, now holding 95 seats out of the two-house total of 148. That left the G.O.P. with only 53 seats. Emil grasped all too well what a seismic shift that was, fully aware that Republicans had dominated both Houses by a total of 81-63 going into the election.[231]

"I could see voters wanted a more balanced government, party-wise," Emil said in retrospect, recalling Governor Romney's sizable win in face of an otherwise Democratic sweep. "Like it or not, that's how we got out of the doldrums," he said, referring to the fiscal reform agenda.

From the Republican Senators' standpoint, it meant a big adjustment, however, suddenly operating as the minority party. But, because their party held the Governorship, and the Lieutenant Governorship, they would play a more significant role than that which often accrued to a minority caucus. This fact made the post of Senate Minority Leader even more desirable to Emil. It was time to make his move.

Emil carries away old senate chair, purchased from state for $15 following massive refurbishing of House and Senate. UPI, Lansing (MI), December 20, 1964. *Family album, newspaper unknown.*

EMIL CATAPULTS TO SENATE MINORITY LEADER

In "Emil-ese," the selection process for legislative leaders—and their responsibilities—is like a cross between a close wrestling match and a high stakes poker game. Legislative leadership posts, in Emil's day and now, are filled by a majority vote of each caucus. In the Michigan Legislature, that means there are four party caucuses—a G.O.P. and Democratic caucus in both the Senate and the House of Representatives. The party that enjoys a majority of members in the Senate elects the Senate Majority Leader. In the House, the counterpart of the Senate Majority Leader is the Speaker of the House. The minority party in the Senate elects a Senate Minority Leader, while the House minority caucus follows suit by also electing a House Minority Leader. Each caucus, in addition, elects a Floor Leader, who typically controls his party's debate on issues during legislative sessions.

"All of them," Emil said of the four top leaders, "got to name committee members from their caucuses. They also set legislative priorities, and gave the go-ahead for staff and office assignments. They got to approve expense accounts, too. That really came in handy sometimes."

Ideally, Emil recounted, these four leaders met frequently in various combinations to strategize, negotiate, complain or compromise. They also met with the Governor and his key advisors from time to time for the same purposes. The leaders' length of service, knowledge of issues, reputation, command of the intricate legislative process, personality, and relationships with the other players largely determined their effectiveness. That is, except for one important ingredient: the size of their caucuses. This clash of alternate interests and odds-making constituted a strategist's delight for someone like Emil.

"I did a fairly good job of making deals," Emil remembered, "but I was lucky a lot of the time, too,"[232]

He knew, for instance, that if party caucuses in the Senate were close in size, the power would likely be shared a good deal more than if the majority caucus greatly outnumbered the minority. Republicans in the Senate elected to serve in 1965-1966 faced the latter predicament, a reality that made the game more interesting for Emil. Republicans were outnumbered 23-15, and since it took a majority vote of only 20 (of 38 elected) to organize or control action in the Senate, Emil and his colleagues supposedly held a distinct disadvantage. Visions of the Kemper wrestling mat come to mind, as the details unfold of Emil's deft handling of his minority caucus against a much larger foe.

Thirteen of the 15 eligible Republican Senators were on hand at the Jack Tar Hotel across the street from the Capitol for their crucial post-election leadership vote. Unlike the Democrats who unified behind Senator Ray Dzendzel (D-Detroit) and his slate of other caucus officials, G.O.P. Senators selected their leaders on "a discordant note," according to Bill Burke of the Lansing *State Journal*.[233] The Republican caucus vote in the Senate would be the first of several close calls that Emil would confront during the remainder of his tenure in the Michigan Senate.

At this fateful meeting, the coast was clear for anyone to try for Minority Leader especially because last term's caucus Leader (Thayer), and Floor

Leader (Milliken), were no longer in the Senate. Any Senator who thought he could rally more than half the votes would make a try for the top post, or one of the other caucus posts. Emil decided to go for broke, as he had done so many other times in his life.

His main opponent was Senator Thomas F. Schweigert (R-Petoskey) who had first been elected to the Senate in 1960. Two years earlier, he and Senator Vander Laan had joined Emil and others to narrowly control the caucus by a 12-11 vote, electing Stan Thayer as Majority Leader. But now Schweigert and Vander Laan thought that Emil hadn't backed Governor Romney's legislative programs and reapportionment plans enthusiastically enough. Their effort failed to derail Emil's all-out bid for the post of Minority Leader, however. After a heated debate, Emil won easily by a vote of 9-4. Schweigert maneuvered a consolation prize of sorts. He was given the post of Minority Whip, a new party office in the Senate. Senator Garry Brown (R-Schoolcraft) won the post of Minority Floor Leader.[234]

When confronted by the press after the vote with accusatory quotes from the losing side, Emil characteristically played the controversy down and refused to retaliate.

"I told them I was sorry to hear of unhappiness in my caucus," Emil said, and then reaffirmed his attention to work closely with both his G.O.P caucus, and the Governor.

After the caucus vote, Emil told the press, he had met with Romney, and described the meeting as "cordial." Significantly, in a foreshadowing of one of the most prominent traits shown during his leadership tenure, Emil added that he not only planned to work closely with the Governor's office, but he also would establish communication ties with the majority Democratic leadership.[235]

Emil adapted easily to his party's top leadership role in the upper chamber. The two-year apprenticeship he had served on the important Appropriations and Taxation Committees prepared him well. His first advice to his caucus members was, "Do your legislative homework and don't miss committee meetings." The Lansing *State Journal* observed that "he made this formula work to perfection . . . in the Tax Committee on which he serves, and on the Senate floor as he teamed up with Democrats, headed by Sen. Raymond D. Dzendzel, D-Detroit, on a 'workable' senior citizens tax relief bill."

Emil admitted openly that he had learned how to get ideas across, even though his party was in the distinct minority, from Senator Garland Lane (D-Flint) with whom he had served on Appropriations during the previous term. "Democrats were always outnumbered three-to-one on the Appropriations Committee," he told the *State Journal*, "but Gar was always able to get most of his amendments on budget bills."[236]

Emil continued preaching this strategy, and also demonstrated how it worked in action. He knew that the most important work of any legislator is accomplished in committee. If a committee member really does his home-work—knows the issue at hand, and tears down imaginary partisan fences—the lawmaker can often win enough support for his point of view. With his or her important amendments incorporated into the bill that the committee re-ports to the floor, it is much easier to win a majority vote when the measure is considered for passage by the entire Senate.[237]

Emil implemented some key reforms within his caucus during the 1965-1966 session, a couple of which he had recommended to no avail in 1963. The first arose out of the outright caucus battles that had occurred during the previous session over the need for closer communication with the Governor on key issues. Emil, as Minority Leader, took it upon himself to maintain close contact with Romney, and advise his caucus of the Governor's posi-tions. To help implement this initiative, he had analyses of bills prepared, including positions of the Governor, and other key players. Before action was taken on a bill, the analyses were distributed to all members.

"It was obvious," Emil noted, "but it was so basic nobody saw it."[238]

After Emil implemented the new procedure, appreciative Senators ac-knowledged that the initiative provided important information easily, and in a timely manner. Today, in an almost overly informed Information Age, legis-lators take it for granted.

Emil also put into effect another reform to expedite legislative action on the Senate floor when bills were being debated and voted upon. He persuaded the caucus to agree to delegate authority to control action on the floor during debate to one individual, the Minority Floor Leader, who in this case was Senator Garry Brown.[239] This eliminated a lot of confusion, according to Emil, as well as distracting competition among members who wished to speak, or introduce amendments during often-heated floor debate.

The political landscape had shifted radically in a short time. It was a pe-riod of change in many important ways, big and small. The Michigan Legislature found itself forced to adapt to the times. Beginning in the mid-1960s, the legislature began to reflect what was going on in the broader soci-ety. Historically, it had been dominated by economic considerations, largely built around agrarian interests. Even the seven terms when Democrats Wil-liams and Swainson occupied the Governor's chair didn't make much of a dent on the conservative, farmer-small-town oriented, Republican dominated legislature. Nevertheless, with the election of an overwhelmingly Democratic legislature for the first time in decades, the convincing re-election of a moderate Republican as Governor, and the new Constitution, the legislature's agenda changed. Now the nexus of power to get things done lay in the compromises that could be ironed out between the Governor, aided by the Republican Minority Leaders in both houses, and the Democratic leaders in both Houses.

At even a whisper of the need for deal-making, we can almost hear the wheels turning beneath a certain lawmaker's brush cut.

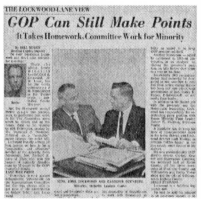

THE LOCKWOOD-LANE VIEW

GOP Can Still Make Points
It Takes Homework, Committee Work for Minority

Friendly conference with the opposition—GOP Senate Minority Leader Lockwood and Senate Majority Leader Dzendzel confer on statewide fiscal reform. Lansing *State Journal*, April 4, 1965.

The long pent-up Democratic agenda further complicated the landscape. Along with the fact that freshmen accounted for half of the new legislature, it resulted in an unprecedented demand for new legislation, with a sizable amount directed at problems involving cities, labor, welfare, employment discrimination, and other social issues. This in turn dictated that the Michigan Legislature needed more staff, office space and equipment. The trend in Michigan, mirrored in many other large states at the time, would continue well into the 1970s and beyond.[240]

Beefing up staff and facilities, of course, takes a fair amount of loose change, and that means an appropriation by the legislature. This inevitably invites scrutiny by the press corps who camp out in the Capitol building. Bill Kulsea, a long-time member of the Capitol press corps—and a respected if not at times feared one, at that—took note of the legislative expansion in his regular report for the Booth Newspapers in March 1965. He called attention to the fact that the current legislature was shaping up as "the most expensive, the most political and the most interesting in the nation—and the best paid."[241]

"Apparently he had neglected to compare it with sheep farming," Emil may have been overheard commenting during a 2 a.m. hand of poker at the City Club.

To back up his claim of the Michigan Legislature being the most expensive, Kulsea pointed to the legislators' $12,500 combined salary and expense money, plus the $4 million the legislature would likely spend that year, including large supplemental appropriations recently passed to accommodate their growing needs. To gain office space for members of both houses and their staffs, legislative leaders prevailed on many office-holders from the executive branch to downsize, or vacate the Capitol altogether. Up until this ecutive branch to downsize, or vacate the Capitol altogether. Up until this point, all three branches of government housed some of their most important functions in the Capitol itself. For instance, in addition to the two legislative chambers, the 19th Century landmark housed the Supreme Court hearing room and chambers, the governor and his staff, the Attorney General and the Secretary of State.[242]

"Legislators didn't even have personal offices or secretaries until then," Emil

recounted, "except for a few leaders." They had to accept phone calls, he said, at a few phone booths located just outside each chamber.[243] To achieve at least some progress in this vital area, the legislature cleared out the entire ground floor of the Capitol to make more room for members, secretaries and other staffers. Even then, only 68 legislators could squeeze into the one floor—six to a room at that. Upstairs on the first floor, only

Leaving on a jet plane—Emil (center) leaves for six European countries and England as part of Gov. Romney's trade mission, "Operation Europe." Lansing (MI), 1965.

"Operation Europe" sends trade delegation of 73 Michigan business and political leaders to six Common Market countries and England. Emil (2nd top right). Detroit (MI), 1965.

the actual offices of the Attorney General, Secretary of State and State Treasurer themselves remained, minus their executive office staffs. The Governor and Lt. Governor were allocated generous amounts of space to carry out their duties.[244] It would take several more years to find space and funds to apportion offices and staff to each member of the House and Senate.

The legislature had also been looking for space to accommodate the new Constitutionally-mandated Auditor General's office, and the bipartisan Legislative Service Bureau, which would draft bills and maintain related services.[245] In retrospect, Emil thought this upgrading of legislative members' staff and facilities—for the first time in the history of Michigan Legislature—was overdue, and far from adequate. At the time, however, it represented a bold and precarious political move, especially given the state's financial condition. Yet it constituted but a small down payment on changing a part-time legislature into a modern, self-sufficient, full-time body. As a newly minted legislative leader, Emil participated in this first major foray into the future, and within a short time, would become a high profile supporter of modernization of the legislature.

Congressman's key supporters—(from left): Frank Kropschot (Pres., Bank of Lansing), Cong. Charles Chamberlain, Edgar Hardin (Pres., Northern Michigan Univ.), Emil, and C. John Holmes. Lansing (MI), 1965.

In regard to Kulsea's claim that this legislature would likely turn out to be the "most political," the reporter pointed to the legislative Democrats summarily dismissing Romney's entire state budget, and substituting their own. This brought the public ire of the stubborn Governor, which then required an equal blast from the Democrats. The duel of the partisan powerbrokers alone wouldn't warrant Kulsea's assessment, since such is the lot of both federal and state governments that are divided on a partisan basis between the executive and legislative branches. The more over-arching point was the opportunity for Democrats to make Romney appear weak in his ability to lead Michigan, thus making him lose his re-election bid the following year. If they could succeed in doing so, it would end Romney's chances to run for President in 1968. It would be a payback for Republicans causing former Governor Williams to lose national prestige in the 1950s.[246]

The stage was set for a major battle over tax reform, again the issue that would dominate Emil's second term in office.

13

EMIL LEARNS LEADERSHIP ROPES

The labor-liberal coalition that dominated the Democratic side of the legislative aisle in the Williams-Swainson era had repeatedly clamored in vain for the enactment of a graduated income tax. But when Governor Romney tried to gain legislative support during his very first year in office for an income tax bill featuring provisions that made it less onerous on lower income people, minority party Democrats joined with some Republicans to soundly defeat him. The Democrats' lust for an income tax had not dissipated one bit, but two realities stood in their way then, as well as now in 1965.

The first obstacle facing Democrats was a clause in the new Michigan Constitution, which narrowly passed by a statewide vote of less than one-half of 1% in April 1963. The provision plainly outlawed a graduated income tax in Michigan. Thus Democrats, following the lead of another Ottawa, Illinois native—August Scholle, head of the powerful AFL-CIO—refused to vote for an income tax before the state's voters had a chance to repeal the Constitutional prohibition against a graduated income tax. They felt strongly that any income tax passed by the legislature while such a prohibition was in place would be unacceptable. Thus their earlier opposition to Romney's proposal.

The second obstacle confronting legislative Democrats was the fact that, in order to put such a measure to a vote of the people, they would have to muster a two-thirds vote in both houses. Given the strong opposition by Republicans to a graduated income tax, and the lack of enough Democrats to constitute two-thirds of each chamber, such a strategy was doomed to failure. Ironically, it was not until two years later, when the Republicans gained control of both houses again in 1967 with Emil leading the Senate, that an income tax, largely the same as today's law, was passed by the legislature.[247]

"We wanted to do it in '65," Emil recalled, "but the unusual political balance of power produced a stand-off."[248]

The resulting firestorm of pent-up legislation, along with the perennial maelstrom surrounding fiscal reform, bestowed on Emil a kind of baptism by fire in his new role as caucus leader. In addition to tending to his duties as Senate Minority Leader, he took on active participation in the Taxation, Agriculture, Insurance and Public Utilities Committees.[249] Even though he and his fellow Republicans didn't have enough votes to get their way when key issues reached the Senate floor, Emil at least could make a significant contribution by getting his ideas incorporated into the bill in committee. Meanwhile, he honed his skills in building coalitions—both within his Republican caucus, and between his caucus and the Democrats. There was no lack of important issues requiring broad coalition support in the 1965-1966 session.

A sampling of some front-burner issues enacted into law in the 1965-1966 legislative session amply demonstrates the broad range of interests addressed. Among these issues were: complete reorganization of the Executive branch; family planning programs; anti-age-based employment discrimination measures; homestead property exemptions; standards for the physically handicapped in public buildings; funding for community health programs; establishment of the Michigan Consumers Council, the State Housing Authority and the Michigan Arts Council; election reform; and the complete restructuring of social welfare programs in the state.[250]

As Emil and others knew, the actions of the legislature reflected, in many ways, trends that were evident in the society as a whole at the time. The legislature was also heavily impacted by the activism of the Kennedy-Johnson administration in Washington. As the pressure cooker of conflict mounted over civil rights, the escalating Vietnam War, and urban blight, to name some of the more controversial issues of that time, the need for strong, decisive and principled political leaders at the state level was never more apparent.

Emil possessed the right qualities for a leader in those turbulent times, it seems. New and unprecedented challenges to citizens and institutions cried out for leaders who could quickly grasp their implications, and put together new political partnerships to address them successfully. Emil's leadership style as Minority Leader foreshadowed the approach used later, as he rose to the challenges of Majority Leader when the G.O.P. retook the Senate.

Guy Vander Jagt, who joined the Senate in 1965 for one term before serving in Congress for 27 years, said that Emil's leadership style was similar to the way he played cards. "I remember Emil often playing pitch at the Lansing City Club with fellow Senators for 25 cents a game and ten cents a hit," Guy remembered. "Emil was the champion. He played by instinct, and most of the time he was right. He took risks. He'd have an ace and a jack, and no low card, but he'd bet anyway because he gambled that his partner did. He was a great bluffer. I never saw Emil get emotional or angry, not in cards, or in the legislature. He had no highs and no lows."

Guy chuckled over how he and Emil first met, recalling the early days of what would become a close friendship that continued nonstop until Emil's death. Guy had a background almost as eclectic as Emil's. Just before running for the State Senate, he had served as news director of WWTV in Cadillac. Before that he had been a foreign news correspondent, and held degrees from Yale Divinity School, and the University of Michigan Law School. One of Guy's campaign themes had been running in solidarity with Governor Romney against the incumbent Senators whom Romney had dubbed "the Five Quizlings". Ironically, Emil had been included in Romney's pejorative because he had not enthusiastically supported all of the Governor's positions, especially legislative reapportionment. So, it is perfectly understandable that Guy had some misgivings when Emil invited him to be his roommate, along with Senators Haskell Nichols, Harold Volkema, Charles Zollar, and, sometimes, Milton Zaagman. Emil's friendly and open manner soon won Guy over. And, he ended up voting for Emil in his bid for Minority Leader to boot.

Guy attributed Emil's successes in his first legislative leadership role to several characteristics. One of Emil's uncanny abilities was to put the pieces of a political puzzle together to make it go, according to Guy. "He knew every Senator's hot button, what meant the most to him, what committee he wanted, the street where he lived, the bridge he wanted built. Democrats too. He was very pragmatic, and could trim down his own goal to something the Senator could vote for."

Another one of Emil's defining traits, Guy remembered, was his honesty. "He was as honest a politician as I have ever seen," he said. "There was no double talk. His word was his bond, and everyone knew that. He was very straight forward, on the level. This held true for the news media as well."

Emil also exhibited his lifelong ability to keep accurate mental tallies, first learned at the card table playing with his Grandma Augusta. "Emil walked a razor thin edge in dealing with that Senate Republican caucus," Guy said. "But I always had confidence that Emil knew who was going to vote 'yea' and 'nay' before any important vote."

Guy gave high marks to Emil's overall leadership during this phase of his career. "He was one of the most incredible leaders I have ever witnessed," he said. "A lot of leaders wait for the crest of the wave, and then ride it. Emil didn't do that. He led his colleagues where he wanted to go, even when it was unpopular."[251]

The next several years would surely test these leadership skills as Emil's role in the Senate expanded. But first, like all elected officials, he had to run for re-election. So, as the legislative session went into high gear in the spring of 1965, Emil once again declared his candidacy for Senator from the 30th District.

EMIL BARNSTORMS FOR HIS THIRD SENATE TERM

Much of the rough hoeing had been accomplished during Emil's first two campaigns. Now he could campaign in a Senate District unchanged since the last election. He had served successfully as Republican Leader in the Senate. He had produced results for his district. And, he had always made it a point to keep in constant touch with his District, even as his Senate duties in the Capitol had mounted. His chances for victory could not look better.

This time, only one Republican dared to oppose Emil in the primary. He was one of the two Meier candidates from the 1964 primary, whose combined total nearly matched Emil's. Not to worry. Emil campaigned vigorously, as usual. He knew enough not to ever take re-election for granted. Constituents wanted to know—and Emil believed firmly that they deserved to ask—what their legislator had done for them yesterday, not last term. When the Senate primary results were tallied, Emil scored a runaway victory: Emil—11,072, Victor H. Meier—3,963. Three months later, Emil would again face Joe Kurka Jr. in the November election.[252]

Due to the plethora of legislation addressed during the last legislative session, and the ongoing policy debates between Republicans and Democrats, Emil had a lot to talk about during the general election campaign. He loved barnstorming through his district's towns such as Carson City, Greenville, Stanton, Charlotte, Potterville, Grand Ledge, Eaton Rapids, Owosso and Williamston. Trading stories and viewpoints with the voters back home energized him, and helped him keep the right perspective when he had to wheel and deal in their behalf in the Capitol.

At the same time, however, it was difficult for Mariella Lockwood to cope with the frequent absences of her increasingly in-demand husband. Insecurity was the unfortunate result. Many of Emil's Senate friends took him aside during this period, confiding in embarrassment that Mariella had phoned them— even in caucus meetings—claiming that Emil was sleeping with their wives. "They of course knew that it wasn't true," Emil recalled, "but all my reassurances to Mariella seemed to fall on deaf ears."[253]

As predicted, Emil won re-election to the Senate by a lopsided vote: 42,738 to 22,391.[254]

Now it was good-bye to the home fires once again, and off to Lansing to catch the train to his political future.

14

EMIL SETS THE STANDARD FOR SENATE MAJORITY LEADER

Michigan general election results created a lot of excitement for the state's Republicans, Senators in particular. Governor Romney had successfully withstood a heavy barrage of criticism from the Democratic controlled legislature, out polling his Democratic opponent, Zolton Ferency in the general election by a whopping 527,000 votes. Romney's vote count this time signaled yet another personal mandate, since the only other independently elected statewide officials under the new Constitution—Secretary of State, and Attorney General—were Democrats.

Such a resounding victory, along with the memory of 1964's nearly 400,000 plurality in the wake of the President Lyndon Johnson landslide, was more than sufficient to keep Romney in national news as a yet undeclared candidate for U.S. President.[255] Romney's first four-year term, to be cut short by his growing national aspirations, would become inextricably intertwined with Emil's term in the top Senate post.

What made Senate Republicans happiest was that the 1966 elections threw control of the upper chamber to them, after two years of operating as a distinct minority. Republicans had won 20 seats (of 38), the minimum number for them to claim an outright majority, and organize the Senate in accord with their wishes. But, as Roger Lane of the *Detroit Free Press* remarked, "One bad case of the sniffles and [the Senate Republicans] . . . lack the 20 G.O.P. votes it takes to pass a bill."[256] Add to this the wild card that no less than 10 Republican Senators—a full half of the caucus—were freshmen, with no history of allegiances in the Senate. Who could play cards better than any one in the Senate? Emil, of course.

So, following the usual skirmishes and mating dances that accompany such political rituals, few were surprised that Emil emerged as the winner. Senator Robert Vander Laan of Grand Rapids was elected Majority Floor Leader under Emil as Senate Majority Leader. Thus Emil had achieved the top post in the State Senate at a time of fiscal, political, and social turmoil, heading a caucus that held on to a slim margin of control over the chamber. To further complicate Emil's task, he knew that he could not always count on party solidarity among members in his own caucus when it came to high stakes issues. It was a lesson he had learned all too well in his term serving as Minority Leader.

When it came to certain caucus members, Emil knew he would have to count on Republican Governor Romney to use his muscle and persuasive power. In other cases, he would have to rely on his own ability to forge coalitions between select members of his caucus and various Democrats. He felt that he had as good a chance as anyone to build winning coalitions for two good reasons. First, he had maintained close relationships with several Senate Democrats throughout his tour in the Senate. Second, he was acutely aware that the strict, ideologically driven nature of political parties in Michigan during the Williams-Swainson era had dwindled in the years since.

Now hanging in Senate Conference Room, with portraits of all past Senate Majority and Minority Leaders, Emil places call under his official photo. Lansing (MI), 1967.

Typically, Emil began his four-year run as the majority party leader relishing the precarious gamble, not realizing what an indelible mark he would make on Michigan history in that position. Three-term Republican Governor John Engler (1991-2002), who served as Senate Majority Leader in the 1980s himself, agreed with the assessment of Emil's contribution, commenting in an interview for this book, "Emil set the standard for the post of Senate Majority Leader."[257]

Another curious result of the 1966 general elections was the 55-55 party stand-off in the House of Representatives. There existed no electoral mandate for either party to organize the House. Such is a rare occurrence, to say the least, Emil acknowledged, in that it had happened in the House only once in the state's history—in 1959.

The election of leadership positions takes on an aura of high drama in instances such as these. The parliamentary maneuvers, and deal-cutting that transpired over election of Speaker of the House is still talked about by old-timers in the Capitol. But that story more properly belongs in a book about the House. Suffice it to say that, when the dust settled, Emil's fellow Republicans in the House had elected Robert Waldron of Grosse Pointe as Speaker, due to the infamous defection (to Democrats at least) of Democrat E.D. O'Brien. Waldron, dubbed "Mr. Republican" by some members of his caucus, became the ever-sociable Emil's Lansing roommate. Another player who would interact productively with Emil in the coming years was the new House Minority Leader William Ryan of Detroit.[258]

"Do you solemnly swear . . . ?" Judge T. John Lesinski swears in Emil after '66 election, which threw Senate to GOP and cast Emil into defining role as Senate Majority Leader. Lansing (MI), January 1967.

Bipartisan Happy Birthday—Senators Basil Brown (D-Detroit, left) and Ray Dzendzel (D-Detroit, right) present cake to Emil and fellow GOP Sen. Tom Schweigert (R-Petosky). Lansing (MI), 1966.

With both houses of the legislature so evenly divided between the parties, it was difficult to envision the marshalling of enough political consensus to tackle the mounting problems of the state. The biggest challenge before lawmakers still remained to overhaul the state's financing mechanisms. Emil and everyone else remembered painfully that three Governors, over ten years, had been rebuffed by the legislature in efforts to pass an income tax into law.[259]

In the 1967 legislative session, moreover, the stakes had been raised higher. Each year had passed without a solid tax base in place, even in the light of increased spending, and a souring economy. To make the political mess even murkier, lawmakers faced the new Constitution's mandate to produce a balanced budget every year.[260]

In facing up to this challenge, Emil would pull off one of his most amazing legislative feats to help get Michigan back on its fiscal feet again.

FISCAL REFORM: WIZARDRY WINS THE DAY

Romney led off in February 1967 with an urgent message to the legislature for enactment of tax reform. It contained adjustments in the state sales tax and property tax, along with an imposition of a 2.5% personal income tax, and a 5% corporate income tax. The onerous business activities tax would be repealed.

Predictably, Democrats railed against the plan, still calling for a graduated income tax, and, generally, an overall reduction in working people's share of the tax burden. Legislators dug in, largely along party lines. The Senate and House Taxation Committees promptly disbanded their joint hearings, and adopted rival tax overhaul plans, which were soon voted down by the opposite chamber. As the June 29 adjournment approached, the state Democratic Party chief, Zolton Ferency, announced plans to wage a statewide campaign to put the question of an income tax on the ballot.[261]

In the middle of this melee, Emil had to come up with enough votes to get the Governor's tax program passed in the Senate. Otherwise, the Republicans would lose bargaining power with the House. With his slim partisan advantage, and several recalcitrant G.O.P. Senators, he faced near impossible odds. But Emil built an unusual yet victorious faction to pass the tax measure in the Senate with 22 votes, a group that included 6 Democrats.

Roger Lane of the *Detroit Free Press,* observed Emil's mastery of the legislative process in this, and several other such resourceful victories. Lane said that Emil "wins with his wits rather than by force of Republican numbers," and further remarked that "his wizardry lies in putting together endlessly different combinations of Republicans and Democratic votes to win."[262]

Following heated negotiations among the Senate, House and Governor Romney, a final version of fiscal reform passed both houses, and was targeted for immediate effect so that sorely needed tax collections could begin October 1. Such a vote requires a two-thirds majority vote in both houses, a perfect chance for opponents to play obstructionist. In the Senate, that meant that Emil had to produce 26 "yea" votes in a hurry. Teaming up again with Democrats, lead by Minority Leader Sander Levin, who had earlier replaced Senator Dzendzel as Minority Leader, Emil produced seven Democrats to join with Republicans. Immediate effect of the act was achieved.

Romney publicly hailed Emil as a hero, affirming that Emil's "was the most skillful leadership job I've seen in five years in the Capitol."[263] The long awaited fiscal reform became fact in Michigan by July 1. By now, it was clear to everyone that Emil Lockwood was the man to see in the Michigan Senate.

EMIL TAKES STAND ON OPEN HOUSING

The ink was barely dry on the new tax package when another, even more critical crisis erupted in July. Race riots raged in Detroit, Grand Rapids, Flint, Saginaw, Benton Harbor, Muskegon, Kalamazoo, Albion, and Pontiac. Over 40 deaths, and thousands of arrests resulted, along with massive personal injuries, and $500 million in Detroit property damage alone. The Michigan National Guard was called out to restore order to the streets of Detroit, Michigan's largest city, and the car capitol of the world.[264] The atmosphere that engulfed state lawmakers was tense and foreboding. The legislature would reach many significant milestones in improving equality and opportunity among the state's races during the next few years. But Emil's sterling victory in leading the charge in the Senate to pass the controversial Open Housing law will sufficiently make the case for both his commitment to fairness, and his brilliance as a legislative strategist.

The urban riots shook all levels of government around the state, but most visibly affected were the Governor's Office and the Michigan Legislature. They were the only public entities that could make laws, and appropriate monies for statewide law enforcement, and remedial socioeconomic programs. The problem, however, as could be observed in the income tax fight, was that there existed a wide range of viewpoints in both the Senate and the House.

Emil was not surprised, then, that matters such as racial equality in housing, put before the legislature in a fall Special Session called by Romney, touched a raw nerve in many legislators. Some lawmakers emotionally attacked the rioters with verbal bombasts, calling for more law and order. Other legislators called for more education, housing, jobs and enforcement of new, tougher civil rights measures. With all the threats being leveled by multiple players, against the background of smoldering inner cities, it seemed for a while the odds were no better than a crap shoot that a genuine compromise could be reached.

Governor Romney had canceled his out-of-state travel aimed toward a presidential bid, in order to deal with fiscal reform, and now the post-riot crisis. He looked to the leaders of the Senate and House to help him fashion a workable approach.

The first step in achieving more equality for black people in Michigan, according to the consensus of the pro-civil rights forces, was to ensure every citizen's right to live where he or she wants to live, and to set up an apparatus that would enforce the law with enthusiasm—and teeth. Such a step, it was believed, would open up access to better public education, increase job opportunities, and speed integration of many hitherto inaccessible institutions. Enforcement authority would be housed in the Michigan Civil Rights Commission.

The legislative measure that emerged from this cauldron of decision-making was called the Open Housing bill.

This new legislative vehicle became a political football during the fall 1967 session—and, it turns out, during the following spring session as well. The issue frequently dominated the state's page-one headlines. A major newspaper in Emil's Senate District, *The Owosso Argus Press,* selected Civil Rights, including Open Housing, as Michigan's biggest story of the year.[265] In fact, Emil helped make it a hot issue in Owosso when he spoke to the Rotary

Club there on December 6. The incident reveals several personal traits that accompanied Emil into any political battle.

Emil had accepted the invitation for two reasons. He had long been a faithful Rotarian, and these particular Rotarians were his constituents. They were mostly local business and professional men, like him. He knew going in, that they were not supporters of Open Housing. Realizing this, would Emil beguile the eager listeners with humorous stories from the Capitol, and carefully leave himself wiggle room on the question of racial equality? Or, would he do what he always did—lay it on the line? Knowing Emil, the answer is easy. He didn't hold back one bit.

During his remarks, Emil boldly stated that he was 100% for an Open Housing law, and predicted passage in the spring legislative session. In the Q&A period, the club president asked Emil if he minded a show of hands to indicate how many supported the civil rights measure. Emil, of course, said he didn't mind at all. "There wasn't one person in favor of Open Housing, and there were at least 50 there," Emil recalled. "The head guy asked me in front of the group, 'We're your constituents, and you mean you aren't going to give us your vote on this?' And I said, 'No, I'm for it, and I intend to get it passed.' He didn't know what to say."[266]

The Owosso Argus Press reported in bold type in a front page article that Emil supported the controversial measure, defying the wishes of his constituents. The newspaper story bellowed: "Lockwood conceded that 70 per cent of his constituents, primarily in Shiawassee, Clinton, Gratiot, and Montcalm counties oppose a state open housing law. 'But,' he added, 'I'm enough of a realist to know that senators don't run for re-election until 1970 and maybe by that time you'll forget how I voted.' "

Emil also predicted that there were going to be riots in Detroit and other major Michigan cities whether an open housing bill passed or not. He further pointed out that the Michigan Supreme Court was supposed to rule early in 1968 on whether Open Housing was already guaranteed in the new state Constitution. Obviously, Emil believed it was an assured constitutional right.[267]

Emil's deft handling of what could have been for many elected officials a blatant act of political suicide, highlights both his innate sense of fairness, and his disarming frankness. Emil never flew under false colors, so people trusted him, even when they didn't agree with him. He believed that it was the fair thing to make sure every citizen could live where they wanted to live. He was not afraid to tell anyone that, even fellow Rotarians who had more than likely voted for him. And, he used humor to couch his stiff message. He didn't take himself too seriously, so it was hard for opponents to get too mad at him.

Lastly, of course, Emil's stance enjoyed the additional benefit of being true. The Supreme Court was going to assert the right to Open Housing. There was going to be further unrest, because one bill would not right all the wrongs previously done to the minority community. Further, he had promised

Romney that he would deliver the necessary votes in the Senate, so he was committed to the bill's passage. Finally, the next election was three years off, and he remained confident that, should he decide to run again, he would have brought the goods home for his district several times over by then.

EMIL ENGINEERS PASSAGE OF HISTORICAL BILL

It is telling that Emil, in an interview for this book, refused to take credit for standing tall on behalf of wronged minorities. He felt uncomfortable with any implication that he might have been ahead of the times, or a leader who operated from lofty principle alone. The most he would own up to is that he fought so vigorously for Open Housing because "it was the only fair thing to do."[268] Humility, those who knew him agree, was always one of Emil's hallmark traits.

The legislative battle over Open Housing reached its fevered pitch in the Senate on April 4, 1968, coincidentally—and somehow appropriately—the same day that Dr. Martin Luther King, Jr. was assassinated. The issue had become a constant lightning rod as numerous attempts were made to forge a bill that could attract the necessary 56 (House)-20 (Senate) votes for passage. An attempt to gain final passage of the measure had already been defeated in the House just before Christmas.[269]

Controversial efforts were underway in numerous Michigan cities to pass local open housing ordinances, creating intense pressure on the legislature to act on uniform standards and procedures at the state level. Violent eruptions responding to the unthinkable Dr. King assassination began in several Michigan cities, as well as across the country on the very same day. It was now or never for the newly seasoned Senate Majority Leader.

In momentous legislative floor battles such as the one Emil faced, the Majority Leader had his work cut out for him. He had to have Senate members lined up for various preliminary and follow-up votes, not only for final passage. Emil recounted for this book many examples of other roll call votes requiring various numbers of votes, depending on the stage of debate going on at the time: To amend the bill; send the bill back to committee; substitute the bill for another version; overcome delaying actions by opponents; and, as seen in the case of the income tax measure, to give the bill immediate effect once the bill has been passed.

Shrewd tacticians, such as Emil, know that some colleagues in their own party might be willing to support leadership on all procedural motions, for instance, but not on final passage. Others might agree to vote with the Leader only in the event that one last vote is needed to pass the bill. To complicate things further, often a colleague from either party may offer a certain kind of vote in return for reciprocal support for a measure he or she wants to pass into law. Other examples of such tradeoffs come in the form of a concession on travel, or staff, or a committee assignment, to name a few of the more obvious.

The trick, Emil knew, was to spend as little political capital as possible to reach the magic number of votes in any given situation. It requires an uncanny ability to retain enough rapport with members across the political spectrum to win their support, however minimal, in tight situations. Moreover, the Leader has to keep all this in his head during the dizzying machinations of parliamentary maneuvers, emotional debates, defections, unsuspected success of hostile amendments, and a cornucopia of delaying tactics. It helps to possess an ability to "thrive in times of confusion, always a jump ahead of most others," as Roger Lane of the *Detroit Free Press* described Emil during times like these.[270]

For this historic battle, Emil knew he had to form an alliance with the minority party in the Senate. With outright opposition by at least nine members of his own caucus, he would need to deal with the Democrats to assure safe passage of the Open Housing bill through the Senate. It is only necessary to point out the final vote tally to underscore what has been said so far about Emil's ability to form coalitions, and maintain control of the floor action with minimal support from his own Republicans. The final count among the 22 votes in favor of passage: Republicans-11, Democrats-11.[271] Emil had pulled off another seemingly impossible feat, delivering a victory with half of his caucus opposed to the measure. The House underwent its own share of controversy, but finally reversed its earlier failure, ultimately passing the Open Housing bill before session's end.

While it may seem sacrilegious to some to introduce a note of levity into such serious proceedings, a certain anecdote relating to a key vote in the Senate during the passage of the Open Housing bill can be instructive. The incident highlights brilliant vote-getting tactics, the tenuous hold a Leader often has on a member's vote, and the grateful reality that humor can be found in even the direst of legislative standoffs.

"It was incredible," said Emil's son Eric, an MSU student at the time. "My Dad invited me along with him and Democratic Senator Coleman Young that night of the vote, and when a UPI reporter joined us somewhere for coffee afterwards, I heard the whole blow-by-blow."[272]

In the heat of battle in the Senate over Open Housing, as Emil told it, he desperately needed a key vote. Eye witnesses disagree over just which vote it was. Suffice it to say that the upcoming vote had the aura of life or death of the measure hovering over it. Emil had nearly exhausted his magic tricks on every member who had the least inkling to support the controversial bill. Yet he still needed a vote. So, he turned to Senator Stanley Novak, a Caucasian Democrat who hailed from a district entirely within the City of Detroit. The

Senator's nickname was "Stash," Polish for Stan.

Emil put the maximum squeeze on Stash for that final vote, and got a halfhearted commitment. Yet when it was finally time to vote, low and behold, Stash didn't take the plunge after all. Instead, the stubborn Senator cast a "nay" vote, and reserved the right to explain his no vote. The Open Housing Bill momentarily bit the dust. With a gruff and somewhat righteous manner, Stash Novak approached the microphone on the Senate floor.

Every Senator and staff person there knew that Stash roomed in Lansing with two black Senators from Detroit—Coleman Young, and Basil Brown—and one white Senator, Roger Craig. Emil, along with the press, and everyone else was curious as to what possible rationale Senator Stash might have to justify his logic in voting to defeat Open Housing under such obvious conflicting circumstances. When he was recognized by the presiding officer to explain his no vote, Stash tried to explain his thinking to the hushed chamber. He blurted out, "I voted no, because I don't mind living with them, but I don't want them living next door to me. . . ."

When the tense laughter died down, Emil moved to reconsider the vote by which the bill had failed, and slipped over to ask the somewhat confused Senator if he had totally reneged on their bargain. When Stash sheepishly said he might give it another try on the next vote, Emil told him he would "make it easy" on him. Instead of Stash voting in the usual alphabetical order, Emil would arrange it so his name would be called last. "Easier" or not, Emil arranged it. He knew that Stash would be under maximum pressure to vote as promised, since the tally would still need one more vote when it got to him. The whole world would be watching Stash Novak.

By the time the Secretary of the Senate called out "Mr. Novak" at the very end, right after "Mr. Zollar," Stash—sweating profusely—succumbed to the pressure, and voted to pass the bill. Emil got his vote. He and other insiders will never forget how really close it was. Later in life, Emil still chuckled when he talked about the incident, and confessed a fondness for "the Senator who made a difference in passing the Open Housing Bill into law." Turns out, he recalled ironically, that Governor Romney even acknowledged Senator Novak's contribution with a letter of thanks, a document which Stash kept framed on his office wall for years thereafter.[273]

◆

WALTER REUTHER SAVES HENRY FORD'S BACON

In those days, as one of the most powerful political figures in Michigan, Emil had his share of front row seats to history. Another case in point was his appointment by Governor Romney to the New Detroit Committee's prestigious Board of Trustees, a group comprised of a Who's Who of the Detroit area. New Detroit had been created almost instantly following the July 1967 riots in that city. Emil joined corporate chieftains such as Henry Ford II, organized labor's legendary Walter Reuther, financier Max Fisher, and the future Mayor of Detroit and fellow Senator, Coleman Young. Dozens of members represented the auto industry, other businesses, labor, universities, churches, local elected officials, and community activists. Their mandate was to seek solutions to the rising unrest in the three county area that held as its political and economic center the City of Detroit. Emil was the only member from outside that area asked to serve.[274] Those in the know recognized that they needed Emil on their team if they hoped to have a lasting impact in the Capitol.

Emil is sole non-Detroit area **legislator serving on New Detroit Committee** following July '67 Detroit riots. Shown (upper right) with members Jack Wood, Mrs. Jean Washington, and Brock Brush, M.D. Detroit (MI), 1969. *Published by New Detroit, Inc., with acknowledgments to* Detroit Free Press, Detroit News, *Safran Printing Co., Campbell-Ewald Co., The Thos. P. Henry Co., and Art Place.*

Emil told a story of the first meeting of New Detroit, which characterizes the aura of tension that existed among many of its members. "One of the militant black activists wanted to bring his gun into the meeting, and, of course, they wouldn't let him," Emil remembered. "That made the guy really mad, from the looks of it. So, later on, during the meeting, the same guy got up from his seat, and stood right behind Henry Ford. Henry was Chairman of Ford Motor Company. His nickname was Henry the Deuce, because he was grandson of the founder who had the same name. Anyway, the militant called out to Henry, 'Next time, we're coming out to Grosse Pointe to get you where you live. We don't give a damn whether we burn the whole place down—so you'd better put out here, or we're going to #*@%&* you!' I thought he was going to throw Henry right out the window.

"You can imagine how that brought the conversation around the table to a halt. We all wondered whether we were going to have to wrestle this guy down, or what," Emil recalled. "So, Walter Reuther, who might have been one of the toughest negotiators on earth at that time, stood up and walked behind the black guy. Walter said to him, 'Who the hell do you think you are, you little squirt? I've been trying to get money from these bastards since before you were born, and I've managed to get a hell of a lot more than you'll ever get . . . so go and sit down.' " Emil said that the belligerent guy did sit down, probably because Reuther had earned the right to speak as champion of working people, black and white. "As far as I'm concerned," Emil speculated, "the only thing that scared Walter Reuther was hell itself."[275]

Emil ended up contributing his considerable expertise to New Detroit during the remainder of his Senate term. He believed that, overall, the group helped the deep wounds begin to heal in Detroit. He did not recall, fortunately, any more public confrontations occurring during meetings while he served on the Committee.

15
WHY EMIL VIEWED AS CONSUMMATE LEADER

E mil's unique style of leadership in the arena of the Michigan Legislature, and politics in general, marched boldly among the many styles of leadership on parade there. But no easy turn of phrase or handy label can answer the question, "Why was Emil viewed as the consummate leader?"

The Byzantine workings of the Michigan Legislature have bewildered many of the great and would-be great, since Michigan won statehood in 1837. But obviously it did not bewilder Emil. Why? One clue lies in Naval Lieutenant Emil Lockwood's deft handling of his LST's unwieldy pump and anchor navigation system while under attack by Japanese kamikazes. Compared to that ordeal, he experienced considerably less trouble mastering the labyrinthine nature of the Legislature, even though Emil testified that it may have come close once or twice at that.

Another insight can be gained from a noted American philosopher—William James—who defined a truly American trait in the late 19th Century. To describe the genius he observed inherent in the nation's greatest achievements, he coined the term "pragmatism." Unfortunately pragmatism today has taken on connotations of acting to achieve an end at any cost, often with little regard for the ethics involved. This assuredly was not James's notion. He described pragmatism as "a method of mediating between the extremes of competing conceptions of reality and truth, between rationalism and empiricism, between contrasting temperaments. . . ." He believed that a pragmatist acted with a goal in mind largely unencumbered by preconceptions, ideological rigor, or narrow intellectual barriers.[276] That is why American leaders, free of their old country's social, political, religious and economic structures, soon surpassed the accomplishments of their homelands. Emil surely qualifies as an American Pragmatist in the original sense of that term.

His later business partner, Jerry Coomes, worked with Emil on several issues during his term as Majority Leader. He underscored this notion about Emil by noting that "perhaps his greatest strength was his ability to cross the aisle to develop personal relationships and, what I call, a position of trust with the other side, in this case, the Democrats. . . ." According to Jerry, "Emil was not a typical Senate Majority Leader from a rural area. He absolutely did not embrace the conventional position of rural Republican legislators on civil rights, public housing and public accommodations. He believed in those causes just as deeply as any member of the minority community."

Emil's future business partner, Jerry Coomes (center) moderates panel at Michigan Catholic Conference legislative conference. Left to right: Sen. Maj. Leader Lockwood; Sen. Min. Leader Coleman Young; Jerry Coomes, Exec. Dir. MCC;. House Minority Leader Robert Waldron, and House Speaker William Ryan. Lansing (MI), 1968.

Jerry elaborated on this point. "Emil used a very focused, practical method for rounding up votes. He was like a hunter stalking a rare animal," Jerry remembered. "Emil would know the issue substantively, and politically. And then he would be endlessly patient with that person, and endlessly generous if that person needed some kind of tradeoff. He didn't bluster, or pound the table, or threaten the legislator. He was more like a spider enclosing the prey in his web so slowly that he hardly noticed."[277]

Former Senate colleague, and long-time G.O.P. Congressman Guy Vander Jagt agreed in an interview for this book that "Emil was very pragmatic. He could trim his legislative goal down to where it was saleable." Guy described Emil as "the greatest leader the Senate has ever had. He was the closest thing to LBJ that Michigan ever saw, only not as irascible, or crude. Emil was more low key, but equally effective."[278]

Richard Whitmer acted as legislative counsel for both Governors Romney and Milliken during many of the same years. He later served as Director of the Commerce Department while Emil briefly worked there. Now CEO of Blue Cross Blue Shield of Michigan, and also a long-time friend of Emil, Dick remembered those days well. "Emil was a pragmatist," he said, "and he worked from dawn to dusk. He got a lot of things done. Then at 2:00 a.m., after a full day, he'd still be playing cards at the City Club."

Dick said that Emil treated legislators the same way he treated the press, and that was one of the keys to understanding his effectiveness. "Emil treated everyone the same," according to Dick. "He was honest, and not partisan. He saw problems and ideas, not a man or a woman, or other differences. He worked harder than anyone else to boot. He was very ethical, and at the same time, he was charming and direct. He knew the issues, and had a good sense of humor. He charmed people with his personality, his knowledge of the issues, and his work ethic."

Dick summed up his take on Emil's leadership style this way: "Emil was a John Wayne type. He didn't notice gender, or race, or political differences, and didn't take credit for hardly anything."[279] A more fitting tribute to a political leader from his colleagues and friends can hardly be imagined. But why did a prominent member of the Capitol press corps compare Emil to Machiavelli? Did Emil take his pragmatism too far at times?

WHY COLUMNIST CALLED EMIL "MACHIAVILLIAN"

Bill Kulsea, a close observer of Senate Majority Leader Emil Lockwood, called him just that in his regular column for Booth Newspapers in July 1969. His exact words were: "There is a Michigan Machiavelli after all. His name is Emil Lockwood and he is a Republican state senator from St. Louis."[280]

In *The Prince,* the Rennaissance Italian Machievelli "denies the relevance of morality in political affairs, and holds that craft and deceit are justified in pursuing and maintaining political power."[281] After reading Kulsea's largely complimentary article, one can speculate that what he really meant by the comparison was that it was a mystery just how Emil was so successful in the Senate. He operated in full view of everyone, yet nobody but Emil really knew how he did it.

"Lockwood is an enigma to many," according to Kulsea's column. "He is tricky, in a seemingly simple way; a political prince who works best in an atmosphere of confusion. Only he knows what's going on when everyone else is grappling for answers, for motives why that bill or this bill is being killed or passed. He trades, deals, compromises on bills that the governor may not want passed, and lets the world know about it. And he gets what he wants."

So far, this sounds like a brilliant tactician, not a devious, amoral power-seeker.

"Whatever his enemies say about him," Kulsea continued, "they do admit that he keeps his word and is frank in his assessment of whether a bill can or cannot pass. Many in both parties don't like his tactics but they respect his ability." Again, Kulsea seemed to deny his own description of Emil as "Machiavellian" by testifying to his colleagues' admission that "he keeps his word." It appears that Kulsea used the comparison as an attention getting device, not a literal portrayal.

Almost marveling at Michigan's "political prince," Kulsea again praised Emil. "He always seems to be a day or a week ahead of his opposition and characteristically carries his widest smile when deepest in trouble. Worry seems alien to his nature and he never frets or sulks if he loses one or two bills, or if legislative problems appear."[282] It should be clear by now that Kulsea could not make a good case for his "Machiavellian" charge. He did portray an effective and ethical pragmatist, however.

On Senate floor with John Bowman (D-Roseville), Emil discusses upcoming Senate session. Lansing (MI), circa 1968.

EMIL'S BAG OF TRICKS

Emil can definitely be said to have possessed a big bag of tricks when it came to maneuvering in and around the Legislature. The fact is, his bag of tricks was even deeper than most people knew. Former Senator Robert Vander Laan, a colleague of Emil's during the entire time Emil served in the Senate, and his successor as Majority Leader, had some interesting insights on the way Emil carried out his always-challenging duties.

"Emil was an adept politician," Bob said in an interview. "You might even call him a political junkie. He was 100% committed to his role in the legislature. The only person who came close to his total dedication as Majority Leader was (future Governor) John Engler. Emil was not only an adept politician, he had a keen intellect, and great political insight. The members respected him for his knowledge, and his memory of facts. It was just like when he played cards—nobody wanted to play against him, because he was so good at it."

Bob Vander Laan revealed a particularly effective technique Emil used for gaining support from some recalcitrant members of the Senate: "Emil kept a list of each Senator's campaign contributors, and how much they gave," Bob said. "So when a vote came up that might affect that contributor, he wasn't averse to calling the contributor up to get some help if he needed the

Senator's vote."

"Man in Motion" at home in command—Senate Majority Leader Emil Lockwood at Senate podium. Lansing (MI), 1967.

One of the things Emil excelled at, Bob remembered, was his ability to forge close one-on-one relationships with all kinds of people. "Emil invested in relationships," Bob said, "he didn't show up just when he needed someone. For instance, he would often invite a small group of fellow Senators over to his Lansing place at night to play cards. He reached out to Democrats too, such as Ray Dzendzel, and Stan Roszycki. Black legislators respected Emil too, because of his record of voting for minorities. Senators saw Emil Lockwood as a man of the world, not just a guy from St. Louis,"[283] he said.

A good example of Emil's ability to forge bonds with other Senators, regardless of their party or race, lies in the Coleman Young incident. When the black Democratic Senator, who would later become the legendary Mayor of Detroit, was accused wrongly of once belonging to a Communist group, Emil rose to his feet in the Senate Chamber to fiercely defend his friend. Emil believed, as illustrated in this instance, that friendship always trumped playing for destructive partisan advantage.[284]

Emil didn't like to make speeches on the Senate Floor, or preside over the proceedings, he recalled in an interview. His style was to work as quietly as possible with individual members. He said the real job of the Leader was to "get results, not make noise." He did, however, allow as how "sometimes certain members might need a pat on the back, and then again, other times they might need a kick in the pants." When asked about his well-known strategy of frequently reaching out to Democrats for votes instead of battling them at every turn, Emil said, "It's simple. You can't assemble an army if you shoot them all first."

To keep tabs on members he needed for different upcoming votes, Emil used another technique that is not taught in political science classes. "There was a barber shop in the hotel across the street from the Capitol where a lot of legislators got their haircuts," Emil recalled. "I got mine there too—sometimes more often than I really needed it. I used to ask the barber who he had down in his book for haircuts in the next day or two, and if it was somebody I wanted to talk to, I scheduled my haircut right before or after his. I could get a good twenty minutes or a half-hour to talk to the guy when he was captive in his chair. I got a lot of help that way," Emil chuckled.[285] That about sums up Emil's no-nonsense approach to running the Senate from his point of view. He did what he thought was best, and let others do the talking about it.

Members of the Capitol press corps had a few more choice tidbits to add. Roger Lane, Lansing Bureau Chief for the *Detroit Free Press*, may have had the best take on Emil's methods for keeping the lid on the Senate in contentious times, and coming out a winner. Lane described Emil as "a crew cut, one-time collegiate wrestler [who] is considered to be by his admirers a master of the legislative art." He noted that Emil's "influence is spreading. Savvy Michigan Republicans consult him before making a big political move."

In face of the closely divided upper chamber, Lane said that Emil's fellow G.O.P Senators—"princelings all as committee chairmen—are split a dozen ways: A jealous, contentious, ambitious crew forever breaking ranks." So, Emil had to use his wits, according to Lane, rather than force of numbers, to be effective as the Governor's "field marshal."[286]

Stopping by the "Breakfast Roundtable" was another of Emil's techniques, according to Lane. Emil usually showed up early, about 7:00 a.m., in the Jack Tar Hotel coffee shop across South Capitol Avenue from the Capitol. There, a random, revolving number of legislators and lobbyists gathered each morning during the legislative session to "swap and sort overnight political intelligence."

One time Emil was confronted by a reporter and asked how he could justify being hosted every morning for breakfast by lobbyists. Emil just shrugged nonchalantly and replied, "I've never lost sleep over a cup of coffee."[287] No place was off limits to Emil, according to the reporter. After a long day of meetings, and a legislative session, Lane said that Emil was "a sure drop-in at any sizable legislative social gathering, paying his respects and picking up the scoop."

"To many, Lockwood is an enigma, to others he is a chameleon," Lane wrote. "His flexibility is a key trait. He is smart, tireless, resourceful, and a conniver and yet strictly a man of his word. He's a regular Republican with a host of Democratic friends, a fast man with a favor." Lane likened Emil to a "parish priest" counseling his diverse political flock.[288] This may be an apt comparison to a keen observer like Roger Lane, but it is a sure bet that Emil never looked upon himself as one particularly suited to wear a cassock and collar.

◆

WHY THE PRESS RESPECTED EMIL

Emil enjoyed extraordinarily good relations with most news reporters, as numerous accounts have shown so far. Why? It was an era before Watergate, of course, after which most political reporters felt compelled to emulate the famous investigative journalists, Woodward and Bernstein, who broke that sinister story.

So it is certain that reporters who covered the State Capitol in the 1960s had not yet adopted the more cynical attitudes of their successors in the post-Watergate era. But they still thought politicians were fair game, and never hesitated to point out their foibles. Emil was not exempt from being targeted by the press. It is just that a review of a cross section of daily metropolitan newspapers, and selected smaller dailies and weeklies, particularly in Emil's district, demonstrates an unusually high percentage of articles favorable to him, or at worst neutral. Furthermore, it is even more interesting that after Emil became a high-profile lobbyist—an occupation not known for attracting favorable press coverage—his press treatment remained uncommonly favorable.[289] What was his secret?

As Emil's contemporaries have said, Emil treated everyone the same. He was honest, fair, frank, knew his issues, had a good sense of humor, did not take himself too seriously, handled his responsibilities with deftness and achieved unusual success. And, probably the trait that should go to the top of this list is—*he never tried to hide anything.* Reporters knew that what they saw was what they got. No hidden agendas. No contrived, superficial statements. No resentment of the reporter's intrusion into his business. If Emil told a reporter something, he could take it to the bank. Unfortunately these traits did not describe those of the average elected official, at least in the eyes of the press.

An example of Emil's forthrightness in dealing with the press was the annual voluntary disclosure of his income tax returns and statement of net worth to the Governor, Secretary of State, and senior Capitol news correspondent. Recipients of the documents were invited to raise questions about the information, but not to disseminate it—a request dutifully honored, ostensibly because they never found any dubious transactions, or conflicts of interest. The most laudatory aspect of Emil's disclosure was that, not only was it not a requirement, but no other legislator did so.[290]

Another story Emil told about these years as Senate Majority Leader highlights his rare relationship with a particularly influential political columnist known among Lansing's political class for his razor sharp pen, and his acerbic wit, Bill Kulsea.

It is fair to say that Emil and Kulsea had developed a healthy respect for each other over the years that Emil served in the Senate. They could even be called "more friendly than not" to each other, though each of them knew very well the limits that existed between reporter and elected official. Emil knew that if Kulsea ever ran into something that smelled fishy, he would not hesitate to write about it. His column appeared in several Michigan cities, such as Grand Rapids, Kalamazoo, Jackson, Flint, Ann Arbor, Bay City and Saginaw. Many a legislator had felt the sting of Kulsea's sharp pen in the past. With this background, Emil's story involving the eagle-eyed Bill Kulsea can be better appreciated.

"One Friday after session," Emil liked to recount, "I was wrapping things up on the Senate Floor—just about everyone else had already left—when a Senator came up to me. He looked kind of sheepish. He was a Democrat, and somebody who occasionally gave me a vote on something or other. He told me in kind of a hushed voice that he had a big problem, and he needed my help to get him out of a jam. He flashed $200, and asked me if I would hold on to it for him until Monday. Seems he had just learned that his wife was about to show up any minute. He said that whenever his wife drove up from the district, she hit him up for all his cash, and that meant that he wouldn't have any money to spend in Lansing until the next payday. But, turns out he had worse problems than that.

"His second problem," Emil revealed with a broad grin, "was that his wife wanted to go to lunch, and he had already asked his girlfriend to go to lunch before he knew his wife was coming. She was also due any minute. So, the guy asked me if I would do him another favor—intercept his girlfriend, and take her out to lunch. He was in a real pickle, and while I didn't necessarily cotton to what he was doing, I said I would help him out.

"Just as he was handing me the $200, out of the corner of my eye, I saw Bill Kulsea watching us like a hawk. I knew I'd better think fast, or this whole thing could come to no good. The $200 he had just handed me was a fair amount of cash in the 1960s, and I realized that it didn't look too good for the Majority Leader to be accepting a handful of cash on the Senate floor from a Senate Democrat.

"Anyway, I sent the guy on his way, and I made a beeline for Kulsea," Emil continued. "I asked Kulsea right out if he would do me a favor, and hold on to the $200 until Monday. He looked at me kind of skeptical. I told him the pickle the Senator was in, and that I agreed to help him out. But, just so that Kulsea didn't get any wrong ideas about me accepting cash on the Senate floor, I thought it best for Kulsea to hang on to it over the weekend.

And—I'll be damned—Kulsea agreed, and gave it back to me on Monday. I also went and found the Senator's girlfriend, told her the story, and took her to lunch. I wasn't that happy about it, but that was nothing compared to the poor Democrat—he had both of the women right there in the same restaurant."[291]

It is safe to say that few men—elected officials or not—could duplicate such presence of mind, such display of trust, and such disarming rapport with a skeptical reporter. It is clear that Emil had not developed Kulsea's trust the day before yesterday.

There is no such award from the Capitol Press Corps as Favorite Senator. But they do designate annually the Most Influential Member of the Senate. Emil deservedly won that very award in 1970. Even a cursory scan of his press coverage during his four-year tour of duty as Majority Leader, clearly demonstrates why he won such a prestigious award. This relationship of trust with the Capitol Press Corps would carry over to his years as premier lobbyist in the 1970s.

16

EMIL FACES FIRST "DUMP LOCKWOOD" ATTEMPT

Not everything was coming up roses for Emil, however. Newton's law of physics that states "for every action, there is an opposite and equal reaction" applies equally to politics. As Emil's success skyrocketed, so did increasing resentment of his leadership by some of the more conservative Senate G.O.P. caucus members. Two well-publicized attempts at deposing him, or at least clipping his wings, were launched in 1968 and 1969, while Emil served as Majority Leader. A look into these incidents, and how Emil confronted them, demonstrates how complicated and politically life threatening such hijack attempts in a 20-member Senate caucus can actually become.

The first real challenge began to gather steam following the November 1968 general election. That fall the U.S. President, the Congress, and Michigan's House of Representatives were elected, but not Michigan's Governor, other statewide officeholders, or the State Senate. Emil, accordingly, did not have to run for re-election, thanks to the new state constitution. Senate caucus leadership elections, however, were on the docket for November 25-27, 1968 in Cadillac, a resort town in northern Michigan.

Reporters picked up some grumbling by a few disenchanted G.O.P. Senators that they might try to elect a new Majority Leader to serve for the next two years, thus replacing Emil. There was a growing list of reasons it seems, for why they thought this might be the appropriate time to act.

The main substantive issues that had drawn displeasure from some of the dissident caucus members were Emil's siding with Governor Romney, and championing both the state income tax and the Open Housing Law. Perhaps an even more overarching development was the election of President Richard Nixon. There was rampant speculation, not unfounded, that Romney would soon be appointed to a Nixon cabinet post, causing Lieutenant Governor William Milliken to succeed him as Governor. It also forecast the likelihood that the post of President Pro Tem of the Senate—the official who presided over daily Senate legislative sessions, now held automatically by Milliken—would have to be filled by a Senator of the majority party.

In turn, caucus members anticipated that the chosen G.O.P. Senator would most probably vacate an important committee chairmanship to devote full attention to the task of presiding over sessions. The Senator likely to be elected to that post was Thomas Schweigert, from Petoskey. If he got the job, this would leave the State Affairs Committee without a chairman. A spirited competition for that post, along with the need to replace newly retired Appropriations head, Frank Beadle, meant that a kind of musical chairs would probably ensue. The Majority Leader thus would enjoy a unique midterm opportunity to appoint new key committee chairmen.

Moreover, since Emil had served as Nixon's hand picked state campaign chairman, and was viewed as having been a "major power and leader" in that role, he was expected to receive a job offer in the Nixon administration. Such an appointment would leave the recently juggled Senate leaderless.[292]

With all of these balls of uncertainty bouncing in the air at the same time, the potential was rampant for something just short of chaos developing at the upcoming Cadillac caucus. Emil, in fact, revealed to Bob Stuart, a Capitol correspondent from the Lansing *State Journal*, that there might be a "Dump Lockwood" plan being cooked up for the meeting, adding that "it has been talked about for two years." But he told Stuart that he didn't know of any concrete schemes underway.[293]

Less than two weeks later, the Cadillac *coup* had failed to materialize. In a secret ballot, Emil was re-elected Majority Leader. No public statement was made by anyone regarding whether the anticipated Dump Lockwood plan materialized. Some of the underlying causes had not been addressed to the satisfaction of the dissidents, however, and it would only be a matter of months until they boiled to the surface again.

STRONG LEADERS STEP UP: LOCKWOOD AND RYAN

Interestingly, as Emil recalled all too well, on the Democratic side of the Senate aisle, following the Open Housing decision, Senator Dzendzel had been deposed several months before as Minority Leader, and replaced by Senator Sander Levin (D-Berkley). One of the purported reasons for Dzendzel's downfall was his close relationship with Emil in cooperating on a wide range of legislation. Emil, in fact, had even lent his endorsement in a radio advertisement in behalf of Ray Dzendzel that was aired in Dzendzel's district during the fall campaign.[294] Emil explained that he was "awfully sorry to see such a close collaborator and good friend as Ray Dzendzel suffer defeat in his caucus, especially if his relationship with me had anything to do with it." Relations between Emil and the Senate Democratic leadership in the Senate were never quite the same after that, according to Emil.[295]

In the House of Representatives, Democrats won 57 seats to the Republicans' 53 seats in the November 1968 election, throwing rather precarious control over the lower chamber to the Democrats. William A. Ryan (D-Detroit) was elected Speaker, while Robert Waldron (R-Grosse Pointe) got the nod from his caucus to serve as Minority Leader. In effect, these two leaders merely swapped roles as a result of the November election results. The close House elections, teamed with the razor thin partisan split in the Senate, and the increasing breach between conservative, moderate, and liberal members in both houses, meant that strong leaders would have to come to the fore to bring more order to the legislative process.

On its face, it is difficult to find more opposite legislative leaders than Emil Lockwood and Bill Ryan serving at the same time. Ryan hailed from Detroit, to many the state's epicenter economically, socially and politically. Ryan had completed only high school, grown up politically through the powerful United Auto Workers (UAW) labor union, was very much a New Deal Democrat, and a devout Catholic devoted to using government to help bring social and economic justice to all levels of society.

Emil, on the other hand, held an M.B.A. from the University of Michigan, had paid his dues in the world of the small-business entrepreneur, represented small towns and farming areas, and took a dim view of government intruding in areas that more properly belonged to the individual and the private sector. Without knowing their skills, dedication and willingness to search for solutions instead of battle slogans, many might have justifiably assumed that these two men would be genetically wired to be political adversaries. To those who knew Emil and Bill Ryan well, however, it came as no surprise that they found ways to get things done in spite of the many obstacles they faced.

In two respects, Emil held an edge during the next two years. First, he had already served as Majority Leader for the two prior years, while Ryan had only just risen to the Speakership. In addition, Emil belonged to the same party as Milliken, the brand-new Governor. Emil planned to help him, just as he had his predecessor, George Romney. Since the Governor introduces each year's state budget, can use his "bully pulpit" to steer public opinion, and significantly, holds the power of the legislative veto, Emil's role as Governor Milliken's field marshal in the legislature gave him clout, in many instances, not enjoyed by other leaders.

Majority Leader Lockwood and Speaker Ryan, while often disagreeing on legislative initiatives, did find enough common ground to shepherd the adoption of many important laws, and in the process, grew to regard one another with esteem. Important legislative initiatives adopted during the 1969-1970 session, among others, included continuation of the modernization of legislative support systems, creation of a state administrative procedures act, prohibition of automobile insurance redlining, creation of a state bureau of youth services, creation of a state construction safety commission and local building authorities, adoption of a shoreline protection act, establishment of a civil service system for county employees, and an increase in minimum wage.[296]

Romney's U. S. Presidential pre-campaign strategies tossed around after hours—Romney (left), Emil (right), with Rep. Russ Strange (later upset by future Gov. John Engler), and others. Lansing (MI), 1969.

U. S. Congressman Guy Vander Jagt (and former State Senator) confers with long-time friend and Sen. Maj. Leader Lockwood. Lansing (MI), 1968.

"Lockwood Keeping Busy During Recess"—Capitol correspondent Marcia Van Ness interviews Emil, following stormy caucus-leadership standoff. Lansing *State Journal*, August 10, 1969.

One of the most prominent and contentious measures that the legislature faced during this period was whether the state should (or, even could, constitutionally) grant non-public school students government aid for their education. Emil and Ryan did agree on that one, but found, after several bold attempts, that it could not be resolved within the legislature alone. The effort brought together, however, a triumvirate that would work together on many issues in the future, albeit in different roles. The aid to non-public school initiative, called "Parochiaid" by the press, teamed up Lockwood, Ryan, and then powerful lobbyist for the Michigan Catholic Conference, Jerry Coomes.

Emil always chuckled when he recalled the Parochiaid effort, engineered by Jerry Coomes. The *Wall Street Journal* described accurately the unparalleled effort to get state government to approve $40 million to aid secular aspects of non-public schools. In a front page article on March 26, 1969, the *Journal* reported: "Francis J. Coomes is a man to be reckoned with in political matters here. . . . He can rally thousands of volunteer workers, tens of thousands of letter writers, and more than a half-million voters to back up his efforts at persuasion."[297]

Emil remembered well the thousands of letters of support for Parochiaid that rolled into legislators' offices. "Jerry really had that thing organized," Emil said. "I got so many letters, I had to hire two extra girls just to open them. I can tell you though there wasn't any money in the envelopes. I checked myself. I thought it might be nice if they sent some money—I could have used it to pay the girls. If there had been a ten dollar bill in each envelope, I would have been a millionaire overnight."

Emil continued the story with that certain Emil glint in his eye. "There must have been a few atheists in those churches," he said, "because once in a while we'd open an envelope, and there wasn't a darn thing inside. The priest must have asked all the parishioners to send a letter of support, and some just couldn't do it. Then maybe they felt guilty, so they addressed an empty envelope, and sent it anyway." In any event, Emil said he developed even more respect for Jerry, because of his adept handling of Parochiaid, and the emerging abortion issue as well.[298]

17
EMIL'S STOCK GROWS IN MICHIGAN G.O.P.

E mil's clout in the Michigan Republican Party had grown steadily from the time he was elected Minority Leader in the Senate. His relationship with Governor Romney had blossomed into a warm and productive one from that point forward. He delivered the goods repeatedly for the charismatic, moderate Republican, who was trying to wrest control of the Republican Party apparatus, put the state on its feet financially, deal with the growing community unrest, and run for president at the same time.

Emil remembered Romney as "one of the nicest guys I've ever met. Talk about clout. He had it, and he used it. He was a strong leader, and I respected him. I guess he thought I was okay, too, because he let me get away with just about anything," Emil said in an interview.

Emil and the hard-driving Governor saw eye to eye on a lot of things. For instance, Romney knew it was important to strengthen Emil's hand with the Senate Republicans, and at the same time demonstrate that he and Emil were close friends and allies. One of the ways the Governor did so was to host selected Senators at his Governor's House on scenic Mackinac Island. Emil gave him names of lawmakers he ought to invite, and the Governor would invite them. According to plan, during their stay he would schmooze with them about legislative matters he was pushing. In some instances, it was better for Romney not to be there. So on some of those weekends Emil hosted a few Senators and their wives, and Emil did his own schmoozing.

As Governor Romney and Emil became friends, Romney often invited Emil and Mariella to social functions, such as to his son Mitt's wedding. "At first, I was kind of surprised that the Governor wanted me to come to those family functions," Emil recalled. "I didn't think that I was all that much of a potentate to be invited, along with all the dignitaries. I remember at one big bash, I got to visit with nine different big shots that I needed to see for various reasons. Anyway, he kept inviting me back, so I guess I behaved myself."

The most famous incident involving Emil and Governor Romney—one that several people interviewed for this book remember—took place in the Capitol hallway outside the Senate Republican caucus. The way Emil told it, it happened during the only time Romney was invited to speak to the caucus.

"I never had any fights with Romney," Emil related. "But a lot of people have kidded me over the years about the Governor tearing off the lapels on my suit jacket. It really wasn't all that big of a deal, but everybody got a kick out of it anyway."

"Senator Lockwood, with lapels"—after Gov. Romney inadvertently ripped off Emil's lapels in heated talk, media long afterwards noted the state of his jackets. Lansing (MI), 1967. *Family album, newspaper unknown.*

Sen. Lockwood, with lapels

Senator Lockwood, without lapels–Emil poses in lapel-less jacket given to him in jest by Senate Democrats after Gov. Romney incident. Lansing (MI), 1967.

Vice President of Belgian Senate visits Michigan Governor due to Emil's friendship with Freddy Van Gaever. Left to right: Emil, Freddy and Lieve Van Gaever, Mrs. and VP Sen. Robert Vandekerckhove, Gov. Milliken. Lansing (MI), 1970.

Ugliest Cheerleader

Never too busy for a neighbor, pep rally guest speaker Emil crowns "Ugliest Cheerleader" of St. Louis High School, Leslie Mead. *Daily Record-Leader Photo,* January 15, 1971.

Emil recalled that Senator Bob Huber was always complaining that he never got to see the Governor, and he ought to come to the Senate Republican caucus to meet and discuss ideas. So, Emil invited Romney to attend the next caucus, and greeted him outside the room where the caucus was meeting. On an issue unrelated to the meeting, Romney was so fired up about a matter that he wanted Emil to look after, that he playfully grabbed Emil's lapels, and started shaking them.

"Sure enough," Emil said, "my old coat wasn't ready for that, and both my lapels ripped right off in his hands. I don't know if George or I was more surprised. Anyway, some reporters and staff people actually saw the whole thing," Emil remembered. "We all started to laugh, and some Democratic Senators saw it too. Later on, the Senate Democratic caucus invited me over, and presented me with a special lapel-less coat in honor of my having to take so much guff from the Governor."[299]

As Emil's visibility and power grew in the Capitol, so did his role in the Michigan G.O.P. Party. Romney, very much a moderate philosophically, had headed up the state party since becoming Governor in 1963. As a result, other moderates, such as Emil, enjoyed an unparalleled opportunity in the party to excel.

There can be little doubt that Emil's progressive brand of politics meshed with the mainstream mood of Michigan's political class in the 1960s. His sometimes stunning legislative victories, that depended on marshaling the middle of the political spectrum, serve not only as reminders of Emil's moderate bent, but also of his winning personality, and his command of the issues.

While Emil's moderate reputation in the Capitol helped propel him to prominence, it most likely was his hard-won stature as the "man-who-gets-things-done" that brought him to the attention of G.O.P. presidential candidate Richard Nixon in early 1968.

Emil was "one of the strongest backers of Gov. George Romney for the presidential nomination," according to Robert Stuart, reporter for the Lansing *State Journal.* Romney had been considered a presidential possibility since first winning the Michigan Governor's post in 1962. His formal campaign, however, lasted only a few months. So, just four days after Emil's friend and close ally formally withdrew, the Nixon camp contacted Emil to ask him to head up the "Nixon for President" campaign in Michigan.

Following a meeting with Romney several days later, Emil met with reporters on March 12, 1968 to announce his decision. "I am looking forward to working for the nomination of former Vice President Richard Nixon, who I feel is the best choice of the Republicans, now that Governor Romney has withdrawn from the race," Emil told the reporters.

The press was eager to know how the Governor had reacted to Emil's decision to support a candidate with whom Romney had recently crossed swords so vigorously. Emil wisely offered only that Romney had made no suggestions "one way or the other—nor did he encourage me to do it." His first task, he told the press, was to set up a state campaign office, and appoint congressional district chairmen across Michigan.[300]

Emil remembered meeting candidate Nixon for the first time that year. "He called me and told me he was taking one of those 'Whistle Stop' train tours," Emil recalled. "Then he asked if I would gather up a small delegation and meet him in Columbus, Ohio," Emil said. "I agreed, so I took three or four cohorts down there. We met at a private club.

"To one of the best guys I ever met"— Emil presents Senate tribute to Governor as Romney leaves Michigan to join Nixon's Cabinet as HUD Secretary. Lansing (MI), February 2, 1969.

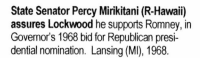

State Senator Percy Mirikitani (R-Hawaii) assures Lockwood he supports Romney, in Governor's 1968 bid for Republican presidential nomination. Lansing (MI), 1968.

Romney accepts Nixon cabinet position in Washington as Secretary of HUD; bids farewell to key legislative strategist Lockwood (right), photographer Harry Fox (left), and Rep. Loren Anderson (R-Pontiac); accepts keepsake of MI Capitol. Lansing *State Journal*, February 2, 1969.

"As far as I'm concerned," Emil said, "Dick Nixon was a real nice guy. Real personable. I got along with him real well from the start. We put together one hell of a campaign in Michigan in a short time.

"We planned a big Nixon visit to Michigan, which included the Capitol City, of course," Emil continued. "I got a committee together to pull the thing off. About 20% of the members were Democrats, if you can believe that. I remember getting a military honor guard from Detroit to greet him. That came off well. We even got the Jack Tar Hotel to lay a new carpet for his stay overnight in Lansing.

"There were a couple of other things about Nixon's visit that stand out," Emil remembered. "He must have had six advance men come in and turn the place upside down before he came. I told them that I might be able to pull a few strings, and get enough people off work early that day, so they could line the street where Nixon's motorcade was supposed to come. They loved that idea. So, that's what I did—it looked great, all those people waving at Richard Nixon.

Emil agrees to coordinate Nixon campaign for president in Michigan, and manage five states for Nixon at Republican National Convention in Miami. Lansing (MI), 1968.

"Another problem the advance team told me about was a train delay along the route," Emil recalled. "They didn't like the security risk of their candidate being trapped by a train crossing. I could see that. So, I suggested that we arrange a stop at an ice cream shop before we got to the crossing. And by.George, that's what we did. You should have seen the looks on the faces of the customers when Dick and Pat Nixon walked in to order ice cream cones. Believe me, the reporters' cameras were flashing away."

At the Republican nominating convention that summer, Emil also served as Nixon's regional floor coordinator for several states geographically close to Michigan. Emil remembered that the hardest part of his job came after Nixon won the nomination for President.

"Suddenly the word came over to me that Nixon wanted somebody I had never heard of to be his Vice Presidential running mate," Emil said. "His name was Spiro Agnew. My job was to get in touch immediately with floor managers from the other states that were assigned to me. Hell, nobody ever heard of the guy. Frankly, the way it turned out, I wish we'd never heard of him, period.

"Anyway," Emil continued, I heard some pretty loud objections. I told them, 'Look, if you support Nixon, it's asinine to reject his choice for running mate. I don't know Agnew; you don't know Agnew. But, we know Dick Nixon, and we trust him. So, we're going to vote for Agnew'."

Emil said that Agnew won over the other candidates for Veep, and he got to invite all the delegates in his region who voted for Agnew to a big party to meet him. "That party was a lot of fun," Emil remembered, "but it sure is a good thing that we didn't know at that time what kind of a crook Agnew would turn out to be."[301]

Five of Nixon's letters to Emil related to the 1968 presidential campaign have survived these many years, and many moves. The first, a March 29 letter, thanks "Senator Lockwood" for his "very effective work in obtaining these [legislative] endorsements." The post victory letter of December 7—on Office Of The President-Elect stationery—was addressed to "Emil" and signed "Dick Nixon". It notes how much the soon-to-be-President "looked forward to the time when I can thank you personally for all that you did during my campaign."

Altogether, the letters provide proof positive that Emil, in his capacity of Chairman of the Nixon for President Campaign in Michigan, held center stage in the state's Nixon campaign effort—from early endorsements, and Nixon's "heartwarming" campaign visit to Michigan in July, to the successful August convention nomination, and the general election blitz itself.[302] It is understandable that Emil would flirt with taking one of the federal posts offered by President Nixon, yet he would never succumb to the allure of Washington, D.C.

"DUMP LOCKWOOD" REVISITED

As Emil and the Senate racked up legislative victories in 1969, the grumbling against Emil's leadership peaked again. This effort was led openly by the increasingly vocal Senator Robert Huber (R-Troy). In May, Huber published a campaign-style newsletter, and sent it to over 14,000 Michigan residents, many outside his Senate district. In it, he took on the entire Michigan Republican establishment. Senate sources told Al Sandner, reporter for the *Detroit News,* that Huber was gearing up to run as the conservative candidate either for Governor, or U.S. Senator the following year.[303] Leading a successful drive to replace the otherwise popular Emil Lockwood as Majority Leader, of course, would put a huge feather in his cap, and give him a perfect platform from which to challenge the as yet untried Governor Milliken.

Huber and his band of dissidents, however, found themselves on the horns of a strange dilemma. They did not object to Emil's failures—a more common gripe in any group setting. They objected to Emil's victories. Huber *et al* could not very well disapprove openly of Emil's unrivaled skill in engineering victories against difficult odds. Leaders who do that, they knew, were usually acclaimed—rightly so—for their leadership ability.

The dissidents, therefore, attacked Emil's allegiance to the two successive Governors he had served under—Romney, and Milliken. They reasoned that the Senate Majority Leader should not run the legislative show for the Governor, even though the state's chief executive was also the leader of their state political party. Rather, they felt, their caucus leader should represent the wishes of a majority of the caucus, and disregard the positions of the Governor, as well as his own, if they disagreed with the caucus position.

As in a high stakes poker game, Emil had been counting the cards that had already been dealt. He knew this frustration had been building for years. But, Romney, with his convincing election victories, his personal charisma, and his widespread popularity—not to mention his having been responsible for defeating some rebellious incumbent G.O.P. Senators—helped to keep the disenchanted lawmakers under control. So Emil bided his time. Now, however, Governor Milliken, not yet elected in his own right, and without the public acclaim enjoyed by his predecessor, could not exercise the same degree of discipline.[304]

Huber objected to assembled reporters that his efforts were being characterized as a "Dump Lockwood" movement. Rather, knowing that an outright collision did not enjoy a ghost of a chance to win the day, he told them another interpretation was more appropriate. "The question as I see it," Huber said, "is whether any individual has the right to obviate the will of the majority; whether any person outside the Republican Senate caucus has the right to dictate to the majority; and whether the Republican Senate caucus will operate on principle or expediency."

Huber's only hope was to round up 11 or more caucus votes (a simple majority of 20 members) to adopt such a rule. Apparently, by resting his argument on principle, he sought to avoid attacking Emil head on.[305]

Adding fuel to the dissidents' flames of revenge, was the result of a caucus fight the previous week over the Milliken appointment of a "Negro attorney, Myron H. Wahls," to the Michigan Employment Security Commission Appeals Board. Most Senate Republicans initially opposed the Milliken appointment, which they were asked to confirm under the "advise and consent" clause of the state constitution. They criticized Wahl for past involvement with "organizations listed as subversive by the U.S. Justice Department, and past association with Democrats." Moreover, Wahl reportedly lacked MESC experience according to the opposition.

Milliken's office defended Wahl on all counts, and per usual, enlisted

Emil's aid in securing the Wahl appointment. When the votes were cast, there were 18 votes to outright reject the nomination, 15 of them Republican. Thus, they came up 2 votes short of the 20 needed to ditch the Milliken appointment.[306] That means that Emil convinced 4 other Republicans to stand by him and the Governor.

The conservatives were unhappy to say the least. Emil had won again, this time going contrary to 15 members of his 20-member caucus. They had again forgotten two important traits that characterized Emil: He keeps his word, and he rarely gets beat when the incident involves numbers. Within a week, they would again receive a stinging reminder that Emil is at his best when everyone else exists in the state of confusion.

According to the *Detroit News*, Emil's detractors met at dinner on the night of July 14, and called a Republican caucus. All 20 members showed up for what would turn out to be a 2 ½-hour heated debate over how the caucus should be run in the future, and by implication, who should run the show. Outside the closed-door session, Senate business came to a standstill. Would Emil finally catch his comeuppance from his opponents?

Word got to Governor Milliken who had already left the Capitol for the night. He was obviously concerned that an insurrection of sorts was taking place that involved one of his appointees, and his staunchest Senate ally. He also realized that, should the dissidents win, there was an inherent message in it to him that in the future he must treat the dissidents with kid gloves in their new majority status. So, Milliken rushed back to his Capitol office to be on hand to help in any way he could.[307]

Marsha Van Ness, of the Lansing *State Journal*, reported that during the caucus, the disgruntled faction offered a rule change that would "require the majority leader to fight for and express the majority sentiment of the caucus." So far, this was not a direct challenge to Emil himself. But it was clear to Emil that he would never be able to function under such a puppet rule.[308]

So, Emil's instincts dug in deep to ponder, how could he: 1) Keep his own supporters enthusiastically backing him; 2) At the same time, allow the dissidents to have their day in court; 3) Accustom his opponents to the fact that while they might have a legitimate idea, they did not control enough votes to prevail? And, oh yes, 4) Keep them in the caucus without bearing a giant-size grudge against Emil? Tall order indeed, yet his solution was another prime example of what some members of the press called Emil's "wizardry" in action.

Emil confessed to the caucus that he could see merits in both sides of the argument, even though he himself would find it rather difficult to conduct business that way. Nevertheless, knowing that the conservative faction had 9 votes, and that it took 11 votes to adopt a caucus rule, *Emil sided with Huber and voted in seeming capitulation to adopt the rule*. The resulting vote tally showed an even 10-10 split, and therefore lacked one vote to become caucus policy.[309] Now to their chagrin, his opponents knew exactly where they stood, and of course, were still unsatisfied. Time for the next move.

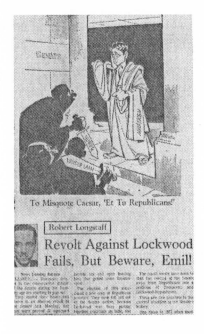

To Misquote Caesar, 'Et Tu Republicans!'

Robert Longstaff

Revolt Against Lockwood Fails, But Beware, Emil!

"Revolt Against Lockwood Fails, But Beware, Emil!" article headline under political cartoon. *Saginaw News,* September 19, 1969.

According to Bob Longstaff, Capitol reporter for Booth Newspapers, the embroiled caucus came to a head when Emil quietly slipped a note to Senator Huber. The note read: "If you will move, I will second that we take a vote for majority leader (secret ballot). Top two will then be secret for 11 votes." Emil's overture to Huber seemed to reveal, on the face of it, a heightened desire for self-destruction.[310]

Why would a caucus leader invite such a vote at this time? This was a serious offer, after all, because Emil offered to second the motion, meaning that he was willing to signal that he had agreed to such a vote.

Emil calculated that no other candidate could muster the 11 votes required to elect a new Leader. A few names for Emil's successor had been circulating quietly. But each of them had strong opponents. Emil had also let it leak that he might be willing to form a coalition with certain Senate Democrats. After watching Emil in action, few doubted Emil's ability to do just that if he were given no other alternative. Such a move would shift control from Senate Republicans to a coalition of Democrats and "Lockwood Republicans." This meant also that chairmanships of some important Senate committees would change hands, further leaving the dissident conservatives out in the cold.[311]

Huber and his group finally caught on, apparently also calculating their low odds for winning. Accordingly, Huber declined Emil's offer expressed in the note. The caucus ended with Emil still in charge, and with his opponents admitting once again that they did not have enough votes to do anything about it. Emil had outmaneuvered them . . . again. He was more powerful than he had been walking in the door 2 ½ hours before. As for Huber, he told the press that until the caucus rule was changed, he "cannot in good conscience participate in the Republican caucus."[312]

Emil, with typical understatement of his own accomplishments, shrugged all this off in interviews for this book. His take on the intricate maneuvers he employed to outwit his opponents boils down to this: "Every now and then one of the guys in the caucus would make a claim that he knew how to run the caucus better than I did. So, I kind of said, 'Okay, go ahead.' Thing is, none of them ever seemed to get enough votes to get rid of me."[313]

Governor Milliken, relieved by the outcome, issued a statement praising Emil. In it, Milliken said that Emil "has my greatest admiration for the way he has conducted himself both in the caucus and in this year's legislative session. I support Sen. Lockwood because I think Sen. Lockwood has done a responsible job and in many ways a courageous job."[314]

The Lansing *State Journal* editorialized a few days later that the "senator survived another 'non-dumping' movement last Monday. It is just as well for Republicans who now control only the Senate. . . . It would be difficult to find another leader who could equal Lockwood's agility and persuasive abilities."[315]

This attempted *coup* constituted the dissidents' last attempt to overthrow Emil during his tour of duty as Senate Majority Leader. Emil continued to work as hard as ever with both Democrats and Republicans to "get things done."

ROMNEY HEADS FOR WASHINGTON; MILLIKEN NEW GOVERNOR

In January 1969, Romney accepted newly installed President Nixon's appointment to a cabinet position, as anticipated. Romney would serve as Secretary of Housing and Urban Development (HUD). Milliken automatically ascended to the Governorship, while Senator Schweigert took on his duties as President Pro Tem, and Senator Vander Laan was elected once more as Majority Floor Leader.

Emil champions low and moderate income housing—Milliken (left) signs Lockwood bill to aid Michigan residents in substandard housing. *Daily Record-Leader,* June 5, 1970.

Following Nixon's victory at the polls that fall, it was widely believed that Emil would pack his bags for Washington, too. Everyone connected to the Michigan-for-Nixon effort praised Emil for his stellar performance. For the next several months, the newspapers regularly speculated on when Emil would leave. Emil was offered a federal appointment, but he refused it—at least until the end of his current Senate term.

Despite the fanfare over Romney's cabinet position in Washington earlier in the month, by the end of January Emil's life temporarily took a more somber turn. Jane Durand Lockwood, age 49, had died on January 27 of a debilitating rare form of cancer, an illness that might have been avoided with surgery and medical care. At her request, and in a show of support for his son, Eric, Emil served as one of the pallbearers at her funeral.[316]

In the ensuing months, Emil admitted to himself and others that he was not interested in leaving Michigan. "I never really seriously considered taking a job in the Nixon Administration," Emil later said. It never appealed to me, like it appeals to a lot of people. I enjoyed my work as Senate Majority Leader, and I was beginning to give some thought to running for statewide office. If I decided to run, I couldn't very well do that from Washington. At that point, the next election year was coming around in just over a year."[317]

Emil had connections to another President besides Nixon. Jerry Ford had served in the U.S. Congress since first being elected in 1948. The well-respected and affable Republican,

Gov. Milliken (right) gives 1st pen of administration to Emil (center), on signing Emil's bill correcting illegal organization in County Boards of Review. Sen. Geo. Kuhn (left) co-sponsor. *Daily Record Leader,* March 28, 1969.

who represented Grand Rapids, Michigan, had risen to become an effective Minority Leader in the House of Representatives in 1965. Mr. Ford had gained a sterling reputation in the Congress with both political parties, a trait that figured heavily in his being tapped by President Richard Nixon to take over the duties of Vice President following the forced resignation of Spiro Agnew. As the world watched in utter dismay, Gerald Ford assumed the Presidency in 1974, when Nixon resigned under the weight of the Watergate scandal.[318]

Emil crossed paths with Jerry Ford numerous times during the 1960s and 1970s. Emil said that their encounters took a variety of shapes, but usually were centered around Republican planning and strategy sessions, as well as fundraisers, political conventions, and issue specific meetings.

"I can't count the times I met with Jerry, or chatted with him at some Republican shindig" Emil recalled. "Jerry's Congressional District, of course, was not so far from my State Senate District, so that gave us something in common there. But, when I became the Republican Leader in the Michigan Senate, and he became Republican Leader in the U.S. House, we had even more things to talk about."

Emil well remembered Jerry Ford in those years—and his tenure in the White House, too. "I think highly of Jerry Ford," Emil said. "He had his feet on the ground, and he never let his fancy titles go to his head. He always made time for the folks back home. He was a genuine human being. And I think Jerry was a lot smarter than some people gave him credit for. There weren't very many people in Washington who could step into the Presidency in the midst of Watergate, and gain enough respect from both political parties to govern the country," Emil recalled.[319] Numerous pictures in Emil's photo album attest to their ongoing relationship over the years.

Emil had risen in the galaxy of state Republican politics as the decade of the 1960s came to a close. He had made his indelible mark on the Senate. He was respected by his colleagues, his district's voters, the press, and the Republican Party apparatus. This serendipitous confluence of factors could only mean one thing to the restless Senator from St. Louis. It was time to roll the dice again.

18
EMIL WAVES GOOD-BYE TO THE SENATE

The holiday season had been fraught with discord in the Lockwood family.[320] The long-term prognostication for Emil's marriage, he knew, was not good. It seems that more than his public life was about to change.

Emil publicly broke the news that he would not seek re-election to the Senate at a fundraising breakfast in Ithaca on January 6, 1970. He had publicly hinted now and then that the current term might be his last, but he kept his real plans away from reporters until he was ready to deal with the many-layered consequences of his decision.

Emil was ready now. He told Marcia Van Ness, reporter for the Lansing *State Journal*, that while he would not run again for Senator, he would "remain in public life." He announced that a bipartisan event to honor him would be held at the Lansing Civic Center on January 15. Obviously, an event that big had been in the works for some time. Somehow, Emil and his planning committee managed to keep the preparation under the radar screen for some time.[321]

The next day a flock of potential successors hurried to make it known that they would be the best candidates to replace Emil. Many were current or past officeholders at the county or State Representative level. The persons considered holding the edge in such a race were already serving in the House of Representatives. Among the House members whose districts included part of Emil's Senate District—an area that encompassed some or all of six counties—Representative William S. Ballenger, a 28-year old Republican from Ovid serving his first term, was considered most likely to throw his hat in the ring.[322]

Emil thought highly of Ballenger, telling Tom DeWitt of the *Gratiot County Herald* that Ballenger had done "an excellent job as a member of the House of Representatives and has always had my support and admiration for his dedicated service."[323] Press speculation turned out to be correct. Bill Ballenger not only ran to fill Emil's vacated seat, he went on to win, and served in the Senate with distinction.

Lockwood won't run

Won't seek re-election, Emil announces at GOP breakfast, seated with Sen. Robert Vander Laan (R-Grand Rapids). Standing: Rep. Dick Allen (R-Ithaca, left), GOP County Chairman Anna Weaver, and Breakfast Chairman Larry Trexler. Ithaca (MI). *Gratiot County Herald*, January 8, 1970.

Rep. William S. Ballenger III (R-Ovid) consults Emil on his campaign for Emil's Senate seat. Ballenger won. Photo by Hal Leffingwell at Allen centennial farm, Ithaca (MI). *Daily Record-Leader*, 1970.

1,500 people honor Emil at testimonial dinner—Emil (center) with dinner Co-Chairmen, Stephen S. Nisbet (left) and Murray D. Van Wagoner. Lansing *State Journal*, January 16, 1970.

'Salute to Lockwood Dinner' Program cover. Lansing (MI), January 15, 1970.

About one thousand people had been expected to attend the January 15 event. So, when the festivities began, and more and more people showed up, the Civic Center staff could barely set up more tables and chairs fast enough to accommodate them. The actual size of the crowd was estimated at about 1500, the largest testimonial to honor a legislator in memory.

Despite Emil's problems at home, he made every effort to include his children in his whirlwind life. His son Eric was serving in the Navy and stationed in Korea that January, but it was important to Emil that his daughters Lori and Lorette attend the event. They stood by his side and basked in the accolades, despite deeply conflicting emotions over the all-but-certain divorce of their parents. They had a front row seat to their father's statewide appeal and bipartisanship, enthusiastically on display in the diverse cross-section of attendees.

Proud daughters, proud father—Emil's daughters Lori (left) and Lorette share place of honor with Dad at testimonial dinner. Lansing (MI), January 15, 1970.

In addition to Emil's legislative colleagues, guests included the present Governor and past Governors, present and former mayors from many regions of the state, Congressmen from both parties, college presidents, businessmen, members of the news media, and neighbors from Gratiot County.

Governor Milliken praised the man who so often had delivered the goods in the legislature. "Emil Lockwood has consistently stood up on open housing, court reorganization, taxes, and many other issues. . . . [He] is standing up to be counted now on education reform," Milliken told the banquet crowd.[324]

The Detroit contingent attested to Emil's skillful assistance to that city while serving on the New Detroit Committee. Mayor Roman Gribbs, his predecessor Jerome Cavanaugh, and J. L. Hudson, Chairman of Hudson Department Stores, praised his involvement. Hudson called Emil "an exceptional servant of the State of Michigan," and recalled that "when the call went out in the trying days of 1967 [following the riots], Emil was one of the first asked and one of the first to serve."

The Latter Day Soapy Singers, a singing group of four Capitol reporters headed by Bob Longstaff, serenaded Emil with hilarious lyrics that took good-natured potshots at Emil and assorted pooh-bas from both parties. Emil's birthplace, Ottawa, Illinois also honored him, noting that the small town had sent two other men to Michigan who had become prominent—former Governor Harry Kelly (1943-46), and AFL-CIO President Gus Scholle. President Nixon and HUD Secretary Romney headed a long list of dignitaries who were unable to attend, but sent telegrams of tribute to be read at the event.

The memento from his testimonial that Emil prizes the most, however, was the book of letters from both Republicans and Democrats serving with him in the Senate. The highly complimentary letters go beyond the usual perfunctory, obligatory send-off letters politicians often write for such occasions. They reveal an uncommon respect and admiration for the often hard-driving Senate Majority Leader who sometimes was called "the Lockwood train." *

Days before SOS announcement—Emil (2nd lower left), HUD Sec. Romney (2nd lower right) and Alma College president Robert Swanson (lower right) at Highland Festival hailing college's Scottish heritage. Alma (MI), May 23, 1970. Family Album, Unknown Paper.

Attendees at the testimonial seemed to look upon the "size and warmth" of the gathering as proof that Emil Lockwood was now marked as a "formidable candidate" in 1970 should he decide to run for statewide office, according to Bob Pisor, political writer for the *Detroit News*.[325] Emil still would not definitely tell the press his plans for the future. In a generous gesture, however, Emil donated the proceeds of the affair to Mother Waddles for her work in helping the poor people of Detroit, rather than fold the funds into a political campaign fund for possible future use in a statewide election bid.[326]

Emil knew that his public announcement of plans to run for Michigan Secretary of State should coincide with his stepping down as Majority Leader. Trying to pass the state's budget, and wrap up other pressing legislative matters, while slugging it out with Republican opponents in the G.O.P. primary, if not downright impossible, would create a nightmare at the least. Also adding pressure to this decision was the fact that Senate Minority Leader Sander Levin (D-Oak Park) had already stepped down from his leadership post when he declared his candidacy to challenge Milliken for the Governorship. Levin

---

* NOTE: *Excerpts from these letters appear as a special addendum at the end of PART 3.*

was replaced by veteran Senator George Fitzgerald (D-Detroit) as Democratic leader of the Senate. Appropriately, Emil decided to announce his candidacy for Secretary of State (S.O.S.) on the same day he formally resigned his leadership role in the Senate.

Bob Longstaff, correspondent for the Booth Newspapers, predicted a "bloodletting" on Monday night, June 1, when Emil would formally announce his withdrawal in a closed-door caucus meeting. Dissident members in the caucus, the same ones who tried to oust Emil as Majority Leader, were expected to demand a stronger voice in running the Senate. There were no expectations, however, that Senator Robert Vander Laan, who had won wide respect for his role as Floor Leader, would be challenged for the top post. Nevertheless, skirmishes would most likely take place over positions such as Floor Leader, a reinstated Caucus Chairman who presided over caucus meetings, and Chairman of the powerful Appropriations Committee—if Senator Charlie Zollar, current occupant of the job, decided to challenge U. S. Representative Edward Hutchinson in the Republican primary.[327]

Emil shrewdly chose a Detroit breakfast meeting of an estimated 300 civic, business and political leaders from throughout the state to launch his campaign for the Republican nomination for Secretary of State. The long-awaited announcement came on the morning of the same day as the Senate caucus was scheduled.

In addition to the diverse demographics of the meeting's guests, Detroit represented Michigan's most concentrated mass of voters, the state's media center, and the home base of Emil's most likely opponents from both the Republican and Democratic parties. Moreover, as exhibited at his retirement testimonial, Emil was very much appreciated by many opinion leaders in Detroit.

At the Cobo Hall breakfast, Emil was lauded by Chrysler Board Chairman, Lynn A. Townsend. Townsend said that the meeting's announcement format resembled Emil himself. "This program fits Lockwood's character," he said. "It begins early and it will be businesslike and brief." In paying tribute to Emil's work on the New Detroit Committee, the Chrysler executive told the crowd, "Many times he arose early to drive from Lansing to Detroit. When we needed him, he was there."[328]

When it was Emil's turn to take the podium, he addressed the assembled leaders in his unpretentious, self-confident style. He said that any candidate who wanted to seek the Secretary of State post "must want to serve the people of Michigan, must put forth constructive methods for improving the department's service, and must have proven experience in administration and leadership."

Emil told the group that his background and desire to serve measured up to the challenge. "This is why I'm here today," Emil continued. "I do care and want to serve the people. I can improve the service of the Department of State. I have proven that I have the leadership and administrative ability necessary . . . ."[329]

Emil was aware of the enormous challenge he faced. Not only did he

All on program

1,500 pay tribute to Senator Lockwood

Lockwood Seeks Hare's Seat

Bi-partisan "Who's Who" lauds Emil and his run for Secretary of State nomination. Gov. Milliken (left), Alma College President Robert Swanson (right). *Daily Record-Leader*, January 17, 1970.

have to win the delegate vote at the August Republican convention to gain a place on the ticket in the November general election, he also had to battle the Democratic nominee head-on in the fall for a majority of the state's votes. If victorious in both contests, he would join the Governor, Lieutenant Governor, and Attorney General as the top elected officials running the state.

The perennially popular Democrat James M. Hare had served as S.O.S. for the past sixteen years, eight of them under two popular Republican Governors. He had turned the department into a user-friendly operation, and a patronage gold mine. Although Hare had announced his retirement from the office, and such a move left the post up for grabs, the patronage system in place could be construed as potentially favoring a Democratic replacement. On the other hand, an incumbent Governor Milliken heading the G.O.P. ticket in November could fairly be said, under normal conditions, to favor a Republican candidate for statewide office running on the same ballot.

The prize, should Emil win the S.O.S. job, was two-fold. First, he would head a highly visible state department with 1,800 employees, and a $28 million annual budget. Second, if he were so inclined in the future, he might think about using the post as a stepping stone to yet higher elected office.

The Department of State issued two million automobile titles, registered nearly six million cars, and issued about two million drivers' licenses. Various divisions administered and regulated elections, administered the motor vehicle accident claims fund, and oversaw the Michigan Historical Commission. Emil, in fact, strongly felt that of the numerous state agencies, the Department of State alone was the "agency of state government most directly affecting the people."[330]

Under the Capitol dome in Lansing, Senate Republicans resolved enough of their differences, at least temporarily, to settle on the leadership team that would serve the rest of the year. As predicted, Senator Bob Vander Laan of Grand Rapids was elected without opposition as Majority Leader.

Now it was time to put together a statewide campaign successful enough to win over a majority of local delegates to the Republican convention scheduled for August 28-29 in Detroit. This meant Emil had to travel throughout the state during the next few months, and meet with as many delegates as possible trying to gain their commitment to support him. Michigan consists of 83 counties, some hundreds of miles from each other. There was only one way to reach them: Emil had to become a road warrior again.

Emil's campaign strategy was fairly simple in concept, but most difficult in execution. He would use a self-contained mobile campaign vehicle to do the traveling. That way, he and his campaign driver wouldn't have to worry about staying in motels in Northern Michigan, most of which were likely booked by tourists for the summer. It also saved money. Significantly for this type of grueling schedule, with someone else driving, Emil could rest between stops, or use the time to bone up on the names, and backgrounds of the delegates and other people he planned to see.

Before launching an 83 county tour, however, Emil, assisted by his small campaign staff, had to line up those delegate meetings, produce campaign literature, appear at political gatherings around the state, seek endorsements, raise money, hold press interviews, and buy billboard space for Vote for Lockwood ads.

The campaign swing through the state constituted the backbone of his primary strategy. It had to be completed expeditiously to leave enough time to accomplish other vital efforts. Accordingly, Emil scheduled the tour for a 26-day period ending August 10. That would leave mid-August open for expected Senate sessions. He also planned to spend as many Sundays as possible with his daughters and son, at his Elm Hall farm—a property he used increasingly as his relationship with Mariella worsened.

The mobile campaign tour began in Howell on a bright July morning, and hit campaign stops in Shiawassee, Clinton, and Saginaw counties the first day, resting for the night in far away Huron County. Emil planned to spend no more than two hours at each county stop, briefly meeting with his supporters, county party officials, newspaper editors, and delegates.[331] Nobody could ever accuse Emil of being a slacker.

Bill McPherson, now a successful insurance company executive, met Emil in 1969 while attending Michigan State University. When Emil asked "Mac" (a.k.a. "Billy Mac" in those days) to be his campaign driver for the 1970 primary, he jumped at the chance. Mac remembered that campaign swing vividly.

Emil drove himself very hard on that tour. He had wrapped up his duties as Senate Majority Leader, participated in remaining Spring legislative sessions, and launched his campaign in a matter of a few weeks. Now, with the demands of the ambitious tour, Emil had to be "up" at every stop. There was no room for a slip-up. He had to convince a majority of the delegates that he was the best Republican candidate for Secretary of State . . . period.

After a while, Mac said, "Emil was practically burned out, but he kept going anyway. Between stops, Emil sometimes took naps on the bed in back. Then we'd arrive at another county seat, and Emil would start all over again.

Emil encourages 1ˢᵗ time state rep candidate and future Gov. John Engler (center), at Isabella County GOP headquarters; former GOP House Speaker Bob Waldron (left). Embers Restaurant, Mt. Pleasant (MI), 1970. *Photo courtesy of Gov. John Engler.*

He'd go into the courthouse, and meet the county clerk, or the register of deeds, and so on. Then, he'd go on to the city hall, and the newspaper office. There was no down time."

Mac particularly remembered an encounter they had at the Embers Restaurant in Mount Pleasant. "We had to go there for a meeting of all the local candidates," Mac said. "After the meeting, Emil offered to put each candidate's bumper sticker on his campaign RV. The RV was covered with banners and bumper stickers. Emil's own campaign theme was, '**Together We Will.**' One of the candidates there was a young guy named John Engler [later Governor of Michigan]. Emil pasted John's sticker on the RV. That was the beginning of a long relationship."[332]

Governor Engler said in an interview that he remembered well meeting Emil in Mount Pleasant for the first time in 1970. "I had just won the Republican primary election for State Representative," Engler said. "I was just starting out in politics, and I had a great deal of respect for him."[333]

Mac gained a lot of admiration watching Emil in action on the campaign trail. "Emil was not the usual political candidate who just turns on the charm," Mac said. "He was more of a doer. Emil wanted to know what the problem was. Then, he'd say, 'Let's fix it.' His definition of intelligence defines the meaning of intelligence as far as I'm concerned. Emil always said, 'Intelligence is knowing the right thing to do.' "

Emil's opponent for the G.O.P. nomination was Weldon O. Yeager of Detroit. Yeager was serving as a State Representative from the state's largest city, and had also directed the Michigan Workmen's Compensation Department. He had been gunning quietly for the S.O.S. post for some time. Emil, of course, knew that Yeager was a hard-working, credible opponent who had been working hard behind the scenes, but he considered him to be beatable anyway. Milliken had refused to choose between Emil and Yeager, something Emil would remember for a long time to come. Emil figured it might go down to the wire, but he never expected the delegate vote to be as close as it was.

Emil pulled out all the stops at the convention. Quintessential Lockwood touches were on display everywhere. Friendly yachtsmen (Lockwood's Navy, headed by Senator Charlie Zollar of Benton Harbor) sailed their illustrious sea craft up to Cobo Hall on Friday afternoon. The more *terra firma*-bound rode in rented mini-buses (Lockwood's S.O.S. Train, or LST, for short) that shuttled convention delegates back and forth from their hotels to Cobo Hall on convention day. On the convention floor itself, Emil engaged a band to lend a festive atmosphere to the celebration of his hoped-for nomination.[334]

In a tense atmosphere, the convention vote for the Secretary of State nomination took almost two hours to cast and tally. That's because the vote total was in question for over an hour after the initial tally, as some county delegations changed their votes, and the 114-member delegation from Oakland County had to be individually polled.

The magic number required to win the nomination was 799 [the convention consisted of 1597 delegates]. When the 799-vote total could not initially be reached by either candidate, nearly a dozen county delegations switched their votes. But, when the final vote was announced, Emil Lockwood-800, Weldon Yeager-790, the convention-goers believed the beaming Emil when he told them, "This is the biggest cliff-hanger I've ever been through."[335]

Headlines appeared in the Lansing *State Journal* on Sunday morning, August 30, proclaiming: "LOCKWOOD WINS IN A CLIFF-HANGER." If Emil had not carried Wayne County's vote—Yeager's home county—he would have lost. Apparently, Emil's experience in working the floor to create ever more imaginative coalitions again came in handy in the confused, winner-take-all atmosphere of the convention floor.

Emil wins SOS nomination in race with Rep. Weldon Yeager (R-Detroit). Gov. Milliken (center) and Lt. Gov. candidate James Brickley (left). Lansing *State Journal*, August 30, 1970.

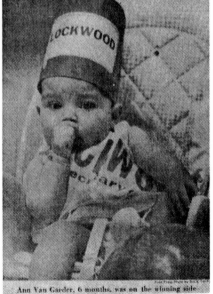

Belgian baby picks winner in Emil's bid for GOP nomination for Secretary of State. Ann Van Gaever, daughter of Freddy and Lieve Van Gaever. *Detroit Free Press*, August 30, 1970.

Governor Engler remembered the close floor fight for the S.O.S. nomination in 1970. He said he got a real education. "I had never been to a Republican convention before running for State Representative that year," Engler recalled, "so I didn't know how they worked. When Emil and Weldon Yeager got into a close race for the Secretary of State nomination, I backed Emil. I don't think Weldon has forgiven me to this day."

19

EMIL SPARS WITH DICK AUSTIN FOR SECRETARY OF STATE

For Emil to win the November general election, a whole different game plan was required. His Democratic opponent was Richard Austin, a successful black C.P.A. from Detroit, who had run unsuccessfully for Detroit mayor, and had served as the elected Wayne County Auditor. As a matter of fact, Emil always considered Austin—another C.P.A.—as a friend. Emil knew he would have to capitalize on his own out-state popularity, and again try to cut into his opponent's Detroit home base in order to win the prize.

Emil also realized that, no matter what kind of a brilliant campaign he ran, his success would depend a lot on how the top of the ticket—Governor Milliken—did against his opponent, Democrat Sander Levin. Milliken's predecessor, George Romney, had won increasing electoral majorities not only because of his charisma, but also because of his successful pioneering of a split-ticket strategy.

Romney's moderate brand of politics appealed to mainstream Republicans, independents, and like-minded Democrats. He gambled that he could make his election contests less about partisan, straight ticket voting, and more about voting for him, the person, regardless of a voter's party affiliation. Since Romney enjoyed success in the gubernatorial races of 1962, 1964, and 1966 using this approach, there was little doubt that Milliken, a moderate himself, would employ the same approach. In fact, Milliken, while calling for party unity at the nominating convention, admitted that he would need support of all Republicans, 70% of the independents, and at least 15% of the Democrats.[336]

Such a strategy created a problem, however, for other statewide G.O.P. candidates, such as Emil, and Attorney General candidate William S. Farr. Lieutenant Governor candiate James H. Brickley, of course, ran on the same ballot as Milliken. The reason it created a problem is due to a simple fact: When the top of the ticket runs such a campaign, it means that in especially vote-rich areas like Detroit and its surrounding suburbs, the party's lead campaigner tends to run more as an individual than as part of the Michigan Republican team. In practical terms, the result is that money, press attention, advertising and campaign volunteers in those essential geographical areas tends to flow disproportionately to the head of the ticket, often ignoring, or at

Emil disembarks SOS campaign tour bus in Ithaca; greeted by county GOP chair Anna Weaver, vice chair Jim Babcock, and others. October 1970. *Family album, newspaper unknown.*

Lenore Romney and Emil discuss their campaigns—hers for U.S. Senate, and his for Secretary of State. Lansing (MI), 1970.

SOS campaign manager, F. A. McCallum, Alma businessman and investor, reviews Emil's ambitious campaign schedule. Lansing (MI), 1970.

Emil, front and center with other GOP candidates—top left to right: David Diehl, Richard Ernst, Paul Goebel Jr., Jack Shuler, Raymond Hayes, Earl Kennedy. Lower left to right: David Robinson, William S. Farr, Jr., Emil, John Dethmers, R. Robert Geake. Lansing *State Journal*, September 1, 1970.

least downplaying, the efforts of other party candidates. This would definitely turn out to be the case in 1970.

The situation that year was further exacerbated by the fact that Bill Milliken—while an experienced, clean-cut incumbent—understandably did not possess, in this first election bid for Governor, the same aura of invincibility as the dragon-slaying Romney. And, even with his vote-getting ability, Emil was aware that Romney had not carried the statewide G.O.P. ticket into office with him, serving with a Democratic Secretary of State, and a Democratic Attorney General throughout his entire term as Governor. In fact, perhaps an even more challenging thought to Emil was the fact that, should he win, he would be the first Republican Secretary of State since Owen J. Cleary held the post in 1953-1954.

Another factor in the general election did not bode particularly well for the Michigan G.O.P. ticket. It seems that the only candidate with name recognition the state party could come up with that year to challenge the heavily favored incumbent—U.S. Senator Phil Hart—was Romney's wife, Lenore. Lenore Romney's only experience in politics had been gained derivatively through her husband.

Although Emil knew this volatile situation inside and out, he figured that the S.O.S. opening was, nevertheless, the best available opportunity to make his bid for higher office. Now it was time to campaign in areas that he had not had time to schedule in the primary, and to go after every registered voter he could.

Emil kicked off his fall campaign on September 17 accompanied by Governor Milliken cutting the ribbon on his statewide campaign office located in Lansing's Jack Tar Hotel. Milliken lauded Emil's contribution to the State of Michigan and said that he "came here to visit the headquarters of what will be a very successful candidate for Secretary of State."

Emil showed assembled reporters his campaign strategy all mapped out on charts detailing exactly how much time he would spend in each county, and legislative district. He said that he planned to work with Republican legislative candidates and other local party officials, plant signs and bumper stickers around the state, and "shake every hand in sight." F.A. McCallum, a long-time friend of Emil's would serve as campaign manager.

Emil predicted victory even though, at the time, polls showed that Milliken barely led his Democratic opponent, and Lenore Romney trailed Senator Hart. Emil admitted, however, that a come-from-behind victory would be needed for the entire G.O.P. ticket to succeed in the November 3 election. He also pointed to the unusual phenomenon of running with a constitutional question related to the controversial Parochiad issue scheduled for the same fall ballot. He knew that it could possibly bring out a bigger vote, but that at the same time it might cause voters to split their tickets even more than usual, perhaps in unpredictable ways.

Emil told the reporters and supporters that he would count heavily on his out-state name recognition, conceding that his opponent, Dick Austin, enjoyed the edge in Detroit. After two days of legislative sessions, he would be off again in his Dodge campaign RV, accompanied by his friend, former roommate, and ex-Speaker of the House, Bob Waldron.[337]

A glimpse at Emil's September and October official schedule, a copy of which he sent to his daughter Lori, shows the ambitious nature of a serious run for statewide office. First, Emil had to make an appearance at big events, so he could gain exposure to large numbers of voters in one fell swoop. To name a few, Emil attended the Michigan State Fair in Detroit, the Michigan Municipal League convention in Detroit, the Michigan Auto Wreckers Trade Fair in Mason, the Michigan-Michigan State football game in Ann Arbor, and the Washtenaw County Ox Roast.

In addition to events such as these, Emil gave speeches to smaller groups, did television interviews, blitzed across the state with other G.O.P. candidates, and debated his opponent, Dick Austin. Television ads touting Emil's qualifications over those of his opponents appeared in strategically important areas throughout the state.

"It was an intense campaign, alright," Emil recalled. "It's the nature of the beast, I guess. But if I had had to choose an opponent, I couldn't have chosen a nicer guy than Dick Austin. We had seen each other many times at C.P.A. gatherings, and had always gotten along."

Emil said that some people outside Austin's and his campaign circles tried to make race the issue in the S.O.S. contest. "Race cut both ways in the campaign," Emil remembered. "In Detroit, it was an advantage to be black. But in some areas outside Detroit, often the opposite was true. Some idiots got it in their minds to play up the fact that I was white, and Dick was black. I can't tell you how sick to my stomach that made me feel. One time, to show some good will, I even asked Dick if he wanted to hitch a ride with me on a private plane I had lined up to travel to a debate we had scheduled with each other. By damn, he accepted, and we flew up there together. We had a good ole time."[338]

The race issue became so hot in early October, that Democratic state chairman James McNeeley listed it as one of three complaints to the state Fair Campaign Practices Commission. Another referred to so-called misleading Lockwood TV commercials, and the third was aimed at Milliken.

It was in keeping with a biannual campaign rite of party chairmen to bash opposing candidates' "outrageous" and "unfair" campaign practices. McNeeley's charges, duly delivered at a Detroit luncheon with great fanfare, were typical of the genre. Nevertheless, Emil understandably took seriously a charge of deliberately using the race card in his election bid. At a speech later the same day—October 8—Emil addressed the charge head on.

"If there is any one issue we have stayed away from it's the color of my opponent's skin," Emil told the crowd. "To me, that is not the difference between Mr. Austin and myself and is not a consideration of a man's qualifications for this or any other job." With that emphatic statement, as well as others like it, Emil tried to make it clear to the public that he supported racial equality, and he inherently warned any supporters who might feel differently that he would not tolerate bigotry in any form.[339]

Larger than life image of Emil appears on campaign billboards around state. 1970.

Emil "hogs" scene with fellow GOP Senator Robert L. Richardson at ox roast in Richardson's senatorial district, during Emil's SOS campaign sweep. Lupton (MI), 1970. *Photo courtesy of Robert L. Richardson.*

Emil remembered that he mostly enjoyed traveling throughout the state meeting new people, matching wits with his opponent, and romancing the press. Probably the warmest memory of that fall of 1970 was renewing friendships he had made over the years as Senate Majority Leader, and as campaign coordinator for Nixon. "It seemed like there were people everywhere that I knew," Emil recalled. "Sometimes, they were local party grandees, but other times they might be somebody I helped out of a jam. And, other times, I couldn't even remember how we met. In any case, it was nice to look out into a crowd and see some friendly faces, and shake their hands afterwards."

Secretary of State candidates respected each other, even traveled together to a debate during 1970 race. Democratic opponent Dick Austin (left), with Emil. Lansing (MI), November, 1970.

As October came to a close, statewide polls showed Dick Austin with a significant lead over Emil among likely voters. Interestingly though, the two shared the "ticket-splitters" about half and half, again demonstrating Emil's bipartisan appeal. At the head of the ticket, Milliken was gaining a small lead over Sander Levin. Attorney General Frank Kelley showed a commanding lead over opponent William Farr, and wide support for U.S. Senator Phil Hart promised a victory of landslide proportions over Lenore Romney.[340] The polls, it turned out, were correct. Emil suffered his first defeat for elective office since the early 1960s, when he ran for delegate to the Michigan Constitutional Convention.

Also as predicted by political pundits and voters' surveys, Democrats swept the statewide offices except for Governor. Governor Milliken barely squeezed back into office by what many called a "cliffhanger." In the face of the Democratic juggernaut, Emil was defeated by 313,201 votes, gaining about 43.4% of the total vote for Secretary of State. The folks back home still loved him, as Gratiot County's vote tally demonstrated. Not only did Emil receive more votes in his political home base than Austin, he even out polled Governor Milliken who headed the Republican state ticket.[341]

There had to be a let down for Emil after the intense effort of running such a campaign. His friends and associates, however—such as the Congressman Guy Vander Jagt, and future business-partner Jerry Coomes—couldn't detect any sorrow or remorse on Emil's part. According to their accounts, Emil moved on without skipping a beat.[342]

Emil himself admitted no sorrow over losing the Secretary of State race. "I enjoyed running that race a lot," he said. "And I couldn't have lost to a nicer guy than Dick Austin. We remained good friends all through the years. I was through with the Senate anyway. I knew it was time for some new venture."[343]

Many years later Mac McPherson, Emil's young driver for the primary and a life-long friend of Emil's, still lamented Emil's loss that fall. "Emil was an extraordinary individual," Mac said. It's a shame he didn't win the Secretary of State election. That could have been a stepping stone. Emil would have made a great Governor of Michigan." Mac said that many of Emil's colleagues in the Senate, as well as many in the Republican Party shared that notion.[344] Fate, however, had other plans for Emil.

EMIL WRESTLES MILLIKEN'S ALLIGATORS

Emil hadn't even formally ended his Senate term, when his newest challenge was announced to the press. Emil was appointed to the position of Deputy Director of the Michigan Department of Commerce in the Milliken Administration. The *Detroit Free Press* reported on December 15 that Emil would have oversight over the state Public Service Commission, Insurance Bureau, Aeronautics Commission, Securities Bureau, and Consumers Council. The annual salary for this position was slated at $24,000.[345] Ironically, Emil had played a major role in passage of the bill that created the Commerce Department five years before.[346]

There was wide speculation, however, that Emil—by now newly divorced from Mariella—had agreed to the post while waiting for a Nixon appointment, or a gubernatorial appointment to either the Public Service Commission, or the state Liquor Control Commission.

For a short time, although appointed to his post with the blessing of Governor Milliken, Emil reported directly to Dick Whitmer, Director of the Commerce Department. Emil had known him well from Dick's days working for Romney and Milliken. Dick remembered those days with a smile on his face.

"It was the talk of the town for a while," Dick said. "Here was 30 year old Whitmer trying to be the boss of Emil Lockwood, who had long been regarded as one of the most important political figures in Lansing. I can tell you that we got along just fine. We remained friends to the end."[347]

Little known to anyone at the time, events would soon sweep Emil back into action in legislative matters. In early January 1971, when the legislature traditionally met in the Capitol for a swearing in, a fight for control of the

Senate was anticipated. That was due to the fact that the general election had produced a stand off of 19 Republicans, and 19 Democrats. The only way that Republicans could retain control of the upper chamber was through the use of Lieutenant Governor James Brickley's constitutionally permitted tie-breaking vote. To make matters worse, Senator Charlie Zollar had suffered a mild heart attack and was confined to a hospital; and, the Ingham County's 24th Senate District's vote had been so close that a recount had been ordered. Members on both sides of the Senate aisle were sure to keep close tabs on each other's health, exact whereabouts, and road and weather conditions. Any lapse in attendance by either party could result in a change in the organization of the Senate.[348] Don Hoenshell, of the Panax Capitol Bureau, called the situation "a period of almost unprecedented political crisis."[349]

Zollar recovered enough to come to Lansing to vote for Senate organization. Philip Pittenger, the Senate Republican candidate from Ingham County, won the recount. So, with Brickley's vote, Republicans continued their precarious control over the Senate. But with such a tenuous hold in that chamber, combined with the fact that Democrats now held a 58-52 majority in the House, the narrowly elected Governor Milliken needed help with the legislature.

Jerry Coomes remembered those days well. "Milliken was out on a limb, with a divided legislature," according to Jerry. "He needed Emil. So, I went to Milliken's office and made the case that he needed him . . . because Bill Ryan [Speaker of the House] had respect for him. He also needed Emil because he didn't have any legislative hammer, so to speak, and because not only the Republican caucus respected him, but the Democrats too. I suggested to the Governor that he should walk across the street to the Commerce Department and offer Emil the job of the Governor's lobbyist."[350]

Such a gesture by the Chief Executive of the state was unheard of. Usually, when the Governor calls, people come running—especially when they already work for his administration. There were extenuating circumstances in this instance, however. Given the nature and outcome of the recent campaign, Milliken probably sensed that Emil might have reasons for not jumping at the chance to be his lobbyist.

Milliken did walk across Walnut St. to Emil's office to offer him the job of Governor's lobbyist. But Emil was not one to carry a grudge for very long. After thinking about it for a while, he said "yes." Emil, a glutton for work in the eyes of some, would now assume the role of Milliken's mouthpiece in the legislature for part of the day, and look after his Commerce duties in his "spare time."[351] Emil quipped to the press, "Maybe a golf cart wouldn't be a bad idea."[352]

Emil told the press that he planned to show up at the Commerce Department at 7:00 a.m., cover the legislative sessions beginning at 9:00 a.m., return to Commerce at 1:00 p.m., then go back to the Capitol to cover the legislative sessions at 2:00 p.m. The Capitol press and politicos all wondered if Emil would still have the same clout in his new position that he had enjoyed as Majority Leader.[353]

"The adjustment from Senate leader to Governor's lobbyist wasn't too hard," Emil recalled. "The only time I missed being down on the Senate floor with a vote was when they screwed up. That was hard to watch."[354]

Still observing Emil like a hawk from the sidelines was Bill Kulsea from the Booth Newspapers. "The rise and fall" of Milliken's legislative program for 1971 rested with two men, according to Kulsea, "One a gregarious type who talks in staccato sentences and the other an English-squire type who listens more than he talks."

The two Kulsea referred to, of course, were Emil Lockwood, and Glenn S. Allen, Romney's former budget director, who now handled legislative and legal duties for Milliken. Kulsea seemed intrigued by the contrast of styles between the two.

"Lockwood," Kulsea said, "mesmerized both Republicans and Democrats with his parliamentary tricks during his six years [sic] as Senate Majority Leader. He cajoled, threatened, compromised, and often employed political pressure to get things done. His philosophy: Get things done, quickly. Never mind the details."

In contrast, according to Kulsea, Allen, during the past seven years in the Capitol, "came on slow, used knowledge of figures and budgets and bookkeeping to make his points, [and] developed friends among lawmakers. They learned to trust him . . . ."

Kulsea, speculating that the new role would be a difficult one for Emil to pull off, nevertheless opined that the Lockwood-Allen team would "do better than any two other guys one could pick."[355] Soon, the team's stellar performance would bear Kulsea's prediction out.

For instance, Emil played the role as deal-maker, on behalf of Milliken, by arranging last minute compromises during the turbulent days prior to enactment of the desperately needed 1.6 per cent income tax increase, and the House passage of a promised tax relief proposal. These constituted the most important linchpins in Milliken's program that year to restore Michigan's fiscal health.

As a result, Capitol correspondent Don Hoenshell reported that speculation was rampant in Lansing that Emil, now 52, would soon be rewarded with a coveted spot in the Milliken administration, such as chairmanship of the powerful Public Service Commission (PSC), or the Michigan Employment Security Commission. Hoenshell added that Emil had already turned down two plumb federal posts that he knew of, despite the fact that Michigan's entire G.O.P. Congressional delegation had recommended him to President Nixon for any job in Washington.[356]

Emil had not changed his mind about refusing to go to Washington, however. "I was more interested in the PSC spot," Emil remembered. "I had every reason to believe right up to the date that it was filled, that my chances for getting it were pretty good, after doing what Governor Milliken had asked me to do for him."[357]

But again, fate had other things in store for Emil. Despite earlier assurances, Milliken appointed somebody else to the P.S.C. chairmanship.

"Most Influential with the Media," Emil interviews with Bill Dansby, then news anchor for Lansing's WJIM-TV. Circa 1970.

On the same day in June 1970, the Michigan Supreme Court refused to hear an appeal to invalidate the Parochiaid constitutional amendment which had passed by popular vote the previous fall. Jerry Coomes, still heading up the pro-Parochiaid effort from his Michigan Catholic Conference base, had been seeking to overturn the ballot vote. Jerry had promised to stay at the helm of the effort until all avenues had been exhausted. With the court denial of an appeal, however, there was no other avenue to pursue.

On that June day, the phone rang in Jerry's office, just blocks from the Capitol complex. Emil was on the line. "Let's take a ride," Emil said. "I have to deliver some hay."[358] Public Affairs Associates was born that day.

❖ ❖

TESTIMONIAL EXCERPTS[359]
JANUARY 15, 1970

"I know of no member of the Michigan Senate who is held in higher esteem than the gentleman from St. Louis."

John T. Bowman (D), State Senator, 26th District

"You have projected an esteemed and envied image characterized by discipline and dedication in the realm of state politics. . . . On occasions [of disagreement] you come as an admired foe, a person to be respectfully heard, your appraisal intently considered. . . . In times of mutual agreement, you come as a friend to support my convictions."

N. Lorraine Beebe (D), State Senator, 12th District

"Although I haven't always agreed with you, I have always been impressed by your consummate political skill and your adept leadership. Few men could have shepherded through the many important but often controversial measures that you have."

Oscar E. Bouwsma (R), State Senator, 33rd District

"Your years of public service have been illustrious, your personal conduct has been of statesmanlike quality. I shall treasure our relationship over the past years the rest of my life."

Joseph S. Mack (D), State Senator, 38th District

"Your ability to coalesce divergent viewpoints into a sufficient consensus to enable the legislative process to move has impressed me deeply."

Gary Byker (R), State Senator, 23rd District

"It has been a rare privilege to serve in the Michigan Senate with you, even on the other side of the aisle. As an honorable opponent and as a conscientious ally on the various matters which have come before the Senate . . . you have always exercised your judgment on behalf of what you felt to be the interest of the people of Michigan."

Arthur Cartwright (D), State Senator, 5th District

"Your responsibilities over the past several years have been trying ones with constant criticisms, pressures, harsh words and few rewards. However, you have handled these problems with patience, a strong will and a positive approach."

Harry A. Demaso (R), State Senator, 20th District

"Even though we are representatives of opposite political parties, we've shared a genuine friendship, nurtured by a mutual desire to serve the best interest of the people of Michigan. Please remember I am, and always will be, your friend."

Raymond D. Dzendzel (D), State Senator
7th District, Assistant Minority Leader

"Even though you belong to the wrong "Party" I have decided to overlook it because that is the only fault I have been able to find with you since 1965."

George S. Fitzgerald (D), State Senator, First District

"Although I may not have always have concurred in the positions taken by you as my majority leader, I have always admired your keen dedication and devotion to getting the job done, as well as the cleverness exhibited by you in the carrying through of your leadership role. My compliments to the 'old gray fox' on the occasion of this dinner in his honor!"

James G. Fleming (R), State Senator, 19th District

"Our differences have of times been profound and the gap between what we perceived as the best course for Michigan has been wide; but when the time came for change you recognized the need and led the battle for tenants' rights, the income tax, and open housing. For this and for your courage and leadership, I salute you. . . . I and your fellow senators will sincerely miss your leadership, your word, and your wit on the floor of the Michigan Senate."

Jerome T. Hart (D), State Senator, 34th District

"I share the view of most capitol observers that you have mastered the art of politics and have learned how to sell almost any program that you have set as your goal. This included such controversial legislative matters as the state income tax of 1967 and the open housing bill of 1968. . . . In my judgment it will be many, many years before anyone will be able to fill your shoes as effectively as you have in accomplishing the magnitude of legislative programs approved."

George W. Kuhn (R), State Senator, 14th District

"Undoubtedly, your [experience in] . . . business . . . on major corporate [and local] boards, . . . your compassionate patient teaching of deaf mute persons, . . . and the hard facts of seven major invasions in the Pacific during World War II, all contributed significantly to evoke and enhance basic elements of your character and abundant understanding."

Garland Lane (D), State Senator, 29th District

"It isn't easy to write a letter to a great friend who is an enigma, possessing the great qualities of infinite agreeableness, coupled with exasperating tendencies. . . . You possess that innate charm of the master salesman and a trigger-like mind that may change mountains to molehills. You are always ready to do kindness or help someone who is in need of assistance but you can be a most provocative individual showing quarter to no one in the intense battle, being charitable in victory and rising again from the ashes of defeat. You possess great administrative capabilities and would thus be an excellent Secretary of State or . . . in fact governor or senator."

L. Harvey Lodge ®, State Senator, 17th District

"There have been times when I could not decide whether you were a Republican or a Democrat. [Yet] . . . I could always come to you for assistance and get it."

Stanley Novak (D), State Senator, 9th District

"Your pledge was always honored and, indeed, that this is so will always stand as a most fitting monument to you."

Michael J. O'Brien (D), State Senator, 8th District

"Since 1965 our association has been constant and our mutual adventures have been challenging, to say the least. . . . You have been a constant friend, an understanding counselor, and sometimes impish humorist who always is able to put a problem in its proper perspective."

Robert Richardson (R), State Senator, 35th District

"All of us admire your ability to accomplish 'what seems almost impossible' in the passage of legislation."

Gordon Rockwell (R), State Senator, 25th District

"Your ability and willingness to serve as an effective 'bridge' between the legislative and executive branches of government, and the manner in which you submerged partisanship in the interests of good government has earned you great respect among your Senate colleagues."

Stanley F. Rozycki (D), State Senator, 3rd District

"Emil Lockwood has gained the respect and admiration of all who have worked with him, . . . performing difficult duties with special adeptness, lending a sense of responsibility and direction to the deliberations of his fellow lawmakers." **Thomas F. Schweigert (R)**

Senate President and Acting Lieutenant Governor

Called "unswerving," "unselfish," and "unprecedented," Emil's leadership is paid "highest tribute" as "both sides of aisle" praise his contributions as GOP Minority and Majority Leader. *Resolution # 172 adopted by Michigan Senate, Lansing (MI), December 17, 1969.*

"You are a dedicated Republican, and outstanding Senator, and one of the most able majority leaders the Michigan Senate has had in its history. You have taken courageous stands. Even though they were sometimes controversial and in disagreement with your constituents and colleagues, we benefited by your decisions and are better off for them."

Jack Toepp (R), State Senator, 36th District

"Your contribution has been outstanding. For five of the past seven years you have been chosen by your colleagues as their leader, and that testimonial shows more support than mere words can do."

Robert Vander Laan (R), State Senator, 31st District

"I can think of no other person among the political opposition to whom I would more readily pay tribute. In the rough and tumble of Senate politics, I have always found you to be 'hard but fair'. Perhaps I can offer no higher praise than to say that within the relatively narrow and myopic confines of our political spectrum, I have always found your word to be your bond."

Coleman A. Young (D), State Senator, 4th District
(Future Mayor of Detroit)

"We have been of different parties and different views on many subjects, but I have listened with respect to what you have had to say and you have gained my support for your position. You are one of the finest and most honorable men that I have had the pleasure to serve with in the Michigan Senate."

Charles N. Youngblood, Jr. (D), State Senator, Second District

"I will never know how you have endured all you have had to put up with in your six years as majority leader. You have always put the needs and problems of your colleagues above those of your own. In my opinion you are one of the most remarkable persons I have ever encountered. You are kind, considerate, understanding, long suffering, patient and, above all, always a gentleman."

Milton Zaagman (R), State Senator, 32nd District

"Senator Lockwood . . . is without peer as a political leader. His competency as a leader has been proven many times in his ability to garner legislative support from members of both political parties in passing programs through the Legislature which benefit all the people of Michigan. His talent to obtain cooperation from legislators who have many diverse views and opinions has been remarkable."

Charles O. Zollar (R), State Senator, 22nd District

"My first-hand experience as your friend of many years and as a President who values your support tells me that the admiration of those who honor you tonight is not only timely, but well-placed. My congratulations on a tribute that reflects a fine record of public service, and my best wishes always."

Richard Nixon, U.S. President *(Telegram)*

"Hearty congratulations . . . richly-deserved tribute . . . outstanding accomplishments."

Bob Griffin, U.S. Senator *(Telegram)*

"Emil Lockwood's . . . personality and character and his dedication to public service have bought recognition to his leadership not only in Michigan but in the nation as well."

Ambassador Robert Ellsworth
Permanent Representative of the U.S. on the Council of NATO
(Telegram)

"It's a personal pleasure to join with your friends and associates in this bipartisan tribute to your outstanding Senate leadership. Usually the Governor's office receives the lion's share of public and press attention. But I know as only a governor or former governor can know that the success of any state administration depends importantly on the quality of legislative leadership. As Governor I was fortunate and the people of Michigan were fortunate to have a Senate leader of your talents and capacity. You were outstanding in getting results [and] you have earned the respect of your associates in the legislative and executive branches and the appreciation of constituents, your party and your state.

George Romney *(Telegram)*
U.S. Secretary of Housing and Urban Development
[Former Governor of Michigan]

"I . . . salute . . . you for your progressive and effective leadership of the Michigan Senate. The real test of that leadership has been the ability to produce sound legislative action."

John B. Martin, Special Assistant to the President for Aging
U. S. Dept. of Health, Education and Welfare *(Telegram)*

"Best wishes on 'your night'. With Jim Northrup and Tom Tresh we will expect you to hit a home run."

Carl Levin, Councilman, City of Detroit *(Telegram)*
[Future Democratic U.S. Senator]

PART FOUR

Lobbying à la Lockwood and Coomes

1971 – 1977

20

LOCKWOOD AND COOMES FASHION
NEW LOBBYING APPROACH

Emil teamed up with Jerry Coomes in 1971 to form a lobbying firm that would soon revolutionize the way lobbyists in Michigan's State Capitol carried out their business. The key to their success, no doubt, lay in their unique combination of personal characteristics and experience.

Both individuals had been considered by the press over the years to be "movers and shakers," but otherwise they were opposites. In fact, they exhibited such opposite resumés that one reporter dubbed them "the odd couple."[360]

Jerry spelled out the contrast between Emil's and his backgrounds, describing their complementary dispositions that provided the alchemy for success. "Emil had a business background," Jerry noted in an interview. "He was a highly respected Senate Majority Leader. Emil was a Republican, and I was a Democrat. I had experience in grassroots movements. His experience came from being a legislator, and having an internal knowledge of the legislature. Our personalities were different, and our working operational methodologies were different. So it was perfect from that standpoint."

Jerry pointed to other areas where their differences meshed. "Just about everything was balanced," according to Jerry. "For instance, Emil's C.P.A. background helped in making 'little' business decisions—well, the ones that might seem little when you're underway, but when you're setting up a business, things like banking, retirement benefits, and insurance are really important. In addition, I was basically interested in serving the clients, and Emil's primary strength was in attracting them. Emil used to always say, 'I'll get the clients, and you keep them.'"[361]

According to all accounts, that's how the new lobbying firm's partners operated. They started small—just Emil and Jerry, and one secretary in a small office at 416 West Ottawa St. across the street from the Capitol. The new firm was to be called Public Affairs Associates. They decided before they officially announced its opening—on September 3, 1971—that they would take no more than ten clients. This arbitrary number would soon be re-evaluated due to the enormous positive response they received, and the changing nature of state government itself.[362]

"We announced at the beginning in our little brochure that we were not going to have more than ten clients," Jerry remembered, "because we didn't believe we could do justice to more than that. We hadn't thought about hiring more lobbyists. So, based on revenue projections from the eight clients we signed up initially, we set an annual budget of $108,000. Emil drew a salary similar to his government paycheck, and I drew the amount I had been receiving from the Michigan Catholic Conference. Business was so good though that when the first two-week payroll came around, we were able to increase our salaries by 20%."

Public Affairs Associates (PAA) soon would revolutionize lobbying in the State Capitol. Several factors accounted for this. First of all, PAA attacked its clients' problems from a bipartisan standpoint, due to the different partisan roots of its two well-known principals. Second, due to Emil's insider knowledge and status, and Jerry's savvy orchestration of clients' supporters back home, the two could cover more bases than the typical solo ex-legislator working on his own in the Capitol.

In addition, Emil's extensive background in private business, as well as in dealing with state regulatory agencies, lent great credibility to PAA's efforts to court the private business/corporate sector. Jerry's long and successful history of working in the vineyards of social and educational reform, on the other hand, appealed to a whole other set of possible clients.

There was a central organizing principle, however, that most likely accounted over time for PAA's changing the scope of the lobbying business in Lansing. Emil and Jerry saw lobbying in a broader light than most of their contemporaries. To this pair of veterans, it was better to prevent problems than to have to solve them after they got surprisingly out of hand. This meant continually educating clients in the arcane process of state government. It meant developing issues carefully wherever possible, to appeal to a wide enough range of the political spectrum in order to get them passed into law, and to avoid or defeat destructive amendments.

Modern lobbying, according to the Emil-Jerry play book, meant working with not only the legislature, but the Governor's office, state departments, and state regulatory agencies—whatever mixture was required to achieve clients' objectives.

As the resources and sophistication of both the legislature and the clients' "natural enemies" improved, moreover, PAA introduced other methods as well. They launched programs that could help clients deal with the press, and public opinion, for instance. They advised groups on how to launch and win statewide ballot proposals. And, they developed increasingly more targeted fundraising to support legislators friendly to a client's cause.

Indispensable to the whole process was PAA's talent in developing and maintaining close and helpful relationships with legislators and state officials of all kinds over the long haul. Emil and Jerry both knew that politics is a two-way street. Consequently, they both continued to cultivate lasting relationships with lawmakers and state officials. They realized that they could not just show up and ask for a vote, or a ruling of some kind, without spending time with them in advance, advising them, and possibly getting them out of a jam from time to time.

The only other highly visible multi-client lobbying firm (the preferred description of firms representing multiple clients) that operated in Lansing in the early 1970s was Karoub and Associates, named after its principal, and lead lobbyist, former Detroit area Democratic legislator, James Karoub. "Jimmy" Karoub enjoyed a well-deserved reputation as an accomplished lobbyist, and was considered by many to be the principal competitor to PAA. Emil and Jerry held one big advantage in the short run, however. They offered a bipartisan approach. If a client needed both the Republican and Democratic side covered by its principals, PAA was the only game in town.

When PAA hung out its shingle, the going rate for retaining their services had already reached $1,000 per month, with up to $1,500 for expenses, according to Jerry. That was to rise quickly to $1,500 per month within the next several months. The number of clients rose too. Within a year, PAA served 15 clients, according to the *Detroit Free Press*. Clients included the Michigan Bar Association, the National Bank of Detroit, the Asian Development Bank of the Philippines, the Wine Institute of San Francisco, Blue Cross Blue Shield of Michigan, and the Michigan Road Builders Association. Some potential clients had been turned away, according to the report.

PAA's sterling reputation was reinforced by several newspapers' accounts. The *Detroit Free Press,* for instance, commented on the new firm's progress in glowing terms. "The blaze of success surprised few who knew of Lockwood's uncanny field generalship in the Senate, and Coomes' behind-the-scenes quarterbacking of projects dear to the Michigan Catholic Conference."

Emil explained to the *Free Press* how he looked at his own method of lobbying: "It's knowing who the players are, their special skills, talents, their genuine feelings, political goals, constituencies, that sort of thing." Emil likened good lobbying to managing baseball. "It's like knowing on a baseball team who you should have on second base, the right batting order, and an all-around winning combination."[363] No one in town doubted that Emil "knew the combination."

Emil recalled the early days at PAA. "When Jerry and I went for that ride to get some hay back in the summer of '71, we pretty much cut the deal," Emil said. "We decided to get some clients, and open a little office next to the Capitol. We were pretty sure we'd be able to round up a few clients. I told Jerry I'd do it for five years, then I wanted out."

"My job," according to Emil, "was to get the clients, and Jerry would

Emil and Jerry were the "perfect team" said Congressman Guy Vander Jagt of their work at ground-breaking lobbying firm, Public Affairs Associates. Lansing (MI), 2001. *Photo by Mike Quillinan.*

"Emil always had a smile on his face—no matter what was coming at him. He was the most calm, engaging person I have ever met," said Tom Hoisington, current CEO, PAA. Left to right: Jerry Coomes, Emil, Tom Hoisington. PAA, Lansing (MI), 2001. *Photo by Mike Quillinan.*

"Emil brought a high level of respectability and professionalism to PAA that has lasted through the 30 plus years of our existence," said Tom Hoisington (left), CEO, Public Affairs Associates (PAA). Lansing (MI), 2001. *Photo by Mike Quillinan.*

Public Affairs Associates revolutionized lobbying in State Capitol. Co-founders Jerry Coomes (left) and Emil Lockwood. Lansing (MI), 2001. *Photo by Mike Quillinan.*

look after them. As a matter of fact, Jerry was so efficient that I used to say, 'If Jerry asks you to do something, just wait a few days, and he'll do it himself.' "[364]

Jerry remembered another difference between Emil and him that turned out to be an advantage. Jerry liked to operate in perpetual motion during the day, and go home to his farm at night to be with his wife, Colette, and their large family. Emil, on the other hand, tended to be more office bound during the day, but loved to entertain public officials at night. They consequently covered all the bases.

As the 1970s unfolded, they had to cover even more bases. The decade brought more and more problems before state government. Recession, oil embargoes, the Vietnam War, Watergate scandals, emerging gender and racial issues, ever increasing government regulation, inauguration of the 18-year old vote, and the Watergate-induced militancy on the part of the news media—all created headaches for clients and politicians alike. The new cauldron of political policy called out for well-wired, broadly experienced lobbyists such as Emil and Jerry. A well-meaning ex-legislator who charted his whole lobbying strategy on the inside of a matchbook cover need not apply.

Issues pertaining to the environment, for instance, suddenly raised the stakes for many corporations. Jerry recalled the time that the Michigan Department of Natural Resources started to assess fines on manufacturers for environmental violations. The corporations affected finally recognized the need to be represented at the State Capitol. "When the stakes got higher," Jerry said, "the corporations not only wanted somebody in Lansing to tell them what was going on—they wanted someone who could intervene in the process, and affect the outcome. That's why they wanted to hire a big lobbying firm, a full-service firm that could handle the common lobbying, but also the public relations, the grass roots liaison, and the issue management."[365]

About the time all these exciting new developments concerning PAA erupted, Emil again lived up to his reputation for juggling multiple balls in the air at the same time. If Emil had believed in fortunetellers, he might have heard from a particularly good one that he would soon be jetting around the world with a gorgeous blonde, aided by a handsome Belgian. It did come true, of course. The twists of fate that transpired to make it come true, as usual, make a good story.

21
BELGIAN SINKS ROOTS IN MICHIGAN FARMLAND

Emil's young Belgian friend, Freddy Van Gaever, had been almost as busy as Emil since the two last saw each other. Having interned with Emil's help at a Detroit trucking firm one summer when revisiting Michigan, Freddy returned to Belgium a young man on the move. He purchased two transport trucks of his own, and when the French—just over the border—declared a trucking strike, Freddy Trans was born.

A few years later, Freddy was noted as one of the top 50 business men in Belgium,[366] with spare money to invest. He quickly zeroed in on Michigan, and enthusiastically brought others in on the purchases, explaining to his Belgian associates that he had a friend in Michigan who would help them.

The Lansing Bureau of the *Saginaw News* interviewed Emil about the phenomenon.

Belgians, Emil explained, lived in a country about ¼ of the size of Michigan, with an equal or higher population. They believed in America as an investment, Emil told the *News*, and since the cost of a Belgian acre was ten times as much as rural Michigan's $100 per, it was clearly no-contest.[367]

Freddy's investments in Michigan farmland didn't make him rich overnight, but profits from Freddy Trans were significant, and he expanded his business to include air travel, founding the Belgian airline named Delta Air Transport.[368] Freddy's airline provided KLM's connecting access into Belgium, and he quickly found a way to repay his American friend for all his kindness and hospitality over the years.

"Freddy arranged for my appointment to the Delta Air Transport board of directors," Emil said. "One of the perks was first-class standby status on KLM, worldwide—as long as I went to Amsterdam first," he added. "I really liked going to a lot of far off places in my spare time, although there wasn't much of that until I met Anna."[369]

With U.S. Presidents and old friends alike, Emil's egalitarian, frank approach earned loyalty and respect. Shown with President Jerry Ford soon after Nixon's resignation, and Freddy Van Gaever. Lansing (MI), 1974.

Emil (center) snowmobiling with Belgian friend Freddy Van Gaever (lower left) and others at Lockwood property at Elm Hall Farm (MI), 1970.

Emil's daughters Lori and Lorette Lockwood cheer Freddy Van Gaever on horseback at one of Emil's farm properties near Alma. Vestaburg (MI), 1970.

CONFIRMED BACHELOR MEETS HIS MATCH

Emil expressed his views on marriage in a Leap Year send-up of Capitol City bachelors in early 1972. Mug shots of dozens of affable eligible Michigan bachelors were featured in the Lansing *State Journal* next to interview summaries on a variety of topics including marriage. Emil and long-time friend Stan Thayer had already settled their minds completely on that issue, having helped each other swear that neither would ever marry again, and if one of them weakened, the other was obliged to talk him out of it.[370] So Emil's views on marriage were as clear cut as his signature brush-cut hair.

"It's not for me, I've tried it twice," he told the reporter as the photographer's flash caught his weathered winsome smile.

Emil described his "Sports Interests" for the tongue-in-cheek piece as "playing cards," and what he did in his spare time as "trips to far-off places." He described his home as "neat and well-furnished" but believing that the best defense of a committed bachelor is a good offense, added that he wasn't there much because he worked nights and weekends. Asked to describe his personality, he offered the ambiguous "Adamant in a semi-kind way."[371]

In a follow-up story a couple of weeks later, several of the bachelors reported that they had received some interesting calls and letters from women after the Leap Day article. "Emil Lockwood says a kind woman from a small community wrote to inform him that she's a willing partner when he wants to play cards."[372]

Emil didn't bite on that offer, but—unbeknownst to the reporter—he had started dating someone he wasn't willing to talk about just yet. He was understandably skittish, after two failed marriages, and told the reporter that his kind of woman was someone who "didn't get too serious too quick."

"Originally, Emil was standoffish to me," Anna Weaver Lockwood said, "and I can understand why—I was the Gratiot County Friend of the Court who had to arbitrate child support between Mariella and Emil when they divorced, and I was an appointee of the Governor. I knew who Emil was long before I met him, of course, because I lived in his district, and I saw him at G.O.P. functions."[373]

Other people, in fact, noticed the sparks between the two attractive divorcees almost before they did. Speculation around them abounded, but both Emil and Anna remained wary of commitment. Years later, Dick Whitmer still took credit for fanning the flame between the two, at an off-year G.O.P. Convention on Mackinac Island in 1971.

"Emil and I were staying at (U.S. Senator) Phil Hart's cottage on the Island," Dick recalled. "Anna was at the convention, too, but she was staying at the bottom of the hill. I could tell they had something to say to each other, and somehow I wound up running notes back and forth between them. Eventually," Dick added, "they started seeing each other."[374] Would this turn out to be the imagined fortuneteller's gorgeous blonde in Emil's future?

Emil ran into Anna again in June, this time at his brother Jim's widely attended Bastille Day party. Afterwards, Jim took his brother aside, and asked him if the rumors about him and Anna were true.

"At that point," Emil said, "I finally called her up and asked her to go out with me on a date."[375]

Newlyweds celebrate after whirlwind courtship, despite Emil's vows with friend Stan Thayer that neither would ever remarry. New York, 1972.

Driving an El Camino pickup truck and dressed in a wrinkled shirt and shorts, Emil arrived at Anna's place on July 4th. They drove north past Clare to visit Emil's friends, Guy and Carol Vander Jagt in Luther, Michigan, then on to Lake George for a romantic dinner alone.[376] Not too long later, they rented a houseboat for a long weekend in the Virgin Islands with Jim and Audrie Lockwood. The two women clicked immediately, as Emil and Jim joked over who was the best pilot. "Then Anna and I saw a two foot long lobster while we were snorkeling," Emil recalled. "Jim caught it with a spear gun and it fed all four of us twice."[377]

By November the prognosis wasn't looking too good for Emil's keeping his oath with fellow bachelor Stan Thayer. And he was too busy dating Anna to notice his friend was having the same problem.

"Emil and Anna would pinch each other," Guy Vander Jagt said, "because neither one of them could believe how good their relationship was. The wedding was scheduled for 6:00 p.m. in my living room," he added, "on the day after the November 1972 election."

As Carol Vander Jagt's memory and photograph album attest, the wedding preparations were well underway at 5:57 p.m., and so was Emil—playing Pitch in the kitchen with his best man, Guy. "It was a wild game," Guy said, "and he was having a ball to the last minute. The photos tell it all."[378]

"The only one who cried at the wedding," said Anna, "was Guy and Carol's daughter, Ginny, who was two years old at the time."[379]

By the following month, the two avowed bachelors were no more, as Emil and Anna accepted an invitation to celebrate Stan and Lee Thayer's wedding at the Persian Room in Rockefeller Center, New York City.

EMIL'S M.O.: IGNORE POLITICAL LABELS

Emil had lost his label as an eligible bachelor, and felt himself fortunate to have teamed up with Anna, a woman with political savvy of her own. They saw a lot of things in the same light. To cite one important example, neither one of them put much stock in partisan political labels.

As they shared their new lives together, it became obvious that neither one of them truly cared which political party a client, public official or neighbor belonged to. It was the same in Duck Key as it was in Michigan, according to Anna. "We always tried to maintain rapport with everybody in all the projects we've been involved with. I always agreed with Emil on that score," Anna said.[380]

Anna's hard-won political credentials made her an exceptionally good partner for Emil from the start. She enthusiastically helped Emil plan for the seemingly nonstop entertainment obligations related to PAA-connected clients, friends, and associates. The newlyweds' first purchase—a 32-foot cabin cruiser humorously christened "Anna's Banana"—guaranteed a variety of adventuresome venues for landlubbers and seafaring folks alike for years to come. Former Senate colleague, and successor to Emil as Senate Majority Leader, Bob Vander Laan, notes that Anna definitely added another dimension to Emil's lobbying activities.

"Anna was a tremendous asset to Emil," Bob recalled. "Emil always liked to entertain a lot, but after they got married, there's no doubt that Anna went over well with the Senators."[381] Emil had a lot of other qualities going for him, but there can be no doubt that having Anna by his side was at the top of the list. Moreover, Emil's and Anna's commonly shared attribute of scorning political labels not only aided their success on the political front, it also netted them many friends that they might otherwise have missed out on in Duck Key.

Many people had marveled at Emil's ability to make deals with all sides of the philosophical equation, at one time or another, while representing a district populated by the traditional conservative bastion of Republicanism—small business entrepreneurs, and farmers. His career and reputation rested on this skill, and it was welcome currency at the newly formed PAA.

Three minutes before wedding ceremony with Anna, Emil (center) plays Pitch card game with Guy Vander Jagt (right) and Marshall Breem. At Vander Jagt home, Luther (MI), November 8, 1972.

Newlyweds have cake and eat it too—after wedding celebration dinner, smiling bride Anna presents Emil with top tier of wedding cake. Luther (MI), 1972.

Emil and Anna celebrate with fellow newlyweds Stan and Lee Thayer in Rockefeller Center. Front left to right: Anna Weaver Lockwood, Stan Thayer, Lee Thayer, Emil, and presiding minister. Back left to right: Mike Doyle, Nan Doyle, Dick Whitmer, minister's wife, and Sherry Whitmer. New York, 1972.

Anna, looking back on 30 years as Emil's partner and soul mate, shed some light on the matter. Long before she knew Emil well, Anna had served as 10th Congressional District Republican Vice-Chair, Gratiot G.O.P. County Chair, Gratiot County Friend of the Court, and President, Michigan Association of Friends of the Court. In these roles she made it her business to know what went on in politics, and who was doing it.

Anna attested that Emil definitely qualified as a "moderate Republican," if that means he never hesitated to get the job done, even if it entailed cutting deals with Democrats and Republicans alike. "Emil worked more from a practical point of view," according to Anna. "He rarely let philosophy get in the way. He never held grudges, either, when people didn't go along with him."

Anna also had an interesting firsthand insight into the political nature of the Senate district that Emil represented for eight years. Unlike today's widespread use of labels such as "conservative," "liberal," and "moderate," Anna said such was not the case at the grassroots level in the 1960s. "Back then," Anna said, "people in our area didn't talk that way. We didn't see ourselves as conservative, or moderate Republicans. We were just Republicans." She said that Emil was popular in the district, "because he was successful at tackling their problems. They were proud of him."[382]

22

DYNAMIC DUO LEARNS DUET

When Emil and Jerry launched PAA, they had to learn how best to work together. Both of them knew the ropes of state government, but they had different sets of skills, and each had a very distinct personality. They had to share important decisions, and develop a way to handle differences when they inevitably arose. Emil and Jerry both testified to the fact that they soon learned how to work together on a daily basis, and truly enjoyed running their business as a duet, rather than dueling tenors.

Jerry remembered the early "roving staff meetings" in which he tried to share concerns about the business with Emil. "We had to find a way to communicate," Jerry said, "because Emil would tolerate nearly anything, and wouldn't complain. So, we agreed to keep a list of concerns during the week, and then, in the car on our way to Detroit every Monday to see clients, we would talk about whatever difficulty we might have with our approaches, or with our agreement, or with any issues we were lobbying."[383]

Jerry said that he always had a list of three or four discussion items on those trips, but Emil never had any. After about eight or nine trips, Jerry's list "pretty much evaporated." He worried sometimes that Emil had difficulties with him, as happens in many partnerships. "But if he did," Jerry said, "I never knew what they were."

"After the first three months or so," Jerry recalled, "we moved around effortlessly, like two astronauts in outer space, changing a piece of equipment outside the Space Shuttle."

For the first year, Chairman Emil and President Jerry went everywhere together. They could do that, of course, because they still kept their client list short. "At the end of the year," Emil said, "I thought we could be more effective, and cover more territory, if we split up."[384] "So, we did," Jerry recalled. "Emil took half of the clients, and I took half. It worked out well."

The two also saw eye to eye on what types of clients they would accept. "We had some very good discussions about that," according to Jerry. "We agreed we wouldn't take clients connected to alcohol or gambling. That wasn't too hard actually, because those issues weren't hot at that time. And when we found out we had a 'bad' client, we would disengage. We both agreed on that as a matter of principle."

Lobbyists take welcome breather between sessions. Left to right: Gus Harrison, Jerry Coomes, Colette Coomes, Emil and Anna Lockwood. Lansing (MI), 1974.

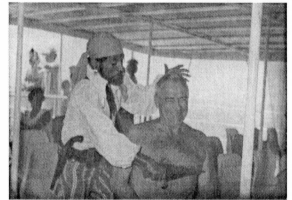

Mutiny in the high seas—Emil plays along with overzealous buccaneer aboard Mexican cruise ship 'El Bonanza' en route to Acapulco with Anna. March 1973.

Emil and Anna stroll down 'Memory Lane'—where Dick Whitmer passed notes between them at prior year's GOP convention. Mackinac Island (MI), 1972.

"Oh, I guess it might be called a principle," Emil added, "but I went more by my gut. If it didn't feel right, I just didn't want to do it."

As a matter of fact, everyone who knew Emil well when he served as Senate Majority Leader must have wondered how Emil would now feel asking his former colleagues for votes—not from a caucus leader's point of view, or from his position as Governor's representative—but as a private sector lobbyist.

Bob Vander Laan, Emil's successor as Majority Leader, had a particularly advantageous view of Emil's interaction with members of the Senate in the early days of PAA. He remembered that Emil adjusted very well to most situations, except one. Emil told Bob that the only thing he really minded was sitting in the balcony during an important vote, and watching Senators "screw up." "It pulls my gut right down to the floor [of the Senate]," Emil said.[385]

CAPITOL PRESS CORPS STILL LOVES EMIL

Odds were stacked high against the usually cynical Capitol press corps continuing its romance with the former Senator from St. Louis. After all, it was unlikely enough that Emil had somehow weathered press scrutiny unscathed for eight years as Senator—most of them in leadership—and another year as the Governor's enforcer in the legislature. But now, how could he possibly continue his usually charmed relationship with the press while being paid by clients to carry out their self-serving agendas in the legislature? It may be hard to believe, but he did.

"Emil's style of working with the press was remarkable," recalled Jerry. "He could teach a lot to modern day politicians on that score. His approach was straightforward and simple, but simply amazing. For a guy who never sought publicity, it was hard for some competitors to figure out just how he always got favorable press. How did he do it? I think it was mainly due to the fact that Emil told them *everything*. He never tried to spin anything. Truth was his defense. It was almost like Little Red Riding Hood strolling through the woods without fear."

Jerry admired Emil's constant ability to reveal all to an inquiring reporter, but that didn't mean that he was always comfortable with such an approach. "It scared the daylight out of me," Jerry remembered about the early days of PAA. "I wasn't ready for that. I didn't really want to talk to the press, but if I had to, I tried to figure out the best way to frame an answer without exposing a weakness. I can't take anything away from Emil, though. None of that stuff bothered him. Most Capitol reporters admired him not only because of his accomplishments, but also because they knew he was telling the truth. In that respect, he reminded me of Will Rogers."

There can be no better example of an encounter between Emil and a reporter, on a controversial topic, that netted Emil favorable publicity, than that reported by veteran Bill Kulsea of Booth Newspapers in September 1972. Kulsea's column appeared on page one, above the fold, in the *Grand Rapids Press*, one of Booth's several metropolitan newspapers that ran the story. Its bold headline declared: "Top Capitol Lobbyist Holds Great Power." Its main subject: How lobbyists gain favor by channeling campaign contributions from their clients to key Michigan legislators. Kulsea set out to show how an influential Lansing lobbyist—namely Emil Lockwood—used holes in the state's lobbying laws to "get influence," and "keep in the good graces of the legislature."[386] Not exactly the prelude one might expect to a glowing account of Emil's methods of gaining and using influence. Yet the following account shows how Emil handled this hot potato by—guess what? Telling the truth, of course.

Kulsea noted right off that PAA listed 15 clients with the Secretary of State, and guessed that, at going rates for top lobbyists, Emil's income should total about $225,000 per year. (It's not clear how Kulsea arrived at that sum). Then, he wrote: "Lockwood readily admitted to being a 'funnel man' between his clients and state representatives prior to the August 8 primary election; in fact, he had counseled his clients to contribute to House members who were seeking re-election."

"I'm sure some people read that," Emil recalled, "and thought we were just raking in big bucks for paying off lawmakers."

But, as Emil explained, he believed in the democratic legislative process, and the right of individuals, groups, legislators, and the press to advance their points of view as best they could—as long as they stayed within the bounds of the law and propriety. He never apologized, or denied, or skirted the issue when it came to facing the music. This time was no exception.

"I strive," Emil was quoted in the article, "to convince my clients that they should have a 'political action' section to further their interests in the legislature. That is one way they can keep their message before the lawmakers and make reasonably certain that their voices can be heard."

Kulsea explained that unlike John MacLellan, a lobbyist for the "dog track interests," Emil registered with the Secretary of State, had his clients make out the contribution check to the lawmaker [instead of cash], and kept a record of the contributions. He explained further that "Lockwood advised his clients to make direct contributions to lawmakers seeking re-election back home, all in the interest of contacts when the legislators make it to Lansing."

Kulsea spelled out how Emil decided who should receive contributions, and how much money each eligible legislator should get. It all depended on the amount of influence a legislator had on the issues important to a particular client, according to Emil's explanation. The four caucus leaders, for example, would be eligible for the top contribution of $500. Committee chairmen, whose panels would review and act on the legislation, would be worthy, of say, $200. Some members of pertinent committees might receive between $100-$200. Kulsea said that one of Emil's well-heeled clients might shell out $7,000 to $8,000 for each election in direct contributions. How's that for full disclosure to the press?

Instead of castigating Emil for such behavior, Kulsea reported that Emil, at age 52, "is the envy of all of the more than 230 lobbyists operating in the statehouse." Moreover, as to the legality of all this funneling of cash to lawmakers, Kulsea admitted that Michigan law allows such actions. There is definitely a difference between bribes and contributions, he said: "The distinction embedded in the law makes 'contributions' clean money. . . ."

This describes yet another instance of Emil confronting potential danger from adverse press scrutiny casually and factually, meeting it head on, and coming out the better for it. "Well, it wasn't bad for business either," Emil said smiling, when major newspapers around the state described him as the "envy" of all other lobbyists, explained his fee structure, campaign contribution strategy, and verified that he played it on the "up and up" legally speaking.

Emil had become a highly successful lobbyist indeed, and was subjected to even greater scrutiny as his reputation grew. Typically, Emil never let the glaring lights of publicity bother him. He continually thought of new ways to go about his business, and never cared a whole lot whether the news media found out about it. He always thought he had good reasons for doing what he did, and didn't mind explaining it if called upon. Interestingly, even as the press began to call for more lobbying and campaign reform, and his former Republican Senate colleagues joined in the clamor for reform, Emil somehow seemed to come out smelling like a rose. A case in point was the G.O.P. caucus in mid-September 1972.

23

EMIL SOLO LOBBYIST AT SENATE G.O.P. CAUCUS

E mil was the only lobbyist to attend—and help sponsor—the overnight caucus in Mount Pleasant in September 1972. His successor, Majority Leader Bob Vander Laan—according to reporter Bob Longstaff—had asked all lobbyists to stay away.[387] Longstaff's article appeared in several Booth Newspapers with headlines such as "Senator Tilts With Lobbyists" (*Muskegon Chronicle*), and "Tight Controls For Lobbyists Gaining Favor" (*Jackson Citizen Patriot*). In it, he reported that Bob Vander Laan's warning to lobbyists to avoid the caucus was part of his effort to rally Senate Republicans to "throw off the 'undue influence' now being exercised by outside groups." Vander Laan hoped, according to Longstaff, to make it easier for the legislature to "take independent action."

"I knew I'd stick out like a sore thumb," Emil remembered about the news media's coverage of the caucus. "And it was fine with me that Bob—he was my friend, you know—announced to the whole world that he was going to crack down on lobbyist influence. He had his job to do, and I had mine."

Longstaff said that Vander Laan "shrugged off" Emil's presence at the caucus, explaining that Emil "was not there in his capacity as lobbyist. Instead, he was assisting a friend of his, Anna Weaver, who manages an apartment complex where the senators caucused." Longstaff noted, however, that Emil evidently "was helpful" in arranging complimentary rooms for G.O.P. Senators who needed to stay overnight. Moreover, Senator Jack Toepp (R-Cadillac) and other caucus members managed to find time to fill Emil in on deliberations in the private caucus.

No wonder Emil was the envy of most other lobbyists. There were no competitors who could have pulled that one off—especially in light of the public prohibition against lobbyists attending. So Emil maintained his insider status, while enjoying air cover from the reform-minded Majority Leader himself. In addition, in a newspaper account largely devoted to Vander Laan's worthwhile lobbyist reform effort, and a cataloguing of current abuses, Emil got away without a scratch.

Vander Laan and everybody else knew there was nothing in the least bit wrong with what Emil did. In their books, it just provided another example of

Emil's totally up front manner, and his Teflon treatment by the press. Paren-
thetically, his close friends also knew how serendipitous the caucus site was.
Located near an apartment complex managed by Anna, it allowed Emil and
Anna to spend a little time together in their hectic schedules. They continued
to pinch each other sometimes to quell their disbelief in the good fortune of
having found one another.

PAA BULKS UP FOR MORE ACTION

Emil and Jerry continued on a roll, piling up more clients, more successes, and more revenue. By 1975, it became more difficult for the two of
them to handle the increasing demand. "We knew it was time to get some
help," Emil recalled, "but we were damn picky."

Emil and Jerry surveyed the political scene in Lansing long and hard to
find their first staff member. They agreed on the candidate's necessary qualifications: the person had to be knowledgeable about state politics, have a list
of relevant, successful experience, possess a pleasing personality, and exhibit
the desire and energy to keep up with Emil and Jerry. They found the right
person in Robert K. Smith, a bright, up-and-coming staff member at the
Michigan Pharmacists Association, then a client of PAA. Bob signed on in
1975, and lived up to his promise.

With the turmoil on the national scene in the mid-to-late 1970s, as well as
the corresponding number of new issues facing Michigan, PAA responded
with the broadening of its services. Emil and Jerry beefed up their full service
menu for clients. They wanted to provide more assistance in areas such as
policy management, research, legal strategy, media relations and fundraising.
To do this right, they felt they needed yet more help. Enter Rick Cole.

Richard T. Cole joined PAA in 1977. Emil and Jerry particularly liked
Rick's unusual blend of talents and experience. Rick had just completed a
stint as top executive aide to Democratic Senate Majority Leader (and gubernatorial candidate) William Fitzgerald. Before that, he had served as aide to
Republican Senator Anthony Stamm, Chairman of the Senate Education
Committee, and lobbyist for the Department of Education. Rick had also received his doctorate in Education along the way. With this background, and a
natural gift for public relations, he lent even more dimensions to PAA's
menu.

Rick, now Senior Vice President for Communications, Michigan Blue
Cross-Blue Shield, offers some insights about those days at PAA. "I liked
Emil very much," Rick said in an interview. "He taught me some lessons in
surviving at PAA. When I first signed on, Emil leaned back in his rickety
chair, smoking nonstop, and told me, 'If you've got a problem, bring it to the

staff meeting in the morning. Tell Jerry you're really worried about it, then go golfing. Jerry will work on it all day. When you come back later in the afternoon, guess what—it'll be taken care of.' "

U. S. President Gerald Ford, with Emil and Anna at Capitol Hill Club. Washington DC, 1975.

U. S. Vice President Nelson Rockefeller with Anna and Emil at Capitol Hill Club.
Washington DC, 1975.

In Rick's view, even though the differences between Emil and Jerry were apparent, the two men had important similarities. "They were alike," according to Rick, "in that they built the firm on long-lasting relationships with clients and legislators. They were also both extremely likable."

Rick said that Emil had a unique style of lobbying, which he called "the bank shot: Setting up a chain of events to achieve a desired goal. Jerry, on the other hand, went more down the middle, was more direct, more willing to be confrontational."

Because of Emil's vast experience and intimate contacts, according to Rick, Emil relied on his wits, rather than elaborate policy papers, or power fundraising—the preferred tools of growing numbers of "new school lobbyists." "It was impossible to outwit Emil," Rick recalled.

Emil gave two priceless bits of advice to Rick during their sojourn together at PAA. The first: "Never ask a public official to do something against his self-interest." The second piece of sage advice: "Never do anything in this town that you don't want to tell a grand jury about." [388] From all accounts, Emil followed his own advice in his many years in the Senate, and at PAA.

PAA STANDARD OF SERVICE
"AS GOOD AS IT GETS"

Public Affairs Associates drew lots of attention from the press, and from Emil's old friends as well. Did Emil and Jerry have the right formula for success? Or, would their magic wear off eventually?

Guy Vander Jagt, the former Senate colleague and Congressman, and long-time friend, called Emil and Jerry "the perfect team." Guy said that "Emil moved with ease among business leaders and educators, but he didn't suffer fools gladly. Emil focused on getting the job done—passing the client's bill, or whatever—but never bothered to tell the client how he did it. He didn't think the CEO should be bothered with details. He never stroked the clients. But Jerry was the best hand-holder in the world, so Jerry kept the clients informed. They were the perfect complement to each other."[389]

Dick Whitmer, Emil's former state Commerce boss, and now President and CEO of Michigan Blue Cross Blue Shield, agreed. Dick noted that "Emil and Jerry created the model for lobbying. They set a standard that's as good as it gets."[390]

At a time when the ranks of lobbyists swelled increasingly with former elected officials, and an unprecedented amount of money backed their attempts to sway public policy, reviews of PAA by the press were usually upbeat and laudatory.

A United Press International (UPI) story, for instance, appeared in the *Detroit News* in January 1975. It named the 12 most influential lobbyists in Lansing, according to legislators and lobbyists themselves. Emil Lockwood and Jerry Coomes were both named, representing 17 clients at the time. [Many clients' needs had been satisfied, and no longer were on the client list.] Others on the short list included: James Karoub, Hiram P. Todd (Chrysler), Harold Julian (UAW), Simon Chapple (AFL-CIO), Robert Perry (Michigan Bankers' Association), Robert Smith (Michigan Farm Bureau), Dan Wellborn (Michigan Education Association), Jack Rose (Michigan Chain Stores Council and Association), Gilbert Haley (Michigan Automobile Association), and William A. Wickham (Michigan Chamber of Commerce). PAA's competitors were well established, and in most cases, much more staff-supported. Nevertheless, PAA continued to more than hold its own.[391]

Patrick Connolly, writing for the Associated Press in November 1975, named several influential lobbyists who had served as high public officials. He especially zeroed in on former G.O.P. House Speaker Robert Waldron (Emil's former roommate), former G.O.P. Senate Majority Leader Milton Zaagman, former Democratic State Representative James Karoub, and former Milliken Chief of Staff William Hettiger. Connolly's angle for the story resided in what he called "chum-ism," meaning that "current elected lawmakers have dealt with some lobbyists for so long that the distinction between buddy and 'special interest flack' often is blurred out of existence." He followed with a detailed example of then current "chum-ism" between House Republican Leader Dennis Cawthorne and Waldron. In the middle of the long, mostly critical article, he mentioned Emil in a complimentary tone.

"Lansing's *top lobbyist* is generally considered to be Emil Lockwood," Connolly wrote, "the friendly, intelligent agent of . . . weighty special interests. . . ."[392]

About a year later, Emil got singled out as the *most successful lobbyist* in Michigan by Jerry Moskel, Capitol correspondent for the Lansing *State Journal,* in an article appearing in December 1976. Although Moskel's article centered on reporting requirements likely to be required under a comprehensive new lobbying law, it led off with a colorful description of Emil, who he said "is regarded as the most influential and successful of the 290 lobbyists registered with the state."[393]

"Lobbying hasn't changed Emil Lockwood that much," according to Moskel, "except to make him richer and more amiable than he was in the days when he served as the Senate's chief head knocker. . . . He still towers above most people. His square jaw, crew cut hair and voice that bellows from deep inside his chest keep him a commanding figure in Capitol circles." Emil told the reporter that he "had no objections" to the reporting requirements, adding, "I have no hang-ups on the reporting of entertainment. It'll mean a lot more bookwork. But I'm used to that."

Emil's C.P.A. background, and reputation for up front, forthright behavior undoubtedly lent credibility to his statement in the suspicious atmosphere hovering over politics in the post-Watergate era.

Not long after Moskel's article, *Detroit Free Press* Lansing Bureau chief Hugh McDiarmid weighed in with his assessment of the lobbying scene at the State Capitol. In a comprehensive column appearing in the newspaper's Detroit supplement, McDiarmid laid it on the line. "When you hire an Emil Lockwood, or a Jimmy Karoub you get more than a mercenary. You get a massacre. . . . These two guys are good. The best."[394]

McDiarmid described the two's specialty as "legislation." "When they want a bill, they usually get it. When they don't, it usually dies," he said. Although both top lobbyists play in the "same big league," according to McDiarmid, Emil's "game is more sophisticated than Karoub's because his [blue ribbon] clientele is a bit more . . . wholesome."

Unlike Karoub, Emil talked freely to McDiarmid about PAA business. He spelled out PAA's fee structure, 90-day cancellation clause, and criteria for signing on with a client. According to Emil, the firm didn't accept just anybody: "We probably turn away maybe a dozen clients a year. The reasons vary but there may be a potential conflict of interest [with another client] or no possibility that we can achieve their objectives for them." Emil also cited two examples of PAA's rejecting clients due to ethical considerations, namely bull fighting, and cock fighting. Emil and Jerry wouldn't represent these interests, so the would-be clients signed on with other lobbyists.

McDiarmid suggests that in addition to top credentials, and client-base, one of the keys to Emil's avoiding problems in the legislature in such areas as campaign financing was his "low-key, affable, country boy charm. . . ." Of all the association and corporation heads with legislative problems at the time, many of them studied Emil's approach, and if they couldn't afford him, they imitated him.

Evidently, things couldn't have been going better for Emil in 1977. But now the seductive call of Duck Key beckoned to him more and more, and it was time to move on.

24
EMIL PHASES OUT OF PAA

Emil had originally promised to stick with Jerry at PAA full-time for five years. Actually, Emil not only stayed a year longer, but promised after that to be on hand when needed, and to serve on the firm's Board of Directors as long as Jerry wanted him to. In order to pull off Emil's phaseout success-fully, they needed a plan. It wouldn't be easy, because Emil had been the lead lobbyist with several of PAA's top clients. In addition, Emil served as the "resident Republican," and the main lightning rod for the ever-present news media.

Jerry remembered those days well. "As the time got closer for Emil to phase out," Jerry said, "it dawned on me, 'What happens if Emil, the former Senate Majority leader, leaves, and clients who saw Emil as leader of the firm leave too?' Won't they just go to another, bigger firm?"[395]

During those two years—between 1975 and 1977—Emil began spending more time in his favorite place in the world, Duck Key, Florida, and gradually turned his clients' issues over to Jerry. "Emil was gracious during the whole transition," according to Jerry. "He allowed me to have more presence with his clients—the C.P.A.s, for instance. He took more and more of a passive position, and let me get to really know his clients so I could service them. I couldn't replace Emil, but gradually some of the old-time Republicans began to trust me—most of all because Emil vouched for me. In the end, we didn't skip a beat."

The partners had agreed from the outset to a buy-out provision when Emil left the firm. Jerry said that it amounted to 10% of the firm's revenue for the first five years of Emil's "retirement." "We were grossing nearly a half-million dollars at the time Emil left us full-time," recalled Jerry, "so he got about $50,000 a year at first. By the time he received his last payment five years later, the check was for $100,000. We had actually doubled our busi-ness over that five years." Following that, Jerry wanted to be able to call Emil up some times to ask him advice on some financial matter or another, so he paid Emil a nominal consultant's stipend of $500/month. "Emil always gave good advice," Jerry said.

Something Jerry said he would never forget occurred several years later. Emil managed the firm's subsequent transfer of ownership from Jerry to

PAA's existing staff. "Emil was magnificent," Jerry testified. "He flew to Lansing in the middle of the winter to help out. He was still on the board—he actually stayed on the board until I left in 1993—so he came here for three board meetings concerning the buy out. His contribution was priceless."

The quality that made Emil such a "perfect partner" was, in Jerry's view, Emil's fairness. Early on, Jerry recalled that Emil came to him one day and said, "I'm spending too much money on expenses. Like this weekend, Anna and I will be in Detroit entertaining on our boat, but you're not doing anything. You've got to join the Lansing Country Club and even out expenses."

Captain of Queen Elizabeth II greets Anna and Emil aboard QE2 bound for Switzerland, Belgium, and points beyond. 1982.

Emil turns tables again— maneuvering waiters into his and Pat Callihan's seats, as Pat (standing, left) serves wine and Emil (standing, right) offers hors d'ouevres for Anna (left) and Coilah Callihan. Queen Elizabeth II, 1982.

Emil remembered that incident, too. "I told Jerry," he said with a broad grin, "you don't play cards, and you don't play golf. That's what these guys do, so you've got to learn to play one or the other. I told him that he should take up golf, so he could invite clients and legislators along and rub elbows with them." [396] Jerry, to the surprise of everyone who knew him well, not only took up golf, but has been a devotee of the sport ever since. "And I did join the Country Club, thanks to Emil," Jerry said. "I never would have thought about it if it hadn't been for him."

Emil's instinctive fairness played a part in another expense adjustment a few years later. "Emil told me that since he was older than I was," Jerry recalled, "corporate payments going into his pension fund were greater than payments designated for mine. So—and this is outstanding—Emil insisted that we cancel my pension fund, and set up a new one so that we could both make equal contributions. I don't know of many partners who would do that. It's a rarity."

Emil's loyalty and fairness, along with his consummate business acumen during their years together, remain one of Jerry's most admiring memories of Emil. Jerry particularly remembered an incident that exhibited all three of these attributes. This one had nothing to do with PAA business. It concerned helping Jerry's father out of an unforeseen financial disaster.

Jerry's father, Lou Coomes, owned a popular upscale dining establishment in Lansing named the Charcoal Galley. One day in 1975, he discovered a note from his stepson who had been managing the restaurant for him. The note said that he had departed for Alaska, and the IRS would be showing up the next day.

"It came as a total shock to my father," Jerry remembered. "He was suddenly left with a huge overdue tax bill, and another $50,000 or so owed to vendors. He didn't have enough money to cover it. His retirement had just gone up in smoke."

"So, I turned to Emil," Jerry continued. "He accomplished the near impossible. He negotiated with four parties who wanted to buy the restaurant, and arranged a lifetime pay out for my mother and father. The payments went on for twenty-four years."

Jerry said that taking on such a complicated task was not a burden for Emil. Rather, he attacked the deal with "enthusiasm and skill." Jerry shook his head with admiration when he talked about it. "When Emil brought back the Charcoal Galley from life-support to a healthy retirement package for both my father and mother," he said, "it almost seemed like Dr. Christian Barnard performing a lifesaving heart transplant with his confident, trained fingers."

"When Emil orchestrated a deal like this one—and he actually helped a number of other people out of jams—Emil was a joy to watch," according to Jerry. "In those situations, he was at the top of his game, like Babe Ruth hitting a home run, with his unsurpassed natural style and grace."

Overall, Jerry said that Emil exhibited "unfailing generosity" in settling PAA's business affairs, as he gradually pulled up stakes. But Jerry also needed to get some first-rate assistance to help make up for the void Emil would leave in the firm's lobbying line-up.

Ed Farhat was Jerry and Emil's "No. 1 Draft Choice." Ed, a former high school coach and school principal, had provided excellent lobbying services in behalf of the Michigan Catholic Conference ever since Jerry had departed to form PAA with Emil. Ed hit the ground running when he joined PAA in 1979, helping to ease Emil's transition.

EMIL'S LAST "LOVE LETTER"
FROM CAPITOL PRESS CORPS

Apparently Emil's presence in and around the Capitol loomed so large that some of the Capitol press corps, at least, wrote about him for some time as if he were still there full-time. The best example may be a full-page Sunday spread about state government lobbying appearing in the several Booth Newspapers on December 31, 1978, long after Emil had started phasing out of PAA. The five articles on the subject were authored by State Capitol Bureau Chief, Robert Longstaff, and four other Booth Newspapers Capitol Correspondents.

The articles duly mentioned all the top lobbyists in the Capitol, but singled out Public Affairs Associates and James H. Karoub and Associates for ruling the top of the power pyramid. These two lobbying firms, according to one of the articles, "are conceded by lawmakers and other lobbyists to have such a tight grip on the legislative process that they can squeeze out what they want for their clients."[397]

The article selected Emil and Jerry as prime examples of successful multi-client lobbyists who had begun to dominate the Lansing scene, describing their backgrounds and partisan affiliations. It notes that PAA's power "is seen throughout state government."

Dominating the middle columns of the full-page spread is was article entitled, "THEIR LOBBYING STYLES DIFFER/*But Both Lockwood and Coomes Operate Effectively.* Emil and Jerry were the only lobbyists to be singled out as main subjects for one of the articles. Their descriptions are priceless.

The Booth reporters' take on Emil and Jerry: They were "Lansing's odd couple in lobbying." Emil swapped "stories and information over breakfast, lunch, cocktails or dinner," according to the article, and related to legislators "like old buddies." Jerry, on the other hand, operated "low-key," and offered legislators "a chance to talk about their worries, their ambitions, their dreams."

Emil "knows exactly what is happening at all times," according to sources consulted by Booth reporters, and "usually is able to predict the outcome of a legislative battle." Moreover, "he knows when to show up at an informal gathering of legislators—and when to leave. He knows when to give his pitch, earnestly and with as much honesty as possible, and he knows when to be quiet."

The Booth article described Jerry as "quietly intense," and added that Jerry's "mixture of political idealism, Catholic politics and concern for his clients—mostly big business and the professions—is fascinating to young politicians." Jerry's style, according to these reporters, was "to build political friendships based on shared ideas and ideals," with the result that "he develops such an ease with them that they seek his advice on almost all political decisions."

Interestingly, both this article and an adjoining one acknowledged that Emil was in "semi-retirement," or "spending more and more time away from the office." Yet they wrote about him as if this were not the case, singling him out—and his now center-stage partner, Jerry—for star treatment.

In the face of such evidence, no one doubted that Emil's reputation—and clout—had become enviable indeed. Moreover, Emil and Jerry's partnership had been a resounding success from start to finish, and Jerry had emerged in the eyes of the press, according to plan, as a worthy solo captain of the PAA ship.

Emil's era of public life in Michigan had finally come to a more than satisfying end, after nearly three decades. His jet-setting and generous entertaining figured consistently into his and Anna's new life together, as they traveled the world via KLM, storing tales of exotic lands to share with their new friends in the Florida Keys. It's a rampant rumor in Florida that snowbirds from the north are known to actually retire when they move to Florida after a lucrative and lustrous career. Not so the *"Man who likes to get things done yesterday."*

PART FIVE

Legendary Mentor and Sage of Duck Key

1978 – 2002

25

"SEMI-RETIREMENT"
IN THE SUNSHINE STATE

The ability to handle ambiguity is often touted as a measure of a person's intelligence or inherent success quotient. Novelists and management gurus alike build it into character analyses to forecast and broaden potential outcomes. Yet it is often that same characteristic that makes predictability an unlikely result, at least on the surface of things.

In the 1960s and 1970s, wearing the mantle of the G.O.P., Emil balanced on the sometimes razor-thin divider between party icons and ideologies, robustly biting into the choicest fruits of each. So it is no surprise when he chucked the fast lane of political lobbying for the supposedly leisurely pace of retirement, that he also concocted his own custom blend of "happiness according to Emil." After all, this was the Navy's "semi-civilian," Root and Nicolai's "semi-senior accountant," the "adamant semi-kind" bachelor, and one of the last of the G.O.P. moderates. It was just a matter of figuring out the mix.

Outfitted with a five-year financial parachute from PAA to serve as board member and advisor, and to host legislators and clients, Emil and Anna transitioned during 1977 and 1978 to their new home in the Florida Keys, for what they laughingly referred to as semi-retirement. There, for half of each year, the new snowbirds set up housekeeping near Jim Lockwood, who had commuted weekly between Duck Key and E.F. Hutton in New York since 1972. Before their suitcases were even unpacked, business deals flew left and right.

"Emil didn't just bring home the bacon anymore," Anna remembered about those heady times. "He brought home entire businesses."

Everything was fair game, from radio stations and banks, to strip malls and strips of sand. They weren't all what they seemed, however, and some unexpected twists of fate called forth a lifetime of Emil's experience, and challenged his endurance, too. Typically, he dug in with both hands to save or grow several businesses. Then after shifting back from warp speed into cruise control, Emil started selling off the businesses and investing his expertise in mentoring many of the new people living throughout the greater Keys community.

Enthusiastic takers included many G.O.P. up-and-comers, as well as his own property owners association, on which he twice served as president, once in order to champion a new tax district. At the same time, he and Anna traveled the world, and snorkeled off the bow of their beloved cabin cruiser, Anna's Banana. They built homes, friendships, and an enduring legend of community involvement.

CRUISING DOWN THE RIVER

Emil and Anna didn't actually parachute into the Florida Keys, when they first moved there, although no one would have put it past them. Friends who remembered the post-honeymoon flyer announcing their whereabouts in East Lansing—after a trip abroad via Emil's handy Delta Air Transport board membership—recalled the picture of Anna's Banana heading toward Villa Montée. So no one was surprised, a few years later, when the ebullient couple said they'd be boating from Michigan to their new home in the Florida Keys. After all, Emil was a veteran of the Pacific Theater in World War II, the Keys were surrounded by water, and they had to get the boat there somehow, didn't they?

Staying afloat aboard Anna's Banana II, Emil and Anna cruised the Mississippi, the Keys and Intercoastal Waterways. Grandchildren left to right: Steven and Ann (Lama) Showerman. Detroit Boat Club, 1977.

"We started from the Detroit Boat Club," Anna recalled, "and the plan from there was to cross over southwesterly toward Illinois."

Emil had mapped out a complex river route, including a nostalgic visit to Ottawa, from where they would head south down the Illinois River, hook up with the Mississippi in St. Louis, and cruise the Mighty Mississippi all the way to New Orleans. After a little revelry in Cajun country, they'd cross the Gulf of Mexico to Naples, Florida, pick up a couple of PAA clients, and entertain their way into the Florida Keys, homefree.

The only reference available to the seafaring couple was a certain Mrs. Quimby's publication, *What To Do On The Way Down The Mississippi.*

"Emil said it had all the main points, like fuel and repair stops and gro-cery stores," Anna said. "He knew exactly how far our boat could travel on a tank of fuel, and according to Mrs. Quimby's annotated maps, we were all set."

What the publication didn't specify, however, was how much flooding the Mississippi had suffered, and—apparently after Mrs. Quimby had penned her maps—that fuel locations were often far inland of the floating docks marked on Mrs. Quimby's quaint maps.

"We had to climb up the embankment, and sometimes a hill or two more, once we tied up," Emil said. "There wasn't even a station at the top—it was more like a phone booth. We'd call and tell them what we needed. Then they'd truck in a fuel line and snake it down the hill—sometimes 20 feet or more," he said. "That was for the birds." After a couple of similar episodes, Emil purchased several portable five-gallon fuel containers, and used them to refuel between the rare dockside stations along the way.

Dodging debris above and below the surface proved more hazardous in the rough water than the explosive fuel on deck. Eventually a pile of rubble snagged and ripped off the boat's strut bolt. Water poured in, and Emil gave the wheel to Anna while he stuffed ballpoint pens in the hole, then leapt ashore to tie a line to a tree branch so they could bail out the water.

"But the rope broke on a branch and Anna started to drift," Emil said. "I jumped back on, but we still had the water to deal with," he laughed later, "so Anna was in the back bailing, while I navigated." [398]

"That trip almost ended our marriage before it began," Anna added mis-chievously.

"Nah," said Emil, "I finally got lucky, marrying Anna." [399]

Maneuvering the steering wheel with one hand, and gripping Mrs. Quimby's map with the other, Emil knew that New Orleans was less than 100 miles away, and he was determined to make it to the homestretch. As good fortune would have it, he located a boatyard along the way and had them re-place the strut bolt, while he and Anna docked overnight. The next day, with Lake Pontchartrain in sight, they were held up in a lock even as the Coast Guard cleared an oil tanker to proceed. In its wake, officials scrutinized the emerging "oil soup" lapping against the sides of Anna's Banana, and desig-nated the battle-weary Chris Craft as the primary suspect for the oil slick.

"As my friend Harry from the Dairy used to say, that makes about as much sense as blaming a thimble for a bucket of spilled milk," Emil said. [400]

Vindicated, albeit hours later and fully dark by then, Emil steered Anna's Banana into Lake Pontchartrain as city lights reflected on the surface of the lake. *Finally*, he and Anna fantasized, *some welcome relief on Bourbon Street!* When they got a good look at their boat's structural damage, how-ever—including a lost rudder—Emil and Anna swiftly agreed to rent a car and drive to the Sunshine State. As far as they were concerned, Anna's Banana could have a long weekend or two in New Orleans and catch up with them by truck in Naples, Florida. There, the Lockwoods would keep their original date with the PAA clients, gather them aboard the spit-polished re-paired boat, and host them in grand style along the western shores of Florida until they landed at their new home in the Keys.

"So we did," Emil said, "mainly, that is."

Two weeks later, Anna's Banana arrived in Naples, and Emil and Anna welcomed aboard the prestigious PAA clients who had been flown by private plane to Naples, for the boating adventure and a stay in the Keys as the Lockwoods' house guests. The clients included John McCabe, CEO of "Old Blue" (Blue Cross Blue Shield of Michigan) and his wife Doris, as well as Pat Callihan, head of Provincial House Nursing Homes of Michigan.

The galley was full of goodies and it was an easy trip, four hours at most. Finally Anna's Banana was cruising. Revelry reigned until mid-afternoon, when the boat conked out—ironically—from an oil leak. Fortunately, Emil was able to make a temporary patch, and a passing boat helped them out with some extra oil. A mere blip on the radar screen, Navy Veteran Lockwood explained to his passengers, as Anna circulated refreshments and they were once again underway.

As the idyllic hours passed, Doris McCabe amused herself by reading numbers on one of the nautical instruments. "Six-six-six," they heard her chortle, as everyone luxuriated in the cool spray of the water under the hot sun. "Five-five-five, four-four-four," Doris trilled, as the wind whipped their faces and Emil piloted through the Gulf, unaware of the significance of what she was reading. "Three-three-three," Doris chirped, when suddenly Anna's Banana ran aground.

"It was the depth finder," Emil said, chuckling at how everyone had tuned out Doris' "civilian" amusement. He and Pat climbed out, planted their feet in the shallow water, and leaned in to heave the boat out of the dune, but it wouldn't budge. "We had to get John McCabe in the water, too, before we made any headway," Emil said, recalling how finally the men pushed the boat out of the sand inch by sweaty inch.

As the sky slowly darkened after sunset, Emil spotted the U.S. Highway #1 bridge, and prepared to cross under it to access the Keys. The area was noted for its fishing and trapping activity, and while it wasn't nearly as haz-ardous as the Mississippi, Emil posted Pat Callihan up front with a flashlight, to spot lobster traps so they didn't get caught in the propellers. Then the Coast Guard called. Emil wasn't surprised, since he and Anna had alerted friends in the Keys about their approximate arrival time, and the oil leak had slowed them down, too.

"This is Anna's Banana," Emil replied, "go ahead."

"Are you all right?" the Coast Guard asked.

"Positive," Emil told them.

"Are you in trouble?" the Coast Guard persisted.

"Negative," Emil said firmly.

"People are worried about you," they said. "Where are you, and what's the problem?"

"Oh, not far," Emil said, surprised that they hadn't spotted his lights by then, "and there's no problem."

"It was pitch dark by the time we got in to our Key," Emil recalled, "but we were still singing when we docked the boat." The tune? "Cruising down the river, on a Sunday afternoon."

26

CASTING FOR GOLD in the "WORLD'S FINEST FISHING GROUND"

After computing the percentages between advertising revenue and expenses, Emil bought the "World's Finest Fishing Ground," WFFG 1300 AM, a radio station built on an unpopulated island across a bridge from Marathon in the Keys. In partnership with Jim Lockwood and Jerry Coomes, Emil had shrewdly set up the purchase package to retain the former owner in a management position. It was a move calculated to magnify profits on an already solid balance sheet. Within six months, however, Kincaid Group—the owner's parent company—whisked the manager away and replaced him, a loophole action that would soon foil Emil's perfect plan.

Unbeknownst to the Lockwoods, who cavorted domestically off the bow of Anna's Banana, and internationally with a cadre of friends and associates, the World's Finest Fishing Ground was losing ground by the day. Maybe the sun went to their heads, Emil speculates about the station's 7-8 employees, but one thing was for sure. Without serious intervention, the station would go down fast. What had he found when reviewing the monthly balance sheets?

"They were charging cat food and a lot else to the station," Emil said. Even worse, when he asked about a stack of fishing poles and boating gear that had appeared in the storeroom, he discovered that they were trading advertising services for merchandise and then absconding with the goods themselves.[401]

"It was like something in a movie," Emil recalled. "The disc jockey banged his head on the wall while he was on the air, and the chief engineer shot himself over his gay lover."

"Overnight, Emil turned from a power broker into someone who had to count nickels and dimes in order to keep the station viable," Anna added. "It seemed like the radio station was the first thing he couldn't conquer immediately."

Emil hunkered down for the count and rolled up his sleeves. He tracked employees' time by the minute, and supervised expenditures down to the penny. Even in his early C.P.A. days he hadn't monitored a business so closely in real time.

"Till then, I thought a log was something you threw into the fire," Emil grumbled good-naturedly to Rick Reason, his C.P.A. of later years, and Rick's able assistant Peggy.

The big challenge, of course, was revenue. "We had to have good enough programs to bring in the advertisers, so when Michigan legislators or my Congressional friends visited us, I'd get them to do a talk on something that was going on in the news. They enjoyed doing it, and people started listening more. Then we had to sell advertising, so I got Anna and my sister-in-law Audrie to sell spots." Undaunted, the two women put on their walking shoes, filled up their gas tanks, and made the rounds in Islamorada and the central Keys, the station's primary market.

"I sold the spots cheaper than I had to, but we eventually made money," Emil said. "It all had to do with the percentages."

Chagrined at getting Jim and Jerry in on a deal that might have gone south, Emil bought out their shares at a good price for them, as soon as WFFG's balance sheets warranted. When at last he sold the station for a modest profit to WMUM-FM, the World's Finest Fishing Ground was again sitting pretty. A few years later it was noted in broadcasting circles as the top station in the central Keys market, and its radio-talk-shows drew anchors from as far as Los Angeles.[402]

"We still had time for some fun," Emil said, even after six to seven hours a day at the station. "I bought a strip mall to fix up at the same time," he said, relishing the memory of the profit.[403] "Well, I guess we did a fair amount of boating, too," he admitted, smiling.

One infamous adventure at sea involved a 50-boat 240-people flotilla to Cuba, as part of Fidel Castro's attempt to improve relations with the U.S.

"It was all very tightly controlled," Anna recalled. "The Marathon Yacht Club was the first to respond to Castro's invitation, and it was a members-only event. We didn't belong," she said, "but we were so intrigued with the opportunity to spend a week in Cuba, that we joined in order to go."

It was a short-lived window of opportunity. Despite the fact that it took place at the tail end of the Cold War, the memory of the Cuban Missile Crisis still lingered in the air, and refugees still streamed into Florida, fleeing the Castro dictatorship.

Emil and Anna were among the last to cast off for Cuba, slower boats having left the day before, in order to time their arrival together. They re-member steering Anna's Banana between two armed gunboats outside the canal. A CNN newsman on one of the first boats leapt to a dock surrepti-tiously, or so he hoped, to photograph the arrival of the Club's U.S. flotilla between the gunboats. His camera was swiftly confiscated, the Lockwoods recalled.

"The paint on the docks was still sticky," Emil said, also recalling that the electrical outlets on the dockside ports were loose in their sockets, they had been so hurriedly installed.

"We saw Cuban frogmen swimming under the boats within the hour," Anna added. "It looked suspicious, but they told us that it was for our own protection, to make sure that there weren't any incidents."[404]

The American travelers had brought along their bikes, but could only go so far into town, and still make it back before an agreed upon curfew. Emil and Anna saw tourist buses from Russia, China, and other countries, and learned that tourism was a large source of income for the island. "So of course they gave us the red-carpet treatment," Emil said, recalling an over-night luxury bus trip to Havana, where they saw Hemingway's and Vanderbuilt's mansions and were entertained at the legendary Copa Cabanna Nightclub. "But it wasn't always a pretty sight," Anna added, recalling a rum-tasting party with the Cubans jealously watching through the windows. "Cubans were still rationed at the time," she explained.[405]

THE BANK DRAFT

Along with twelve other friendly investors in 1979, Emil participated in the purchase of Marathon Bank, a small but thriving bank on Sombrero Boulevard in Marathon, not too far from Duck Key. It was another hands-on deal, he recalled, "but nothing like the radio station."

Hungry to learn something new, Emil booked some time with his brother Jim in New York, for a primer on how to "sell paper," or "securitize mort-gages." With Jim's able coaching, Emil got a several-day graduate course on bundling and selling loans that the bank held, to secondary financiers. "We'd have to discount the loans," Emil explained, "but if the borrowers were good credit risks—and we made sure that all of ours were—then the discount wasn't too bad." With the cash received from the sale of the loans, Emil sug-gested to the board that the bank could leverage its funds to finance a condo development, a marina, and other projects. All of which Marine Bank did—in moves that paid off handsomely in boosting the bank's assets within four short years. Not, however, without some Lockwood hands-on care and feed-ing in the process.

"Emil oversaw the books, and a lot of operations," Anna recalled. "He okayed contractors' work, and most major expenditures, and billed about $1,000 a month. At first I just heard about it over dinner," she said. "Then when one partner moved away, Emil bought his share for me. That made two thirteenth-shares for us, plus—what was even better—as a director I got a front row seat to watch my mover-and-shaker husband in action."[406]

"Emil was at his finest," Anna added. "He could compute alternate sce-narios in a flash, and was quick to sense what needed to be done."

From master plan to talent search, Emil locked in the bank's success. When it came time to fill the comptroller position, the board of directors narrowed down the list of 200 applicants to five finalists, and then asked Emil to continue the process because of his business degree and experience, as well as his C.P.A. expertise. Emil found a way to get the job done, and help a friend at the same time.

"One of my buddies wanted to get his Mercedes from Florida to New Hampshire," Emil recalled, "and one of the candidates lived not too far from there." Emil noted all five candidates' locations lay along the mid-Atlantic seaboard leading northward, and promptly decided to drive the Mercedes up the coast and personally interview them all on their own turf.

"Think how expensive it would have been," he said, "to fly them all down to Florida for a couple of days each, to interview." Instead, Emil narrowed it down to one finalist. "There was nothing to lose," he said. "If the board didn't like him, they could fly the next one in." Within a short time, board members shook hands with candidate "number one" and told him to call the movers. The new comptroller's exemplary performance was just one of a host of factors that put Marine Bank—as it was renamed by then—on the map.[407]

"People started calling it 'The Bank that Grew Up'," Emil said. "We liked the slogan so much we put it on our annual report." Marine Bank expanded to three branches by 1982, and doubled to six by 1983, in locations spanning the full range of the Keys, from Key Largo to Key West.[408] The bank stock, Emil recalled with satisfaction, yielded a hefty return to the investors.

With Marine Bank on a steady growth pattern, Emil had time to spare. He was elected in 1984 to his first term as president of the Duck Key Property Owners Association (DKPOA—pronounced "DUCK-poh"). Emil was happy to serve, but it didn't absorb half enough of his excess energy. When Pat Callihan and Dr. Ron Chase pitched him on the idea of starting a nursing home in the mid-Florida Keys, Emil was primed to go. They had the professional expertise and credentials, and he had the numbers down pat.

The partners studied many choice locations, settling on an attractive seaside parcel in Marathon. The three men put their heads together on a purchase plan and a development design. Permits, however, were not that easily obtained. Regulatory agencies had laid down a few gauntlets to prevent an overproliferation of nursing homes in the benevolent Florida climes. Enter Lockwood—vote-getter and go-getter.

"It almost turned into a march of senior citizens," Emil said of the process for obtaining the Certificate of Need. "Turns out, a lot of people really wanted it."[409]

Many signatures and petitions later, Emil, Pat and Ron set out with permits in hand, to survey their new domain. The sun shone, the sand glistened, and the surf crashed along the boulders and the sand. More sand, perhaps, than they had counted on.

"It was going to take a lot of drilling to find the right rock bed to build on," Emil said, "and the permits only lasted for so long."

The patient trio made frequent visits to the site to confer with the excavation crew, and ultimately celebrated the results—a firm foundation site within reasonable drilling reach. Not long thereafter, they were approached in early 1985 by a developer with an attractive offer. They sold the choice spot to him, plans and all. Today the first class nursing facility named Marathon Manor is a thriving establishment.[410]

Later in the year, Emil and Anna decided to sell their shares in Marine Bank, too, and parlay their earnings into a second home.

"Well, I was 65, going on 66," Emil said. "I thought maybe I'd try dropping the 'semi' off of my 'retirement'."

Having heard about the haunting beauty of the Blue Ridge Mountains north of Ashville, North Carolina in August 1985, they headed north. They stayed overnight in Cashiers, North Carolina, intending to find a realtor, target a purchase, then return to rent it over the Labor Day weekend in September to solidify their selection before making it official. Exiting the Blue Ridge Parkway the next morning—a Wednesday—they stopped for supplies at a store in Highlands. The owner told them about the "cutest little cabin" for sale in an area called King Mountain Club. Emil and Anna saw it, and decided it was almost perfect.

Moving along with typical Lockwood speed, they made an offer to purchase on Thursday, and closed the deal on Friday by phone on their way home. By Labor Day they were back and engaged a contractor to rip out the kitchen, in the process making lifelong friends with Ron Weston and his wife Babs, who in turn visited them in the Keys. Their 3,000 square foot getaway was near actor Burt Reynolds' place, though they never saw him. Instead, they made sure to host Muscott and Lockwood family gatherings, LST reunions, and a host of friends and former clients and associates.[411]

❖❖

27

LIFE ACCORDING TO LOCKWOOD

Some people think fun is what you do after work. Others work so hard at having fun, the fun goes flat, or they're exhausted afterwards instead of refreshed. Still others find all their pleasure in their work, to the exclusion of everything else.

On the surface of it, most people might initially put Emil in the latter category, although opinions might vary between his former spouses, were they alive to tell. Emil and Jane certainly shared a *joie de vivre*, and entertained heartily during their time together, but the relationship did not endure into his public life. Emil's and Mariella's approaches, on the other hand, were so variant as to surprise even new acquaintances.

"The former Mrs. Lockwood was cool and calm," Freddy Van Gaever recalled of Mariella during his early visits to Michigan. "She was soft spoken when she said something, but this was seldom. And she did not like to leave the house. I was not surprised when they separated years later."[412]

In Anna, however, Emil had found a partner with whom he could share his work and his fun. It was a good thing, too, because in his view of things, there was little distinction between the two. He loved it all. Anna Muscott Weaver had earned her own wings in politics, having served the Republican Party in several volunteer and professional capacities. She knew the ropes and enjoyed the dance. And as far as that is concerned, "I'd rather dance than eat," she was known to frequently say with a smile.[413]

"Emil could talk with her about anything," Anna's daughter Franny Showerman said. "Whether it was financial schemes, business, or politics, she got it, and she enjoyed it, too. Emil appreciated her sense of humor, too, and told everybody how for her 60th birthday she had registered at both Tiffany's and K-Mart."[414]

For the first time, Emil had a full-time partner and spouse with whom to share his political and lobbying adventures, as well as his private moments. Before Freddy sold off his first airline, the two KLM jet-setters had dined in castles, casinos and cafes in Vienna, Paris, Istanbul, Caracas, and more. They strolled through the Coliseum in Athens with Jerry and Colette Coomes, David and Jan Hayhow, and Gus and Sue Harrison; they sipped sangria in the same hotel in Madrid where Anna had chaperoned her daughter's dance troupe in the 1960s, and they went native in Nairobi.

PUSH-BUTTON RHINOS IN NAIROBI

"A stewardess and her mother told us about 'Max' after we landed in Nairobi," Emil said. "We were having breakfast with them the next day at our hotel, and they told us there was a native cab driver who could really show us the country. Turns out he had a girl in every village, so he really knew his way around."

Emil called Max after breakfast and the cab driver arrived almost immediately. When Emil told him the itinerary he and Anna had worked out, Max said to scrap it, and that instead, he could take them to all the "real" places. After the Lockwoods thought about it for half a minute they agreed, and by early afternoon they had checked out of the hotel, forsaking the beaten path for Max's adventure in the jungle.

"So we loaded all our luggage and valuables into his Mercedes cab," Anna added, "trusting that the flight attendant wouldn't refer us to anyone bad."

In fact, Max was a gem, and the flight attendant was right about him on two counts. He did seem to know every inch of the bush throughout Kenya and Tanzania. And despite the fact that he didn't seem to bathe very much according to the Lockwoods' olfactory perceptions in close tropical quarters for a week, Max's liaisons were nevertheless as numerous as the number of villages scattered throughout the wild.

After an exciting day-trip through herds of gazelles and villages nestled in the bush, Max got Emil and Anna situated at the Hilton "Salt Lick," thinking how much they would enjoy the up-close viewings of endangered species for which the Hilton had become known.

"We almost got licked at the Salt Lick, though," Emil said with a twinkle.

"We never thought it could be so exhausting to stay at a great resort," Anna added.

The Hilton, Emil explained, had dug a moat around the building, deep and wide enough to prevent large or predatory animals from availing themselves of the facilities or its guests. During the day, a drawbridge was lowered for traffic of the human variety, and after dark the bridge was raised and the grounds secured, so everyone could get a peaceful night's sleep.

"There was something extra, though," Emil said. "The people at the front desk told us we could pick some animals to see, and if they showed up at the salt lick across the moat, a buzzer would go off in our room and we'd be able to see them right off our balcony. Hell, we were so excited we picked them all. I think there were five—elephants, rhinos, giraffes, you know. Then we went to sleep, figuring they'd show up sometime in the morning."

Jetsetting with friends or ordering pizza, Emil and Anna enjoyed lasting friendships throughout their lives. From left: Emil, Jerry Coomes, Gus Harrison. Turkey, 1987.

Calm in the center of the storm—Emil and Anna take a breather in white water near their vacation home in King Mountain Club. South of Highlands (NC), 1985.

Pondering ancient architecture—Emil and Anna in foreground (right center) at Coliseum restoration site. Athens, Greece, 1987.

Belgian connection endures—Emil (far right) views impressive Gránd Plaçe plaza. Brussels, 1992.

"In Service of His Majesty"— Emil and Anna (right) join Van Gaevers at Piz Gloria Restaurant, site of Sean Connery's '007' film.   Lieve Van Gaever (front left). Switzerland, 1980.

Three shrill alarm buzzers punctuated the Lockwoods' sleep that night, after which the novelty of seeing *Rhinocerotidae* in the buff quickly wore off. "I called the front desk and told them to stop, we'd had enough," Emil said.[415]

In the days following, Max took the Lockwoods out on private tours of native villages, or "safari" tours through herds of wild zebras, giraffes, and gazelles. At night, sometimes they stayed in domed huts or motels nestled in the bush. Particularly poignant highlights included a private tour of a native Masai village with Max, as well as an overnight stay in a modernized "hut" at the foot of the majestic Mount Kilimanjaro.[416]

"So don't say I never recreated before 1985," Emil said. "Heck, I went looking for a poker game right away in Duck Key." Within a year of relocation, Emil had identified several comrades-in-arms. He pulled together Jack Schlegel, Dick Sonner, Harry Keller, Webb Gokey, Harvey Hortman, and the incorrigible Sonny Appell—Emil's new best friend and political cohort—into a group known as the "lucky seven poker boys."[417]

"No, wait, Sonny can't be my best friend," Emil said smiling, "because he's a better poker player than I am."[418]

Sonny isn't the only one who beat Emil in the world of wagers, however. Anna's son-in-law, Steve Showerman, has a place of honor in family lore for besting the former Senate Majority Leader at his own game. The Lockwood snowbirds had returned to Michigan early in the fall of 1980, looking forward to some Big Ten football.

"Everyone knew that Emil liked to bet on all kinds of things," Steve said. "He would even bet on a closed door. 'How many minutes before someone opens the door?,' he'd bet with me or Franny. 'Will it be one or two people that come through?' He was always figuring ahead of time, what would happen next, and how it would happen."

The annual MSU vs. U of M football game was always a prime opportunity for bets in the Lockwood family and circle of friends. Emil's loyalty to the University of Michigan, and Steve's to his own alma mater, Michigan

State University, provided the backdrop for a stylistic turning point in Lockwood lore in 1980. The Spartan Stadium was brimming with fans and vibrating with collegiate rivalry. Emil had wanted to bet "even up" and put $100 on the table, but Steve wasn't as confident of his team's ability to win outright.

"Usually Emil would just bet ten cents or a dollar," Steve said, "but this was too high for 'even up' as far as I was concerned. Finally Emil said he'd give me seven points leeway and I took it."

At some point in the game, with the crowd roaring in the background, Emil and Steve were each feeling bullish and the stakes went up, with another—nonmonetary—consequence. Known since his Navy days for his short-shorn brush-cut hair, Emil had told Anna from day one that he would do anything for her, but there were two things she couldn't ask him to do.

Emil sported ubiquitous cigarette, from Senate floor to tennis court. Tennis partner and son-in-law Steve Showerman (left) and Emil. Florida Keys (FL), 1986.

Samson meets Delilah—in reverse, as Emil loses signature brush-cut and $100 in football bet with Steve Showerman (2nd right) at MSU vs. U of M game. Anna (2nd left), Fran Showerman (2nd right). East Lansing (MI), 1985.

In memory of Grandma Muscott (Anna's mother) Emil instigates Muscott reunions in 1973 at his lake bluff "cottage" on Mackinac Island. Showermans' home, Silver Lake (MI), 1995.

Dockside family revelry—left to right: granddaughter Ann (Showerman) Lama, son-in-law Steve Showerman Sr., grandson Steven Showerman Jr., daughter Franny (Weaver) Showerman, Anna and Emil. Silver Lake (MI), 1996.

Rarely was Emil spoonfed, but he made an exception for his great granddaughter Audrey on Anna's side (parents Ann [Showerman] and Dave Lama). Duck Key (FL), 2000.

"Don't ask me to quit smoking," he told her, "and don't ask me to grow out my hair. Period."

She never did, but on that day in the football stadium, Steve had the idea of bundling Emil's hair length into the bet. Emil gamely accepted, figuring he was on the side of the winning team, the invincible Maize and Blue Wolverines.

U of M won the game, but not by seven points. Steve has a picture of Emil handing him $100, but as far as Anna is concerned, the family's photo albums were more enhanced a few months down the road—with pictures of the longer-locked Lockwood.[419]

"He never complained or went back on it," Anna said. "That's just the way he was."

Emil's good humor seemed to keep him going through thick and thin—from times of old, when he bucked up under the pressure no matter what, to his present less harried lifestyle.

"When I think of my Dad," Eric Lockwood said, "I always see his smile."[420]

"Emil rarely could keep a conversation going for over a minute without a laugh for one reason or another," according to Freddy Van Gaever. "He was always in the middle of things, exuberant and joyful."[421]

Emil's exuberance kept him and Anna trotting the globe, even after Freddy Van Gaever sold the Delta Air Transport. In Switzerland with the Van Gaevers they traced "007" Sean Connery's footsteps while filming *In Service of Her Majesty* on location at Piz Gloria Restaurant. They clowned aboard Her Majesty's "Q E II" with Pat and Coilah Callihan, where Emil turned the tables on a waiter, insisting on trading places with him and serving the meal himself. They rendezvous-ed with Jerry and Colette Coomes on Mackinac Island, Michigan, and in Naples, Florida. And they traveled with Jim and Audrie Lockwood to New York City for Broadway shows, catching all-time favorites such as: *South Pacific, The King and I, Victor-Victoria*, and *Oklahoma.*

It wasn't all spectator sports either. Sometimes Emil and Anna worked up a sweat on the tennis or shuffleboard courts. Wherever Emil was, whatever else was in his hands, the red tip of a lit cigarette always glowed between his index and middle fingers. Whether fishing or playing tennis with his friend Bud Carr—even while river rafting in the North Carolina white water rapids with Anna and friends—a close look at the photos will almost always reveal yet another Salem Light Menthol smoldering away. While his Grandmother Augusta might have squirmed in her grave at the sight of it, one thing about Emil was for certain—he was comfortable in his own skin, and as a result, so was everyone else.

Photo collections also reveal another Lockwood trait—loyalty. Emil never left old friends behind, when he made new ones. From Ottawa, Illinois to Pearl Harbor and beyond, familiar faces reappeared even as new ones cropped up. As practiced consistently throughout his life, Emil exuded the sentiments of a simple campfire tune sung in rounds by boyscouts and girlscouts across America:

White-water rapids in Smoky Mountains—Emil (2nd left) steers raft with guide. Freddy and Lieve Van Gaever (1st and 2nd right), Anna (3rd left), and Belgian friend. North Carolina, 1988.

> "Make new friends, but keep the old.
> One is silver and the other gold."[422]

Emil and Anna met new Belgian friends Staf and Simone Coppin through the Van Gaevers, and twice were guested at the Coppins' villa in Marbaya, Spain, on the Costa del Sol. One time they crossed over from Spain, to tour the Rock of Gibraltor with George and Diane Elgis. As a veteran of the Pacific Theater in WW II, Emil was fascinated with the enormous rock that was also a populated island, and one of the key strategic headquarters of the Allies in the Atlantic Theater. They learned all its history from a colorful taxi driver they had hired to drive them within and around the awesome structure. The former football player took them to Eisenhour's bunker, munitions stores, the airstrip and road system, and even a small tourist town.[423]

"Cars had to stop and let planes land," Emil said, recalling being cleared to cross the runway.[424]

Through 1988, the Lockwoods frequently hosted friends aboard their boat, on short as well as marathon jaunts. Once with Harry from the Dairy and his wife, Marion, they boated on Thanksgiving Day from Ottawa, Illinois to St. Louis, Missouri. "Marian had made up a full turkey dinner the day before," Anna said, "and kept it on slow-cook in thermal plates, for a holiday dinner en route."[425]

Another time, celebrating the retirement of Anna's Banana I and the purchase of Anna's Banana II, they attempted a segment of the Michigan to Florida marathon with Jim and Audrie Lockwood, and friends Mike and Alice Pung. Emil and Anna had launched AB II at the Detroit Boat Club and boated through the Welland Canal and Lake Erie, then on to New York. There they saluted the Statue of Liberty, and wended their way to the East Coast Intercoastal waterways to see how far they could make it down the coast before Emil was due back at PAA. It was the transition period before he was permanently "set free" and he and Anna happily mixed work and play aboard their

Boyhood friend Sam Parr and Emil ruminate on rich history of their birthplace, at memorial of Boy Scouts' 1902 American founding. Ottawa (IL), 1999.

LST 478ers relive tales. Left to right: Ray Custer (Engineering Ofcr.), Russell Lake (Commissary Ofcr.), Emil (Deck Ofcr.), Bob Keefe (Navigation Ofcr.). Little Palm Is. (FL), 1993.

boat, hosting a rotating bevy of legislators along the way.

"Come nightfall," Emil said, "we'd stay on the boat, and put the legislators up in a nice marina motel. Some of them would go back home from there, and when they did, new people came aboard." Various people, he recalled, got on and off the boat for a few days at a time, and then he and Anna picked up the Pungs at the Naval Base at Norfolk, Virginia, where Mike Pung had left his plane. After a pleasant jaunt for a few days, the four returned to Norfolk and Mike offered to fly the Lockwoods back to Michigan.

WW II vets beached in Florida Keys,. Left to right: Russell Lake, Ray Custer (Engineering Ofcr.), Emil, Bob Keefe. Duck Key (FL), 1995.

"It was only a two or three hour flight," Emil said, "and I wanted to get back to the office, so we said 'yes.' But a big storm came in and Mike had to put down in Morgantown, West Virginia. He wasn't instrument trained, you see, so we had to wait it out. We had a great time waiting, though."

Three days later, the weather hadn't sufficiently cleared, so Mike hired an instrument pilot for the remainder of the bumpy trip, and the Pungs and Lockwoods landed safely in Michigan. It was all part of the mix as far as Emil was concerned. He was in-the-flow and friends were friends no matter what the weather or the rest of the world did. As a consequence, he and Anna were hosted across the globe; and their home, boat, and properties were always open in return.[426]

"CLUB DUCK KEY" AND THE SENIOR OLYMPICS

Sometimes when Emil was headlong into one of his Tuesday marathon poker matches, or hatching a strategy with one of candidates under his wing, Anna headed North to Miami or Sawgrass for some good old-fashioned shopping with the ladies. Emil knew they were in good hands because their driver was his "personal dental consultant."

"Ted Theodore's a retired dentist," Emil said, "but he wasn't too retired to help me a few years ago when I needed some special work done. Not only did he screen the docs ahead of time, to find the right one, but he drove me up to Miami for the surgery. I guess he likes the drive, because now when his wife Tillie and Anna want to go shopping, they call four or five other gals and off they go, with Ted at the wheel."

"It's always a good guess how far they'll get," Emil added, "and what they'll come back with, too. Sometimes I make a side bet on it with the fellas."[427]

In 1988 Emil and Anna decided they wanted a bigger place in the Keys, and in order to focus on the project, they nostalgically donated Anna's Banana II to a charitable organization. The recipient? A training school for wayward boys, whose residents kept AB II in the water for many years to come. Then the Lockwoods bought four adjoining lots, and put their heads together to design their ultimate home, complete with tennis courts and a heated swimming pool. Their home immediately became the de facto community center.[428]

"Anna wanted a sewing room, and Emil wanted an elevator," said friends Ed and Bonnie Hall, Ed having been the veep of "The Bank That Grew Up," prior to becoming president of five Orion Banks in the Keys, formerly First National Bank. "They designed their home to have combined space, and personal space," Bonnie said. "I'll never forget their housewarming—they celebrated the engagement of two other couples, acknowledging other people, even at their own special time. When you met them, you felt as though you had known them for a long time. They called it 'The House That Love Built,' Bonnie said, "and they shared it with everyone. The downstairs was 'the club' and it was always unlocked, so everyone in the community could come and go whether they were home or not."[429]

Reminiscing about Dad and Starved Rock Park—Lorette Lockwood (left), Lori (Lockwood) Doles (center), Eric Lockwood (right). Park City (UT), 1994.

Emil's daughters and son enjoy reunion out west. Left to right: Lorette Lockwood, Eric Lockwood, Lori (Lockwood) Doles. Park City (UT), 1994.

New branches on Lockwood family tree—Back left to right: Taryn Lockwood Schultz (Eric's daughter), Melissa Barmes (Lori's daughter), Emil, Brandon Lockwood (Lorette's son), Kara Lockwood (Lorette's daughter). Front left to right: Amber Lockwood (Lorette's daughter), Teighlor Lockwood-Koehn (Lorette's daughter, on Anna's lap), Anna, Audrey Lockwood-Koehn (Lorette's daughter), Darian Rider (Eric's grand-daughter), Kory Rider (Tonya's son), and Tonya Lockwood (Eric's daughter). Colorado Springs (CO), 1996.

Reunions burst to overflowing at every location Emil and Anna owned—North Carolina, the Keys, even their six-bedroom "cottage" on the bluff of Mackinac Island, overlooking the convergence of Great Lakes Huron and Michigan. "We were building up a few grandkids by then, too," Emil said, recounting how their combined families spanned international boundaries, living in Oregon, Colorado, Utah, New Jersey, Arizona, Michigan, Florida, and Germany.

The Lockwoods spearheaded another Duck Key innovation—the Annual Senior Olympics, holding the multi-day event on their property each year since 1988. It's a stellar example of their partnership in action—Emil on the brainstorming and barnstorming, Anna on the organization. A host of willing participants helped with arrangements, and enjoyed the hilarious activities as well.

Even their long-standing housekeeper of twenty years, Shari Cronin, leapt in enthusiastically to prepare the grounds for the annual event. "Well, she might have been a little too enthusiastic," Emil drawled, having been driven out of the house more than once by her energetic vacuuming.[430]

"I love everybody in Duck Key!" exclaimed Jim Bicknell, when he and his wife Doris attended the first Senior Olympics at the Lockwoods.

A couple of months in advance of the event, artistically inclined Duck Key residents constructed and decorated plywood horses. Then two weeks ahead of time they auctioned them off to "syndicates," after which the new owners "groomed" them for the race at "Lockwood Downs." Everyone had a hand in the arrangements. Competitive programs included gin rummy, tennis, horse auctions, darts, kite-flying, golf cart racing, mahjong, conch horn blowing, and, of course, shuffleboard.

"Emil could tear you up in gin," Harvey Hortman commented, "but I think he kicked back and went easy on the people at the Senior Olympics."[431]

"Then a year or so ago," Webb Gokey said in September 2001, Emil advised the original planning group that created Club Duck Key. They gave the Lockwoods a lifetime membership in appreciation for the many events held at their residence. Now we're going to take on the Olympics there, as a community tradition."[432]

Finally, the Lockwoods' life was starting to sound like a real retirement—to everyone but Emil, that is. He had his eye on some political candidates in the area, and started calculating with Sonny Appell to see what they could do for the G.O.P. in the Keys. And in the middle of it all, he championed a new tax district for his property owners' association.

❖❖

28

COMMUNITY GUARDIAN ANGEL

"Live in the moment" is a pop psychology phrase Emil didn't cotton to very much, but the truth of it is, he never planned very far in advance. His moments, on the other hand, were like close-up and long-range zoom lenses constantly rotating on interesting possibilities along every inch of his backyard and his horizon. And with rare exceptions throughout his life, once he locked in on a target of opportunity, his instincts for success and his ability to maneuver in complex or simple arenas always seemed to carry the day.

In his evolving take on retirement, Emil began to apply these instincts and skills on behalf of talented up-and-comers around him. He also felt little separation between his own needs and those of his community, investing himself in projects large and small, to benefit the land or those around him.

One year, Duck Key's coconut palm trees were ravaged by leaf-hopper insects carrying a deadly phytoplasma from tree to tree, causing what entomologists called Lethal Yellow (LY) disease. Having destroyed 100,000 palms in Southern Florida in the early 1980s, and 65% of Key West's palms in 1965, Duck Key residents knew not to take the attack lightly. Yet as leaves yellowed and died, and new buds shriveled and blackened, few knew what to do beyond trimming back the infected plants. Tetracycline antibiotic treatments brought on temporary remissions, but after repeated injections, the holes themselves killed the struggling palms.[433]

Emil's simple response was to shoulder bag after bag of LY-resistant coconuts to the lot next to his home, and start digging holes. A palm tree farm, he had concluded, was needed to grow new palm trees to replace the dying ones. Others soon showed up with their own bags of coconuts, and a reclamation effort was well underway.

"Thanks to Emil," fellow property owners Webb and Mickey Gokey recalled, "by the time the leaf hoppers were taken care of, the island had healthy young palm plants growing alongside the dying trees."[434]

EMIL'S GROWING LOCAL CURRENCY

About 500-plus snowbirds comprised the population of Duck Key, an idyllic sun-baked island nestled in the incomparable azure waters of the Florida Keys. Duck Key is divided into five areas—a resort and four residential islands. Each summer Duck Key's population dropped to about 10% of the whole, raising issues about security, among concerned members of the property owners' association.

"In 1991, I was chair of the nominating committee of DKPOA," Webb Gokey recalled. "We had learned that Florida statutes allowed for the formation of Special Taxing Districts, and we wanted to set one up so that security costs would be covered in perpetuity. But it meant getting enough signatures to bring it to the Monroe County Board of Commissioners, and then their passing on it before it could even get to a public referendum. We knew it would be difficult and complicated to accomplish it. So I asked Emil if he would run for president again, and—as a part of his mission—to help us set up a special taxing district for security."[435]

Emil knew that only certain property owners paid the annual security fees to safeguard all Duck Key property, and he thought it was only fair that everyone participate. The new taxing district would provide the mechanism to involve all property owners through their taxes, but first they had to agree to it, and second, the County Commissioners and Assessors Office had to agree on how to allocate the funds—hopefully without raising taxes too much either.

So Emil agreed to run for president, and immediately the wheels started turning. True to his nature, he had befriended folks across party lines even in "retirement," lunching occasionally at a favorite Cuban restaurant with Democrat friend and Assessor, Irwin Higgs. "We got to know each other along the way," Emil recalled, "because I was always dropping in his office to find out one thing or another. After a while, I'd walk in, and the secretaries would say, *Oh, 'L,' what do you want to know now?* The more you know," Emil said, "the more you can do." [436]

Emil's currency with Higgs wasn't limited to schmoozing, either. He had surprised his friend once, by inviting him to a meeting of the Commissioners—all Republican at the time—and walking in with the Michigan Democratic Speaker of the House of Representatives, Bobby Crim. Emil apparently thought Higgs could use moral support from another Democrat. So when Emil asked Higgs' help, his friend was more than willing. First however, he had to get the necessary signatures to bring the issue before the Commissioners.

"Emil was a fire horse going to a fire," said Webb Gokey, who witnessed him in action and shared in the excitement, as the list of signatures grew to the necessary fifty-percent-plus-one, in order to approach the board. Alongside him in the effort, were stalwarts Sonny Appell—a politico in his own right from Ohio—and Harvey Hortman who ably applied his business background to the campaign. People who watched from the sidelines said a new triumvirate had emerged in Keys politics.

Lockwood home serves as de facto "Club Duck Key" for many years—hosting community events, Senior Olympics, and more. Duck Key (FL), 2000.

Silver anniversary—Emil and Anna pose to commemorate their 25th anniversary. Duck Key (FL), 1997.

At GOP notable Peter Secchia's Grand Haven digs—left to right: Peter (in short pants), Carol Vander Jagt, Anna, and Emil (modeling $10 tux 'n tails. MI, circa 1985.

Lockwood sense of humor unleashed in Emil and Anna's attire at annual costume party of DKPOA (Duck Key Property Owners Association). Duck Key (FL), 1989.

"Emil and Sonny were the big cheeses in the Republican Party in the Keys," Hortman said. "I went down with him and Sonny to the County Seat in Key West a few times, and together we cultivated the commissioners, took them to lunch, and made our case. No one had accomplished a security district at the time, and no one knew how. Now a lot of property owners are following suit."[437]

Some might say it was all over but the shouting at that point, but not Emil, despite the "buy" signs he was starting to get. So he called in a reserve player to attend the Commissioners' meeting, on the day they would forward the issue to a referendum vote, or kill it in committee.

Property owners commemorate new tax district—Anna and Emil decked out to celebrate after Emil's successful championing of new tax district for property owners association. Duck Key (FL), 1991.

Irwin Higgs, at Emil's request, met with the board to talk about the assessments, and how tax funds could be spent. "Once they realized a lot of the money was already in there," Emil said, "and they wouldn't lose any votes in the next election, they felt better about it. Just to be sure, though, I told Irwin to alert Wilamena when it was time to vote about our district."

The elderly commissioner Emil referred to was a well-regarded institution on the board by then. But, she was also a Democrat Emil had jumped ship to help elect, crossing party lines temporarily to do so in the closed primary elections of Florida. He knew he could count on her vote, but he also knew she sometimes inadvertently got distracted.

"She might forget," Emil explained to Higgs, who accordingly found a discreet way to nudge her and whisper in her ear just as the item came to vote.[438]

The second wave stood in reserve, even as the measure was approved for a public referendum. Then Emil got buddies Harvey Hortman and Sonny Appell to beat the pavement with him in the weeks prior to the measure's successful passage through popular vote.

"We knew he could do it," Gokey said, "and he did."[439]

G.O.P. MENTOR ON THE ROAM

GOP mentor at large—Emil glad-hands on behalf of his favorite candidates and protégés. Duck Key (FL), 1984.

The Lockwood-Appell "poker boys" worked behind the scenes, too, mentoring and promoting countless G.O.P. candidates throughout the Florida Keys and helping them to organize their campaigns. Fund-raising events were frequent at the Lockwood and Appell homes. Emil told candidates to "come by my house for a while," and when they arrived—to their delight and astonishment—they saw Anna on a microphone introducing them to house full of potential supporters.[440]

"They would pick someone they liked and help him or her, sometimes without the person even knowing it. They did it for me," said Harry Sawyer of his campaign for Supervisor of Elections.

"Sometimes Emil would stop by my office during a campaign, and say, 'Harry give me four or five signs,' and sooner than not they'd be scattered around the Keys. Then he'd say, 'Harry, come over to my house tomorrow, okay?' and when I showed up there'd be a group of people there ready

Best poker player in Duck Key and Emil's dear friend Sonny Appell. Duck Key (FL), 1998.

to support my campaign. If you were lacking any confidence in what you were doing, you sat down to talk with Emil and Sonny, and you walked away feeling like you could conquer the world. If I was worried about not getting out enough to talk with people before an election," Sawyer said, "Emil would tell me, 'Don't worry about it, we're talking *for* you.' If I still brought up problems, Emil would just laugh."

"If you're nervous about something, your days are numbered," Emil told him. "Then it can't be done. But," Emil added, "there's nothing you can't accomplish with a great attitude." [441]

Revisiting yesteryear, Emil checks out his Senate Majority Leader portrait, hanging today in Capitol's Senate Conference room. Lansing (MI), 2001. *Photo by Mike Quillinan.*

As a young police officer who needed to make ends meet in the 1970s, Rick Roth got a part-time job painting the towers at WFFG's World's Finest Fishing Ground. The station was located conveniently for him, next to his department's shooting range. One day on his second job at the radio station in the late 1970s, he met someone who would help him more than he could imagine, several years down the road.

Having held most jobs in his department since 1965, Roth was appointed interim Sheriff in 1990 when the prior Sheriff left. With a scant two years to do his job and run for election in 1992, Roth knew just whom to call. "I was a greenhorn," he said, "not in my department, but in elective politics."

"How does it work?" Roth asked Emil.

"Well," Emil said, "the first thing is you need is about $40,000 to 50,000."

"No!" the shocked sheriff said. "Where will that kind of money come from?"

"People will give it to you," Emil replied, enjoying himself.

"But why, and how?" Roth asked in disbelief.

"You have to ask right," Emil said, and then offered to help.

"Emil was the principal organizer in my first campaigns," Roth said of his 1992 and 1996 campaigns, "and he was a big help to me in 2000, too. He showed me how things happened, and how to approach people."

"Be yourself," Emil told him, "and be honest when you talk to people." Then Emil told him whom to call on, rattling off a bunch of names that Roth

With smokin' shuffleboard stick and cigarette, Emil leaps to victory salute after tournament win with partner, Dallas Phillips (left). Duck Key (FL), 1994.

quickly marked down.

"Emil opened his house for me, too," Roth said. "He hosted contact parties for me for each campaign. I got 70% of the vote, across party lines, and that was due in great part to Emil's help. He might have been 'retired,' but he sure wasn't inactive."[442]

ROBUST AND INCORRIGIBLE

At age 82 and counting, Emil's long-range perspective on things remained pretty consistent. "I still want to get things done yesterday," he said, "and I still like to see my friends. But there aren't as many left now as I'd like. Sonny's sick, and Toni's taking great care of him—she's a nurse, you know."[443]

Emil didn't get maudlin though, recalling the last moments at his brother Jim's deathbed ten years earlier, in 1992.

"You're the only one left," Jim had rasped through his oxygen mask to Emil, "and I finally figured out why." Emil had raised an eyebrow, in a rare experience of not knowing what to expect from Jim.

"Mother must have 'squealed' on Dad the year you were born," Jim had said, relishing the dawning surprise on Emil's face.[444] "Squeal" was their personal shorthand for "getting some on the side," Emil explained, triply hilarious for its incongruous application to their prim and proper mother.

Aside from his hip, and some normal wear and tear over time, Emil's health had been consistently robust throughout the years. He added one caveat, in January 2002, to the authors of his biography.

"The doctor says I'm starting to forget things," Emil told them. "I still remember who you are, though, and I still remember my kids' names. I haven't forgotten my own name, either, and you'd better finish this book before I do!"[445]

Again the crusty, quick-witted man-in-motion had spoken.

EPILOGUE

Portrait of a Farewell

August, 2002

EMIL LOCKWOOD
(1919 – 2002)

Photo 2001 by Mike Quillinan

PORTRAIT OF A FAREWELL

Shortly after Emil made that predictive statement to his biographers, his memory and his health took a turn for the worse. Good days were rare, but he had some. In June his memory and adrenaline kicked briefly into gear, when he met with Governor John Engler to talk shop and old times, reminiscing about their first meeting in 1970, when Engler—a brand new Michigan State grad—had just won his first Republican primary election for State Representative.

"That day in June was his last really good day," said Anna, who had begun attending support group meetings at the Mid-Michigan Chapter of the Alzheimer's Association in Ann Arbor. "It's so difficult to lose someone when he's still with you," she said, "but I had to accept it, and I think Emil did, too, especially after learning that our friend (and former Michigan Supreme Court Justice) Jim Brickley had Alzheimer's. We wanted people to learn from this, and to support the research that's being done."[446]

When he was on, Emil joked about his condition. "I wish I could be around when you're 81 or 82, and someone asks you what you did on a certain day 60 years ago," he said during an interview for this book. "Pretty soon," he added, "you'll know more about my life than I do."[447]

On August 1, 2002, Emil was rushed to the hospital with pneumonia, and later that day suffered a heart attack, both diagnosed as complications stemming from Alzheimer's disease. He died early in the morning on August 2 at St. Joseph Mercy Hospital in Ann Arbor, with Anna at his side. At the State Capitol, the flag flew at half mast. Phones rang throughout the state, and Emil was in the headlines one last time, as the media recorded his passing.

Gongwer News Service credited Emil with "Michigan's first income tax and laws banning housing discrimination." Governor John Engler "called him an outstanding and brilliant legislator."[448] The Alma *Morning Sun* recalled Emil's impact on matters great and "homely," citing former legislative aide Arnold Brandsdorfer's recollection that Emil championed legislation for "signs on the highways pointing out what's located in cities across the state." Friend and local attorney Al Fortino told the *Sun* that Emil was "one of the few who really kept St. Louis going."[449]

"He didn't care what color people were, where they were from," biographer Stan Fedewa was quoted in the *Lansing State Journal*. "He never let those labels get in the way."[450] "The senator made his biggest mark working on legislation to promote fair and open housing after riots hit Detroit," wrote Janet Vandenabeele in a Sunday edition of the *Detroit News and Free Press*, quoting Lockwood as saying, "I thought it was the right thing to do."[451]

Former Senate Majority Leaders reminisce. Governor John Engler (left) and Emil recall political war stories. Lansing (MI), June 17, 2002. *Photo by Mike Quillinan.*

In a show of "lasting esteem for his memory," members of the Michigan Senate rose to their feet *en masse*, to pass a formal resolution honoring their former Majority Leader as a "man of integrity, intellect, and energy" who "provided exceptional leadership during one of the most volatile periods in recent history. . . . Vision and effectiveness in the face of pressure was to distinguish much of his life," the

resolution continued, and "his principled approach to public service earned him the trust of members on both sides of the political aisle." Among many other landmark contributions, the resolution credited Emil as "founder of a groundbreaking public issues company," and as a "talented and committed gentleman" whose "skills of organization, tenacity, and communications greatly benefited our state."[452]

Lights, camera, action—the "Man in Motion" revisits Senate Chamber after legislators' reunion. Lansing (MI), 2002. *Photo by Mike Quillinan.*

Illinois remembered Emil, too. On behalf of the Chicago City Council, Mayor Richard M. Daley adopted a resolution touting their Ottawa (IL) native son as a "legendary member of the Michigan State Senate" who "served with honor and distinction." The resolution cited a long list of Emil's accomplishments, including his bravery in World War II, and called him an "individual of great integrity and professional accomplishment."[453]

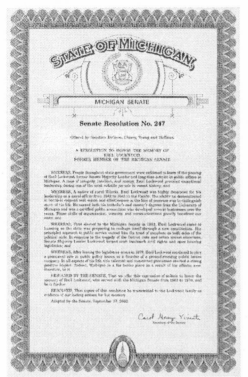

Michigan Senate "honors the memory of Emil Lockwood," in Resolution No. 247 of 91st Legislature. Lansing (MI), September 17, 2002.

Memorialized by dignitaries, friends, and family, in the first floor State Capitol Rotunda on August 14, 2002, Emil is one of four legislators in the history of the Capitol to be accorded such an honor. As reported later, the fervor of the speakers at the memorial service deeply stirred the large group assembled to celebrate the passing of the man who had so affected their lives.

Excerpts from selected memorials are included in the following pages.

Excerpts from Selected Eulogies

Speakers at the Lansing (MI) memorial service included: Guy Vander Jagt, Richard Whitmer, Jerry Coomes, Bob Vander Laan, Mac McPherson, Eric Lockwood, Franny Showerman, and Marilyn Fedewa. Mike Pung also spoke and is quoted in part in the Introduction. Bill Ballenger delivered remarks at the memorial service that were essentially captured in the Foreword which he wrote especially for this book, and therefore are not reprinted here.

"The Very Best There Ever Was"

What Lyndon Johnson was to the U.S. Senate, Emil Lockwood was to the Michigan Senate—the very best there ever was. From the lofty position of Minority Leader, Emil reached down and befriended me when I first came to

Capitol Rotunda echoes with eulogies celebrating Emil's life. Memorial Service speakers, left to right: Richard Whitmer, Franny Showerman, Jerry Coomes, Eric Lockwood, Guy Vander Jagt, Mac McPherson, Marilyn Fedewa, Bob Vander Laan, Bill Ballenger. Lansing (MI), August 14, 2002. Missing from picture: Mike Pung, also a eulogist. *Photo by S. C. Fedewa.*

the state Senate as a very raw rookie. We became roommates. [Then] in one of my life's great honors I was the best man at his wedding to the lovely Anna who gave him so much happiness during the last chapters of his incredible life.

Except when we were playing pitch or backgammon or tennis, when Emil was trying to extract every dollar he could from my thrifty Dutch wallet, [he] was always reaching out to give, to help and to lift me up—just as he did to so many of you. . . . His loss leaves a huge and empty void in our hearts. But this celebration reminds us of how much richer we are because we knew Emil and were the recipients of his generosity and caring and friendship and love. . . . [For] the words that describe Emil Lockwood as leader in the Michigan Senate are the same as the words that describe him as a friend—Emil was the very best there ever was![454]

Presiding Speaker: Guy Vander Jagt
U.S. Congressman (1966 – 1993)

"A Healthy Irreverence for Worldly Things"

It is fitting and appropriate that these services are being held in our State Capitol. This is the building in which Emil's genius reached full bloom. In reality, Emil was the leader of the entire Legislature—both houses, both parties. He did it with an unequaled work ethic . . . with common sense and goodwill for all. . . . He was the most effective public servant I ever met.

Emil Lockwood was not a wallflower, but underneath his commanding personality he was a little shy and very humble. . . . He had a wonderful feel for the mystery of life—how we arrive—our brief experience on this speck of a planet—and how we depart. He had it in perspective in a way few people do. And I believe that allowed him a large measure of peace.

[Emil] had a magical quality about him, and was given many gifts—a brilliant mind, a marvelous sense of humor, and a healthy irreverence for worldly things. . . . He was successful in most everything he attempted and in the very best sense of the phrase, "He did it his way." . . . He was a man of the highest integrity—his word was his bond. If you had it, you needed nothing more. He was fiercely independent—he had a very deep need to be his own man. He was extremely generous, . . . a world-class competitor, . . . an entrepreneur and he was, in the very best sense of the phrase, "The Consummate Politician"—brightly focused on public policy and not on himself. And if Emil was your friend, you couldn't have a better or a more loyal one.

Emil is no longer constrained by the shackles of poor health and . . . we all know [he] is better off having taken the next step. . . . If [he] were here—and who's to say he isn't—he would thank us for coming and encourage us to enthusiastically continue on. He would want us to be light of heart, acknowledging the poignancy of the moment—but leaving here with a com-

mitment to one another to be mutually supportive and to support those family members left behind.

If there is to be sadness, as there must be—let's recognize it is not for Emil—it is for all those he impacted, for all of us who will miss him—for his family first and then for his friends.

Emil Lockwood was one hell of a man.[455]

Richard Whitmer
CEO, Blue Cross Blue Shield of Michigan

"A Moral Giant in the Michigan Senate"

Emil Lockwood was the most important person in my life after my wife and children. A business partner, like a marital partner, will reveal character. And if I could leave you with one thought about Emil, it is that he was a man of rich and abundant character. Honesty, fairness, generosity and loyalty were the essence of his genetic code. In all his dealings with me, Emil put his partner first and himself second. . . . If . . . you asked for his advice or assistance, he never said, "yes, but," or "maybe." He always asked, "how can I help?" and he always did.

Several years after we were in business together, Emil decided that the pension system we had put in place contributed more money to his pension than to mine, even though the pension benefit would have been the same at age 65 for both of us. So he changed it to a pension system with equal contributions, which resulted in a smaller pension to him. That was the way he treated others . . . and those character traits carried over into his life as a public servant.

Here in this capitol, [Emil] exhibited two main qualities that further revealed his character: It was his nature to tell the truth, and it was his nature to treat everyone, regardless of his or her state, with respect and equality. Emil Lockwood was a moral giant in the Michigan Senate. He not only insisted—but he fought ferociously to assure that our laws treated all persons as equals.

Emil, when it came to character, you were one of the wealthiest persons I have ever known. You were a rarity . . . you were more than a business partner to me . . . and it may be a while before we see your likes again. You will be missed, my friend.[456]

Francis "Jerry" Coomes
Co-Founder, Public Affairs Associates

"What Defined Emil as a Man"

Emil understood politics and the role of government. He was a friend of the lobbyist[s] and still voted against them. He was a Republican but was not against supporting Democratic issues if he thought they were right. He rep-resented the Governor in the Senate as Majority Leader, but opposed him if he thought the Governor was on the wrong side of an issue. That defined Emil as a legislator. But what defined him as a man was more important.

There is a text in the Old Testament, in Micah 6 verse 8. . . . It says that "we should act justly and love mercy and walk humbly before God." Emil was an example of that command in action: He voted for Open Housing leg-islation, minimum wage laws, fair school busing, and many others. These will forever define Emil as the man he was.[457]

Robert Vander Laan
Michigan Senator (1963 – 1982)
Former Senate Majority Leader (1971 – 1982)

"A Prayer of Triumph and Thanks for Emil Lockwood"
Lord . . . we thank you today for creating the life of Emil Lockwood. . . . Father in Heaven, all present loved and admired Emil. All are here today to thank you for your love, and to send Emil to you now. . . . We thank you, Lord of the ages, for being there for Emil. . . . We ask that when you greet Emil, you send a special blessing of heavenly love. Send your love to Anna, the children and grandchildren every time they pray to you in memory of Emil.[458]

William G. McPherson, CLU
Four Square Financial Group

"Through the good times, and the difficult times"
My Dad was a proud World War II Navy veteran and Michigan states-man. He was proud of his country, proud of his state, and particularly proud of his children, grandchildren, and great grandchildren—so much so that he just finished telling the story of his life, for a book to be published soon.

His loving wife Anna, known to the family as "Grandma Anna," and his family have been at his side through the good times and the difficult times, and to the end. I'm sure he is looking down from heaven at us at the Capitol today and always. We love you Dad![459]

Eric Achard Lockwood
Son

"Let Me Remember the People I Love"
Emil was my step-dad for almost 30 years. More importantly, he was my Mom's husband for those years. They had a wonderful life together, which they generously shared with us. After meeting my Grandma Muscott, my mom's mother, [Emil] so admired the way she lived her life, having been widowed very young, with five children to raise . . . [he] thought we should have a Muscott

family reunion. We just celebrated our 30th reunion and Emil was there with us last month. Because of those reunions, I know not only my aunts and uncles and cousins, but my 2nd, 3rd and 4th cousins and my grandchildren will know and care about their 5th and 6th cousins! . . .

We can't talk about Emil without acknowledging the horrific disease . . . that took him from us. [The following is] from a poem by Nancy Priff, in a book called Love Is Ageless . . . *about Alzheimer's. . . .*

> The Forgetting is coming . . . .
> From the back of our yard, he stalks me,
> stares unblinking
> to push me off balance. . . .
> At night, the Forgetting creeps closer,
> takes his place at my back door
> like a hobo hoping for a handout.
> "Get away from me or I'll flatten you!"
> But he smiles and waits. . . .
> And I swear he reaches into my dreams,
> pulling out long strings of pearl-gray thoughts
> to decorate his growing nest. . . .
> I've given up shouting and throwing things.
> It makes no difference. . . .
> He simply smiles and waits.
> He gathers all but my oldest memories,
> weaves them into his strong nest.
> "Take whatever you want," I plead,
> "but let me remember the people I love."[460]

Emil was headed for the final, awful stages of Alzheimer's, but he did still remember the people he loved. He could still walk, he could speak, he was still able to live at home with my mom. After he died, my husband Steve said, "he won the card game!" And he did. He died quietly, with dignity, and I'm sure, in a moment of clarity, he had said to himself, "I'm going to win this game the right way, my way!" and he did.[461]

Franny Showerman
Stepdaughter

"A New Vista for Emil"

It's a rare privilege to write the story of a man's life—especially when that person is still alive—and to be chosen for it by the man himself. My co-author and husband—Stan Fedewa—and I soon learned that Emil Lockwood was not a philosopher. He did not wax eloquently about how he wound up as a Naval Commanding Officer in World War II. Or why, after the Detroit riots in 1967, fate picked him as the Michigan Senate's key champion of Open Housing.

For one thing, Emil's list of accomplishments was too long. And Emil— who continually described himself as "the man who liked to get things done

yesterday"—at 81 and 82, knew he was getting forgetful. He also felt something he hadn't felt before, even as kamikazes crashed all around him in the war— Emil was feeling his mortality. . . .

Biographer Marilyn Fedewa recounts Emil's witticisms during writing of *MAN IN MOTION* with co-author Stan Fedewa. Capitol Rotunda memorial service, Lansing (MI), 2002. *Photo by S. C. Fedewa.*

We believe he sensed last year that his own passing was near, and that his urgency about our completing the book was a direct result of computing his own odds—and accurately, at that. . . .

Fortunately, he was able to read the finished manuscript while he still could respond to it—a very rewarding experience for him and us. Because we knew that despite his haste, Emil was just being himself—a gregarious, likable Alpha Male who kept his own counsel and developed his own home-spun brand of fairness from an early age.

Emil never made a fuss, but he was loyal. He didn't pontificate, but he took a stand and held to it. If he said something, he did it. If he did something, he enjoyed it. He computed the odds, counted the votes ahead of time, and seldom lost. When he did, he didn't look back. There was always a new vista for Emil, a new adventure. We believe he is going forward to meet it now.

Marilyn H. Fedewa
Co-Author, *MAN IN MOTION*

BIBLIOGRAPHY

INTERVIEWS

Appell, Sonny & Toni, Interviews with M. H. Fedewa, May 3, 2002.

Cole, Richard T., Senior Vice President, Blue Cross Blue Shield of Michigan. Interview with S. C. Fedewa, September 1, 2001.

Coomes, Francis (Jerry), Retired Chairman and CEO, Public Affairs Associates. Interview with S. C. Fedewa, August 17, 2001.

Doles, Lori Lockwood, Interviews with M. H. Fedewa, August 12, 2001, February 27, 2002; and access to Mariella Coffey's Collected Papers.

Engler, Governor John M., Interview with S. C. Fedewa and M. H. Fedewa, December 1, 2001. Follow-up conversations on June 17, 2002 and September 16, 2002.

Gokey, Webb, Former President of Duck Key Property Owners Association. Interview with M. H. Fedewa, September 5, 2001.

Hall, Ed, President of Orion Banks in the Florida Keys, **and Mrs. Bonnie Bender Hall.** Interviews with M. H. Fedewa, September 13, 2001.

Hortman, Harvey, Interview with M.H. Fedewa, May 3, 2002.

Kandler, William, Partner at Cusmano, Kandler and Reed, Inc., (former Secretary of the Michigan Senate). Interview with S. C. Fedewa, May 14, 2002.

Lockwood, Anna, Interviews with M. H. Fedewa, July 20, 23, 26, 2001, August 9, 30, 2001, September 13, 2001, October 5, 8, 2001, March 18, 2002, April 19, 21, 2002, May 6, 15, 24, 2002, August 19, 2002. Interviews with S. C. Fedewa, March 11, 2002, May 15, 24, 2002. Numerous additional contacts as a result of continual dialogue, fact-checking and source verification.

Lockwood, Emil, Primary Subject. Interviews with M. H. Fedewa, June 20, 22, 25, 28, 2001; July 3, 5, 9, 26, 30, 2001; August 2, 9, 15, 30, 2001; September 13, 2001, October 5, 8, 17, 2001, December 3, 2001, January 14,

2002, March 18, 2002, May 15, 24, 2002. Interviews with S. C. Fedewa, July 20, 23, 2001, May 15, 24, 2002. Numerous additional contacts as a result of continual dialogue, fact-checking and source verification. Also access to EL official USNR Navy papers for USN Personnel Lockwood, # 162914; and Family Archives: Binders #1-6, esp. collected statewide news media articles; and Albums #1-4.

Lockwood, Eric Achard, Interviews with M. H. Fedewa, August 10, 2001, March 16, 2002, May 3, 2002.

McPherson, William, Insurance Executive, FourSquare Financial Group, and former driver for EL. Interview with S. C. Fedewa, August 29, 2001.

Roth, Rick, Sheriff, Monroe County, Florida. Interview with M. H. Fedewa, September 6, 2001.

Sawyer, Harry Jr., Supervisor of Elections, Monroe County, Florida. Interview with M. H. Fedewa, September 7 and 10, 2001.

Showerman, Franny and Steve, Interviews with M. H. Fedewa, October 10, 2001, November 8, 2001, April 8, 2002.

Van Gaever, Freddy, President, VG Airlines. Interview with M. H. Fedewa, September 6, 2001, January 14, 2002, February 10, 2002, March 29, 2002, April 1, 2002.

Vander Jagt, Guy, Attorney and Former U.S. Congressman. Interview with S. C. Fedewa and M. H. Fedewa, August 22, 2001.

Vander Laan, Robert, Former G.O.P. Senate Majority Leader (following EL), Interview with S. C. Fedewa, October 8, 2001.

Whitmer, Richard E., President and CEO, Blue Cross Blue Shield of Michigan. Interview with S. C. and M. H. Fedewa, August 24, 2001.

PRIMARY REFERENCES

Adams, Barbara A. K., *The Unprepossessing Mr. Ryan : Understanding Exemplary Legislative Leadership.* Thesis (D.P.A.)--Western Michigan University, 1994.

Baer, George W., *ONE HUNDRED YEARS OF SEA POWER: The U.S.*

Navy, 1890-1990. Stanford University Press: Stanford, California, 1994.

Benson, Clyde E., Compiler, *Index to History of Saginaw County Michigan, Vols. I and II* by James Cooke Mills. Swartz Creek, Michigan, 1973.

Biographical Publishing Company, *Portrait and Biographical Record of Saginaw and Bay Counties.* Biographical Publishing Co.: Chicago, 1892.

Bordin, Ruth, *The University of Michigan: A Pictorial History.* University of Michigan Press: Ann Arbor, Michigan, 1967.

Bliven, Bruce Jr., *From Pearl Harbor to Okinaw.* Random House: New York, 1960.

Bradford, G. K., Commanding Officer U.S.S. LST 478, Enclosure A: "Factual History from date of commissioning [of LST 478] March 13, 1943 to September 22, 1945," Enclosure B: "Anti Aircraft Action, report of," Enclosure C: "Battle Casualties, report of," Enclosure D: Invasions, participation in," Enclosure E: "Personnel received and transferred, report of". Received U.S.N.R. Office of Public Relations January 16, 1946, Document #159221.

Braithwaite, Joyce, and Weeks, George, *The Milliken Years: A Pictorial Reflection.* The *Traverse City Record-Eagle* and Village Press, Inc.: Traverse City, Michigan, 1988.

Bryan, Jessica, Ed., *Love is Ageless: Stories About Alzheimer's Disease.* Lompico Creek Press: Felton (CA), 2002.

Chambers, John Whiteclay II, Ed., *The Oxford Companion to American Military History.* Oxford University Press: Oxford, England, 1999.

Chicago Bridge & Iron Company, *Our Prairie Shipyard,* Vol. III, No. 10, October 12, 1944: "Launching of a Tank Landing Ship at the Prairie Shipyard, June 5th, 1943" American Society of Civil Engineers, Western Society of Engineers, Chicago Engineers' Club.

Cohen, Herbert J., ed., *Page One: Major Events 1920 – 1980 as Presented in The New York Times.* Arno Press, A *New York Times* Company: New York, 1980.

Colby, C.B., *Fighting Gear of World War II.* Coward-McMann, Inc: New York, 1961.

Denenbreg, Barry, *An American Hero: The True Story of Charles A. Lindbergh.* Scholastic, Inc.: New York, 1996.

Dunbar, Willis Frederick, *Michigan through the Centuries, Vol. IV, Family and Personal History.* Lewis Historical Publishing Company: New York, 1955.

Dzendzel, Ray, *Collected Papers of Former Michigan Senator, Boxes 1,3,15, 31 and 32.* State Archives of Michigan, Michigan Historical Center, 2001.

Grimm, Joe, Compiler and Editor, *Michigan Voices: Our State's History in the Words of the People Who Lived It.* Wayne State University Press and *Detroit Free Press*: Detroit, 1987.

James, William, *Pragmatism,* Introduction by H. S. Thayer. Harvard University Press: Cambridge, Mass., 1975.

LST 1110 Home Port, "Basic LST Information" (including information from the LST 454 website, the *Dictionary of American Naval Fighting Ships*, vol. 7 ed. By James L. Mooney), and the 1998 *Encyclopaedia Britannica, Inc.,* as accessed 5-30-02 at www.xmission.com./~jcander/info.htm.

May, George W., *Michigan, An Illustrated History of The Great Lakes State.* Produced in Cooperation with the Historical Society of Michigan by Windsor Publications, Inc.: Northridge, California, 1987.

Michigan Legislative Council, *A Sesquicentennial Look At The Michigan Legislature.* State of Michigan, 1998.

Michigan, State of, Department of Administration, *Michigan Manual: 1963-1964, published 1965.* Department of Administration: Lansing, Michigan, 1971. [also volumes 1965-1966/pub.1967; 1967-1968/pub.1969; 1969-1970/pub.1971; 1971-1972/pub.1973.]

Miller, Nathan, *War at Sea.* Scribner: New York, 1995.

Mills, James Cook, *History of Saginaw County Michigan, Historical, Commercial, Biographical, Profusely Illustrated with Portraits of Early Pioneers, Rare Pictures and Scenes of Olden Times,* Vols. I, II. Seeman & Peters Publishers: Saginaw, Michigan, 1918.

Mollenhoff, Clark R., *George Romney, Mormon in Politics.* Merideth Press: New York, 1968.

Napoli, Tony, Ed., *Our Century 1900-1910, 1910-1920, 1920-1930, 1930-1940, 1940-1950.* Fearon Education: Belmont, California, 1989.

Nardo, Don, *World War II: The War in the Pacific.* Lucent Books: San Diego, 1991.

Ottawa Daily Times, "About Ottawa". www.ottawadailytimes.com. Accessed July 21, 2001.

Potter, E.B., and Nimitz, Chester W., *SEAPOWER: A Naval History.* Prentice Hall, Inc.: Englewood Cliffs, N. J., 1960.

Public Libraries of Saginaw, *Obituary Index* (referencing Achard and Lockwood birth and death dates). As accessed at Tricitynet.com on July 13, 2001.

Rand McNally, *The Great Geographical Atlas.* Rand McNally & Company: USA, 1991, 1992, 1993.

Reynolds, Clark G., *The Carrier War.* Time-Life Books: Alexandria, Virginia, 1982.

Staebler, Neil, *Out Of The Smoke Filled Room: A Story of Michigan Politics.* Wahr Publishing Co.: Ann Arbor, 1991.

United States LST Association, *LST Scuttlebutt* Sept/Oct 1993.

Upshur, Jiu-Hwa, ed., *World History: Comprehensive Volume,* 2nd Edition. West Publishing Company: St. Paul, Minneapolis, 1991, 1995.

Weeks, George and Braithwaite, Joyce, *The Milliken Years: A Pictorial Reflection.* Edited by Robert D. Kirk. Village Press, Inc., and *Traverse City Record Eagle*: Traverse City, Michigan, 1988.

Wilkinson, Jerry, *History of Duck Key, and Modern Day Duck Key.* As accessed at Keyshistory.org on September 20, 2001.

Williams, Jay, *The Florida Keys.* Random House: New York, 1995.

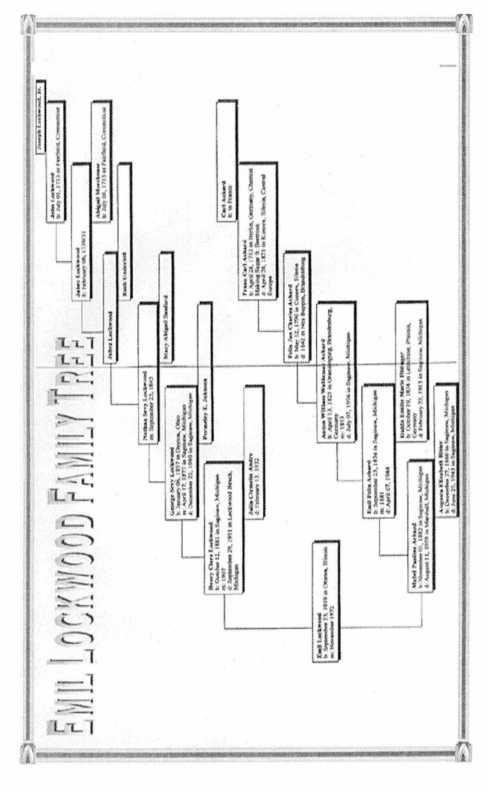

EMIL LOCKWOOD FAMILY TREE

ENDNOTES: Part 1 (Chapters 1-4)

[1] MHF Interview with EL, 6-20-01.

[2] 'National Grange in Michigan' as accessed online 8-3-01 at ancestry.com.

[3] Mills, *History of Saginaw County*, p. 467.

[4] Henley, Robert L., "Sweet Success," as accessed online 8-3-01 through the Michigan Historical Center at http://www.michigan.gov/hal/0,1607,7-160-17451_18670_18793-53367--,00.html.

[5] *Michigan Through the Centuries*, Vol. IV, p. 605.

[6] Henley, "Sweet Success."

[7] *Portrait and Biographical Records of Saginaw and Bay Counties*, p. 800.

[8] *Michigan Through the Centuries,* Vol. IV, p. 605.

[9] *Michigan Through the Centuries*, Vol. IV, p. 605.

[10] *Saginaw News*, 1-1-60.

[11] Mills, *History of Saginaw County*, p. 643.

[12] Mills, *History of Saginaw County*, p. 679.

[13] Mills, *History of Saginaw County*, p. 241.

[14] Mills, *History of Saginaw County*, p. 561.

[15] MHF Interview with EL, 6-20-01.

[16] MHF Interview with Ruth Lockwood, 3-13-02, and 12-31-23 Annual Report of General Motors Corp., accessed at Univ. of Pennsylvania Online Library 3-14-02.

[17] "Pedigree for Henry Clare Lockwood", EL's father, as accessed online 8-3-01 at ancestry.com.

[18] *Michigan Through the Centuries*, Vol. I, p. 262.

[19] Mills, *History of Saginaw County*, p. 700.

[20] Grimm, Joe, Ed., *Michigan Voices*, p. 73.

[21] *Michigan Through the Centuries*, Vol. II, p. 392.

[22] *Michigan Through the Centuries*, Vol. I, p. 263.

[23] Grimm, Joe, Ed., *Michigan Voices*, p. 73-74.

[24] Grimm, Joe, Ed., *Michigan Voices*, p. 73.

[25] Mills, *History of Saginaw County*, p. 701.

[26] Mills, Vol. II, p. 418 (John S. in 1870), p. 346 (Clifford in 1918), and p. 271 (Geo. S. in 1915)

[27] Public Libraries of Saginaw Obituary Index, as accessed online 7-31-01 at www.tricitynet.com.

[28] Eric Lockwood's Father's Day story, 2001, and 3-16-02 Interview with MHF.

[29] MHF Interview with Ruth Lockwood, 3-13-02.

[30] *Ottawa Daily Times* as accessed 7-21-01 at ottawadailytimes.com/abot/htm.

[31] Fearon's *OUR CENTURY 1920-1930*: "Radio Enters America's Homes."

[32] *New York Times 'Page One" 1920-1980*, p. 25 on the Scopes Trial, plus reference to WGN broadcast from www3.mistral.co.uk/bradburyac/tennesse.html as accessed online 3-4-02.

[33] Nostalgic radio programs referenced in Gary Shuster's article, as accessed online 3-4-02 at www.computerbits.com/archive/1998/0800/oldtime_radio.html.

[34] MHF Interview with EL, 7-3-01.

[35] MHF Interview with EL, 6-20-01.

[36] MHF Interview with EL, 6-20-01.

[37] MHF Interview with EL, 6-20-01.

[38] MHF Interview with Ruth Lockwood, 3-13-02.

[39] MHF Interview with EL, 6-22-01.

[40] Ottawa City Schools Monthly Reports, EL personal papers.

[41] MHF Interview with EL, 3-18-02.

[42] MHF Interview with Ruth Lockwood, 3-13-02.

[43] Ottawa Township High School Monthly Reports, EL personal papers.

[44] MHF Interview with EL, 6-20-01.

[45] MHF Interview with EL, 6-25-01.

[46] MHF Interview with EL, 6-25-01.

[47] Gabrielson, Bruce, on Wrestling Rules and Scoring, as accessed online 3-12-02 at www.blackmagic.com/ses/wrest/reference/fsrulesnew.html#ScoringRules.

[48] MHF Interview with EL, 6-28-01.

[49] MHF Interview with EL, 6-28-01.

[50] Gabrielson, on Wrestling Rules.

[51] MHF Interview with EL, 6-28-01.

[52] Handwritten entry on photograph in EL photo album.

[53] MHF Interview with EL, 6-20-01.

[54] MHF Interview with EL, 6-20-01.

[55] MHF Interview with EL, 6-28-01.

[56] MHF Interview with EL, 6-28-01.

[57] MHF Interview with EL, 6-20-01.

[58] MHF Interview with EL, 6-20-01.

[59] Bordin, *Pictorial History of U of M*, p. 112.

[60] MHF Interview with EL, 7-9-01.

[61] *New York Times 'Page One' 1920-1980*, p. 86.

[62] *World History*, pp. 774-780.

[63] *New York Times 'Page One" 1920-1980*, p. 98.

[64] Fearon's *Our Century,* 1920-1930, 1930-1940 and 1940-1950.

[65] USN Annual Qualifications Questionnaire form dated 2-28-45 in "USNR Navy papers for USN Personnel Lockwood," and Emil's original 1941 diploma.

[66] While Emil wanted to honor this person by citing his real name, neither memory nor family archives had record of his identity. "Carter Hale" is an invented name in order to enable the biographers to include this incident.

[67] MHF Interview with EL, 6-20-01.

[68] MHF Interview with EL, 6-20-01.

[69] "At Glen View Pool," *Chicago Sunday Tribune* Society Page, 8-1-37.

[70] Bordin, *Pictorial History of U of M*, p. 111- 112.

[71] Denenbreg, *An American Hero*, p. 218.

[72] Bill Kulsea: for Booth Newspapers in *Flint Journal*, 7-27-69.

[73] EL's 1945 USN Annual Qualifications Questionnaire form.

[74] MHF Interview with EL, 6-20-01.

[75] EL official USNR Navy papers for Personnel Lockwood, # 162914.

[76] MHF Interview with EL, 6-20-01.

[77] EL official USNR Navy papers for Personnel Lockwood, # 162914.

[78] MHF Interview with Eric Lockwood, 3-16-02, and Emil's Navy transport papers.

[79] Under "War News Summarized," *New York Times Page One*, 11-8-1942, p. 112.

[80] EL official USNR Navy papers for Personnel Lockwood, # 162914.

[81] Drawing and caption in EL's papers, from "collection of C.J.Adams, Jr., LST 281".

[82] EL official USNR Navy papers for Personnel Lockwood, # 162914.

[83] EL official USNR Navy papers for Personnel Lockwood, # 162914.

[84] EL's USNR Navy transportation papers show a route via Chicago.

[85] Information included in EL's copy of *LST Scuttlebutt*, Sept. /Oct. 1993, p. 32.

[86] Chicago Bridge & Iron Co., *Our Prairie Shipyard*, Vol. III, No. 10, 10-12-44: "Launching of a Tank Landing Ship at the Prairie Shipyard, June 5th, 1943" American Soc. of Civil Engineers, Western Soc. of Engineers, Chicago Engineers' Club.

[87] Sources for this paragraph include CJ Adams diagram, EL USNR Papers for Personnel #162914; papers on the Seneca-built LSTs; and p. 3, LST 478 "Factual History," submitted by C.O. Bradford, 10-11-45.

[88] Emil places the marriage date after his 90-Day Wonder training, and before he left for the Aleutian Islands, in 1943. Eric Lockwood's records show a notation of "April 1" on the newspaper (a weekly) clipping, which refers back to the previous Thursday, placing the actual date at March 25, 1943.

[89] MHF Interview with EL, 6-20-01. Announcement appeared in *Chicago Tribune.*

ENDNOTES: Part 2 (Chapters 5-9)

[90] Colby, *Fighting Gear of World War II*, p. 3. Also LST diagram in C.J.Adams collected papers, as preserved in EL's personal papers.

[91] Baer, *ONE HUNDRED YEARS OF SEA POWER: The U.S. Navy, 1890 – 1990.*, p. 493.

[92] Miller, *War at Sea*, pp. 451-455 re: MacArthur and Bush at Great Battle of Leyte Island [Oct. 44]; and pp. 485-6 re: Okinawa, both battles at which EL served.

[93] MHF Interview with EL, 6-20-01.

[94] *LST Scuttlebutt*, Sept/Oct 1993, p. 1, in article by Ed Novak.

[95] Chicago Bridge & Iron Co., *Our Prairie Shipyard*, Vol. III, No. 10, 10-12-44; and "Basic LST Information" from LST 1110 Home Port page, accessed 5-30-02, at www.xmission.com/~jcander/info.htm.

[96] *LST Scuttlebutt* Sept/Oct 1993, p. 1, in article by Ed Novak quoting from William Brinkley's book *The Ninety and Nine* (Doubleday: Garden City, NY: 1966).

[97] *New York Times Page One*, 7-1-43, p. 113.

[98] EL official USNR Navy papers for Personnel Lockwood, # 162914.

[99] Colby, *Fighting Gear of World War II*, pp. 20, 28.

[100] MHF Interview with EL, 6-22-01.

[101] MHF Interview with EL, 6-28-01.

[102] Bliven, Bruce Jr., *From Pearl Harbor to Okinaw*, p. 97.

[103] MHF Interview with EL, 6-22-01.

[104] EL official USNR Navy papers for Personnel Lockwood, # 162914.

[105] C.O. Bradford, p. 3, Enclosure "A", LST 478 "Factual History," 10-11-45.

[106] Miller, *War at Sea*. pp. 392-393. Also Chambers, *The Oxford Companion to American Military History*, p. 30-31.

[107] Miller, *War at Sea*, p. 394.

[108] Miller, *War at Sea*, p. 396.

[109] Miller, *War at Sea*, p. 396.

[110] Miller, *War at Sea*, p. 396.

[111] EL schedule, per official USNR Navy papers for Personnel Lockwood, # 162914.

[112] Quote and details of this operation cited from Miller, *War at Sea*, p. 395.

[113] Beaching took place at north side of Bititu Island on 11-24-43, per page 3 of C.O. Bradford's report.

[114] MHF Interview with EL, 6-28-01. Cross-referencing interview and EL official battle itinerary aboard LST 478, pins this incident down to 11-22 through 12-13, 1943, when he was in the Marshall/Gilbert Islands.

[115] MHF Interview with EL, 6-20-01.

[116] Official USNR Navy papers for Personnel Lockwood, # 162914.

[117] MHF Interview with EL, 6-28-01.

[118] Based upon EL's records, 7-9-01 and other interviews with MHF, and integrated with historical background information, per Miller (*War at Sea*, p. 485) and information accessed on 3-27-02 from the U.S. Navy online Office of Information.

[119] Based upon official USNR Navy papers for Personnel Lockwood, # 162914, as integrated with historical background information, per Miller, p. 485, the online USN Office of Information as accessed 3-27-02, and ancestry.com, as accessed online 3-27-02.

[120] USN Office of Information as accessed online 3-27-02 at www.chinfo.navy.mil.

[121] Official USNR Navy papers for Personnel Lockwood, # 162914.

[122] MHF Interview with EL, 6-20-01.

[123] Official USNR Navy papers for Personnel Lockwood, # 162914.

[124] EL Interview, 6-22-01, MHF.

[125] MHF Interview with EL, 8-30-01.

[126] MHF Interview with EL, 6-22-01.

[127] Official USNR Navy papers for Personnel Lockwood, # 162914.

[128] Official USNR Navy papers for Personnel Lockwood, # 162914.

[129] The assignment is listed in official USNR Navy papers for Personnel Lockwood, # 162914.

[130] Official USNR Navy papers for Personnel Lockwood, # 162914.

[131] Denenbreg, *An American Hero*, p. 219.

[132] Miller, *War at Sea*, p. 435-9.

[133] Miller, *War at Sea*, p. 436.

[134] Miller, *War at Sea*, p. 437-8.

[135] Miller, *War at Sea*, p. 437.

[136] Official USNR Navy papers for Personnel Lockwood, # 162914.

[137] MHF Interview with EL, 6-22-01.

[138] MHF Interview with EL, 6-22-01.

[139] Miller, *War at Sea*, p. 447-8.

[140] Miller, *War at Sea*, p. 448-9.

[141] Eric Lockwood narrative, Father's Day 2001, and MHF Interviews with EL, 7-3-01, 7-9-01, and 8-30-01.

[142] Miller, *War at Sea*, p. 435.

[143] MHF Interviews with EL, 6-20-01 and 7-9-01; and Eric Lockwood's 2001 Father's Day paper.

[144] Miller, *War at Sea*, photo insert between pages 352-353, supporting text on p. 453.

[145] MHF Interview with EL, 6-20-01.

[146] C.O. Bradford, p. 5, LST 478 "Factual History," 10-11-45.

[147] *New York Times Page One*, p. 120.

[148] MHF Interview with EL, 6-20-01.

[149] MHF Interview with EL, 6-20-01, and Miller, *War at Sea*, p. 497—re: January 4, 1944 sinking of the *Ommaney* in Sulu Sea where Emil was, aboard LST 478.

[150] Miller, *War at Sea*, pp. 452-453.

[151] MHF Interview with EL, 6-22-01.

[152] C.O. Bradford, p. 1, Enclosure "B", LST 478 "Factual History," 10-11-45.

[153] C.O. Bradford, p. 1, Enclosure "C", LST 478 "Factual History," 10-11-45.

[154] MHF Interview with EL, 6-22-01, and official USNR Navy papers for Personnel Lockwood, # 162914.

[155] MHF Interview with El, 6-22-01, and official USNR Navy papers for Personnel Lockwood, # 162914.

[156] Potter, and Nimitz, *SEAPOWER: A Naval History, p. 816.*

[157] Miller, *War at Sea*, p. 494.

[158] C.O. Bradford, p. 6, Enclosure "A", LST 478 "Factual History," 10-11-45.

[159] EL Interview, 6-22-01, MHF, and C.O. Bradford, p. 6, Enclosure "A", LST 478 "Factual History," 10-11-45, supplemented with background from Miller.

[160] MHF Interview with EL, 6-22-01.

[161] MHF Interview with EL, 6-22-01.

[162] MHF Interview with EL, 6-22-01, supplemented with details garnered from Miller.

[163] Miller, *War at Sea*, p. 498.

[164] MHF Interviews with EL, 6-22-01 and 6-28-01.

[165] MHF Interview with EL, 6-28-01.

[166] Official USNR Navy papers for Personnel Lockwood, # 162914.

[167] MHF Interview with EL, 6-20-01.

[168] C.O. Bradford, p. 7, LST 478 "Factual History," 10-11-45, and official USNR Navy papers for Personnel Lockwood, # 162914.

[169] Miller, Nathan, *War at Sea*, p. 516.

[170] LCI information from Chambers, p. 30, *The Oxford Companion to American Military History,* and Miller, *War at Sea*, pp 518-519.

[171] C.O. Bradford, p. 8, Enclosure "A", LST 478 "Factual History," 10-11-45.

[172] Miller, *War at Sea*, p. 521-522.

[173] Miller, *War at Sea*, p. 522.

[174] Official USNR Navy papers for Personnel Lockwood, # 162914.

[175] C.O. Bradford, p. 8, Enclosure "A", LST 478 "Factual History," 10-11-45.

[176] Miller, *War at Sea*, p. 526-527.

[177] C.O. Bradford, pp. 8-9, Enclosure "A", LST 478 "Factual History," Oct. 11, 1945.

[178] MHF Interviews with: Eric Lockwood, 3-16-02, and Ruth Lockwood, 3-13-02.

[179] MHF Interview with EL, 6-25-01.

[180] MHF Interview with EL, 6-28-01, and official USNR Navy papers for Personnel Lockwood, # 162914.

[181] MHF Interview with EL, 6-20-01.

[182] MHF Interview with Eric Lockwood,, 3-16-02.

[183] MHF Interview with EL, 6-22-01.

[184] MHF Interview with Eric Lockwood, 8-10-01.

[185] From local newspaper clipping, no banner or publication date, citing "Backward Glances," specifically a 7-20-52 event at Lockwood home, via Optimist Club.

[186] MHF Interview with Eric Lockwood, 8-10-01.

[187] MHF Interview with Freddy VanGaever, 9-6-01.

[188] MHF Interview with Freddy VanGaever, 4-1-02.

[189] MHF Interview with Freddy VanGaever, 4-1-02.

ENDNOTES: Part 3 (Chapters 10-19)

[190] Michigan Manual 1963-64, p. 170.

[191] March 10, 1962, Belding Banner-News; Ionia County News.

[192] SCF Interview with EL, 7-20-01.

[193] Michigan Manual, 1963-64, p. 375.

[194] Lansing *State Journal*, 3-8-62.

[195] SCF Interview with EL, 7-20-01.

[196] SCF Interview with EL, 7-20-01.

[197] MHF Interview with EL, 6-25-01.

[198] *St. Louis Leader-Press*, 8-9-62.

[199] *St. Louis Leader-Press*, 8-9-62.

[200] *Kalamazoo Gazette*, 12-3-62.

[201] *St. Louis Leader-Press*, 8-62.

[202] *St. Louis Leader-Press*, 8-62.

[203] MHF Interview with EL, 6-28-01.

[204] SCF Interview with, EL, 7-20-01.

[205] *St. Louis Leader-Press*, 10-62.

[206] Michigan Manual, 1963-1964, p. 448.

[207] Mollenhoff, *George Romney, Mormon in Politics*, p. 4 et al.

[208] Mollenhoff, *George Romney, Mormon in Politics*, p.11 (for issues only).

[209] SCF Interview with EL, 7-20-01.

[210] *Kalamazoo Gazette*, (no byline), 12-3-62, p. 8.

[211] SCF Interview with Robert Vander Laan, 10-5-01.

[212] SCF Interview with EL, 7-20-01.

[213] *St. Louis Leader-Press*, 1-63.

[214] Don Meyers, *Detroit Free Press*, 8-8-63, p. 8-A.

[215] Bud Vestal, Booth Newspapers, 8-8-63.

[216] Don Meyers, *Detroit Free Press*, 8-8-63, p. 8-A.

[217] Lloyd E. Ash letter to 30th District voters, 8-11-64.

[218] SCF Interview with Jerry Coomes, 8-17-01.

[219] Michigan Manual, 1965-66, various pages.

[220] SCF Interview with EL, 7-20-01.

[221] Article IV, Sec. 2, Mich. Constitution (1964).

[222] Michigan Manual, 1965-66, pp. 421, 412, and SCF Interview with EL, 7-20-01.

[223] Michigan Manual 1965-66, General Election results.

[224] Michigan Manual, 1965-66, p. 423, and SCF Interview with EL, 7-20-01.

[225] Michigan Manual, 1965-66, p. 423.

[226] Michigan Manual, 1965-66, p. 489.

[227] SCF Interview with William Kandler, former Secretary of Michigan Senate, 5-14-02 (re: comment on Senate conversion from roll call vote to machine vote only).

[228] United Press International, 12-20-64.

[229] United Press International, 12-20-64.

[230] MHF Interview with EL, 7-3-01.

[231] Al Sandner, Associated Press, circa 12-1964.

[232] MHF Interview with EL, 7-3-01.

[233] Bill Burke, Lansing *State Journal*, 12-64

[234] Bill Burke, Lansing *State Journal*, 12-64.

[235] Bill Burke, Lansing *State Journal*, 12-64.

[236] Bill Burke, Lansing *State Journal*, 4-65.

[237] Bill Burke, Lansing *State Journal*, 4-65.

[238] SCF Interview with EL, 7-20-01.

[239] Both reforms are discussed by Burke, Lansing *State Journal*, 4-65.

[240] Reflects: SCF Interview with Jerry Coomes, 8-17-01; Barbara A.K.Adams, *The Unprepossessing Mr. Ryan,* pp. 79, 88; and author SCF's first-hand experience.

[241] Bill Kulsea, Booth Newspapers, 3-7-65.

[242] Adams, *The Unprepossessing Mr. Ryan*, p. 85.

[243] SCF Interview with EL, 7-20-01.

[244] Bill Kulsea, Booth Newspapers, 3-7-65.

[245] Adams, *The Unprepossessing Mr. Ryan*, p.75.

[246] Bill Kulsea, Booth Newspapers, 3-7-65.

[247] Adams, *The Unprepossessing Mr. Ryan*, pp. 76, 80. Refers to last two paragraphs.

[248] SCF Interview with EL, 7-20-01.

[249] EL's Minority Leader stationary (lists more than Michigan Manual).

[250] Adams, *The Unprepossessing Mr. Ryan*, p. 88.

[251] SCF and MHF Interview with Guy Vander Jagt, 8-22-01. All preceding material related to Guy Vander Jagt's comments come from this interview.

[252] Michigan Manual, 1967-68, p. 424.

[253] MHF Interview with EL, 6-22-01; and SCF and MHF Interview with Guy Vander Jagt, 8-22-01.

[254] Michigan Manual, 1967-68, p. 485.

[255] Michigan Manual, 1967-68, p. 455.

[256] Roger Lane, *Detroit Free Press*, 8-21-69, p. 20-C.

[257] SCF and MHF Interview with Gov. John Engler, 12-1-01.

[258] Adams, *The Unprepossessing Mr. Ryan*, pp. 101-106.

[259] Roger Lane, *Detroit Free Press*, 8-21, 69, p. 20 C.

[260] Adams, *The Unprepossessing Mr. Ryan*, p.108.

[261] Adams, *The Unprepossessing Mr. Ryan*, p. 110.

[262] Roger Lane *Detroit Free Press*, 8-21-69, p. 20-C.

[263] Robert A. Popa, *Detroit News*, 7-3-67.

[264] Adams, *The Unprepossessing Mr. Ryan*, and various Michigan newspaper sources.

[265] *Owosso Argus Press,* 12-31-67, p.1.

[266] SCF Interview with EL, 7-20-01.

[267] *Owosso Argus Press*, 12-7-67, p.1.

[268] SCF Interview with EL, 7-20-01.

[269] *Owosso Argus Press*, 12-22-67, p. 1.

[270] Roger Lane, *Detroit Free Press*, 8-21-69, p. 20C.

[271] *Daily Record-Leader*, 4-5-68, p. 6.

[272] MHF Interview with Eric Lockwood, 3-16-02.

[273] Discussion of Open Housing passage, and Novak story in particular are based on SCF/MHF interview with Richard Whitmer, 8-24-01, and MHF Interviews with EL, 7-3-01 and 8-15-01.

[274] New Detroit, "Beyond the Difference" (An Assessment), November 1969.

[275] SCF Interview with EL, 7-20-01.

[276] William James, *Pragmatism;* quoted in Introduction by H.S. Thayer, p. xxxi.

[277] SCF Interview with Jerry Coomes, 8-17-01.

[278] SCF Interview with Guy Vander Jagt, 8-22-01.

[279] SCF and MHF Interview with Richard Whitmer, 8-24-01. All Whitmer quotes are from this interview.

[280] Bill Kulsea, Booth Newspapers, 7-27-69.

[281] *The American Heritage Dictionary of the English Language*, 1969, p. 780.

[282] Bill Kulsea, 7-27-69. All "Machiavellian" quotes are from this column.

[283] SCF Interview with Robert Vander Laan, 10-8-01.

[284] SCF Interview with EL, 7-23-01.

[285] SCF Interview with EL, 7-20-01; MHF Interview with EL, 7-05-01.

[286] Roger Lane, *Detroit Free Press*, 8-29-69. All quotes on EL's leadership style in this and following two paragraphs are from this article, with the exception of the footnoted comment on Emil never losing sleep over a cup of coffee.

[287] Tom Delisle, *Detroit Free Press*, 2-25-69.

[288] Roger Lane, *Detroit Free Press*, 8-21-69.

[289] Conclusion of Emil's mostly favorable press coverage comes from a review of dozens of articles that mention Emil, usually prominently, during his years in public office, as well as his years as a lobbyist.

[290] Roger Lane, *Detroit Free Press*, 8-21-69. Also, Associated Press, 2-13-69.

[291] SCF Interview with EL, 7-20-01.

[292] Robert Stuart, Lansing *State Journal,* 11-17-68, p. A-4.

[293] Robert Stuart, Lansing *State Journal*, 11-17-68, p. A-4.

[294] Roger Lane, *Detroit Free Press*, 8-21-69.

[295] SCF Interview with EL, 7-20-01.

[296] Adams, *The Unprepossessing Mr. Ryan*, p. 151.

[297] Tim Metz, *The Wall Street Journal*, 3-26-69, p. 1.

[298] SCF Interview with El, 7-23-01.

[299] SCF Interview with EL, 7-20-01. All EL quotes about Gov. Romney in these paragraphs come from this interview.

[300] Robert Stuart, Lansing *State Journal*, 3-13-68.

[301] SCF Interview with EL, 7-23, 01. All EL quotes about Nixon campaign come from this interview.

[302] Personal Letters from Richard M. Nixon to EL, 3-29-68, 7-1-68, 8-2-68, 8-21-68, 12-7-68.

[303] Al Sandner, *Detroit News*, 5-18-69.

[304] Robert Longstaff, Booth Newspapers, 7-19-69.

[305] Marcia Van Ness, Lansing *State Journal*, 7-15-69.

[306] *Detroit News* Lansing Bureau, 7-15-69.

[307] Roger Lane, Detroit Free Press, 7-16-69, p. 4 A.

[308] Marcia Van Ness, Lansing *State Journal*, 7-15-69.

[309] Marcia Van Ness, Lansing *State Journal*, 7-15-69.

[310] Robert Longstaff, Booth Newspapers, 7-19-69, p. A-9.

[311] Robert Longstaff, 7-19-69, p. A-9.

[312] Marcia Van Ness, Lansing *State Journal*, 7-15-69.

[313] SCF Interview with EL, 7-23-01.

[314] Marcia Van Ness, Lansing *State Journal*, 7-15-69.

[315] Editorial, Lansing *State Journal*, 7-18-69, p. A-6.

[316] MHF Interview with Eric Lockwood, 3-16-02.

[317] SCF Interview with EL, 7-23-01.

[318] Michigan Manual, 1969-70, and 1975-76.

[319] SCF Interview with EL, 7-23-01.

[320] MHF Interview with EL, 6-22-01.

[321] Marcia Van Ness, Lansing *State Journal*, 1-6-70, p. A-2.

[322] Marcia Van Ness, Lansing *State Journal*, 1-11-70.

[323] Emil Lockwood, quoted by Tom DeWitt, *Gratiot County Herald,* 12-70.

[324] *Detroit Free Press* (no byline), 1-16-70.

[325] Robert L. Pisor, *The Detroit News*, 1-16-70.

[326] *Grand Rapids Press* (no byline), 1-22-70.

[327] Robert Longstaff, Booth Newspapers, 5-29-70.

[328] Lansing *State Journal* (no byline), 6-1-70.

[329] *Detroit News* (no byline), 6-1-70.

[330] *Detroit News* (no byline), 6-1-70.

[331] Lansing *State Journal* (no byline), 7-70.

[332] SCF Interview with William MacPherson, 8-29-01.

[333] SCF and MHF Interview with Governor John Engler, 12-1-01.

[334] Don Hoenshell, Panax Capitol Bureau, 7-30-70.

[335] Willard Baird, Lansing *State Journal*, 8-30-70.

[336] Willard Baird, Lansing *State Journal*, 8-31-70, p. C-12.

[337] Don Hoenshell, Panax Capitol Bureau, 9-18-70.

[338] SCF Interview with EL, 7-23-01.

[339] Clark Hoyt, *Detroit Free Press*, 10-8-70, p. 11 A.

[340] Associated Press; 10-12-70; *Detroit News*, 10-20-70, p. 13A. (No bylines).

[341] Michigan Manual, 1971-72, pp. 505, 601.

[342] SCF Interviews with Guy Vander Jagt and Jerry Coomes cited above.

[343] SCF Interview with EL, 7-23-01.

[344] SCF Interview with William McPherson, 8-29-01.

[345] *Detroit Free Press* (no byline), 12-15-70.
[346] Mich. Dept. of Commerce press release, 12-15-70.
[347] SCF Interview with Richard Whitmer, 8-24-01.
[348] Marcia Van Ness, Lansing *State Journal*, 1-10-71.
[349] Don Hoenshell, Panax Capitol Bureau, 2-16-71.
[350] SCF Interview with Jerry Coomes, 8-17-01.
[351] SCF Interview with EL, 7-23-01.
[352] Don Hoenshell, Panax Capitol Bureau, 2-16-71.
[353] Don Hoenshell, Panax Capitol Bureau, 2-16-71.
[354] SCF Interview with EL, 7-23-01.
[355] Bill Kulsea, Booth Newspapers, 2-22-71.
[356] Don Hoenshell, Panax Capitol Bureau, 7-7-71.
[357] SCF Interview with EL, 7-23-01.
[358] SCF Interview with Jerry Coomes, 8-17-01.

ENDNOTES: Testimonial Excerpts

[359] All statements are excerpted from original letters and telegrams written to Emil, and presented to him in a binder at the testimonial dinner on 1-15-70.

ENDNOTES Part 4 (Chapters 20 – 24)

[360] Robert Longstaff, Booth Newspapers, 12-31-78.
[361] SCF Interview with Jerry Coomes, 8-17-01. All quotes from Jerry Coomes, and material attributed to him, derive from this interview.
[362] Public Affairs Associates Brochure, 9-71.
[363] *Detroit Free Press* (no byline), 5-28-72, p. 4B.
[364] SCF Interview with EL, 7-23-01.
[365] SCF Interview with Jerry Coomes, 8-17-01.
[366] MHF Interview with Freddy Van Gaever, 7-5-02, who recalls "the book was published by a newspaper man circa 1968 and featured 50 self-made men considered very successful and innovative."
[367] *The Saginaw News* (no byline), Lansing Today Section, 1969.
[368] MHF Interview with EL, 7-9-01.
[369] MHF Interview with EL, 7-9-01.
[370] MHF Interview with Anna Lockwood, 8-9-01.
[371] Lansing *State Journal*, 2-26-72.
[372] Karen Aldag, Lansing *State Journal*, 3-12-72.
[373] MHF Interview with Anna Lockwood, 7-19-01.
[374] SCF and MHF Interview with Richard Whitmer, 8-24-01.
[375] MHF Interview with EL and Anna Lockwood, 7-19-01.
[376] MHF Interview with Anna Lockwood, 7-19-01.
[377] MHF Interview with EL and Anna Lockwood, 8-9-01.

[378] SCF and MHF Interview with Guy Vander Jagt, 8-22-01.

[379] MHF Interview with Anna Lockwood, 8-9-01.

[380] SCF Interview with Anna Lockwood, 3-11-02.

[381] SCF Interview with Robert Vander Laan, 10-5-01.

[382] SCF Interview with Anna Lockwood, 3-11-02.

[383] SCF Interview with Jerry Coomes, 8-17-01.

[384] SCF Interview with EL, 5-24-02. All EL quotes in this chapter derive from this interview.

[385] SCF Interview with Robert Vander Laan, 10-5-01.

[386] Bill Kulsea, *Grand Rapids Press,* 9-14-72, p. 1.

[387] Robert Longstaff, Booth Newspapers, 9-14-72.

[388] SCF Interview with Richard T. Cole, 9-1-01. All Richard Cole attributions come from this interview.

[389] SCF and MHF Interview with Guy Vander Jagt, 8-22-01.

[390] SCF and MHF Interview with Richard Whitmer, 8-24-01.

[391] United Press International, *Detroit News,* 1-22-75, p. 10C.

[392] Patrick Connolly, Associated Press, Lansing *State Journal,* 11-30-75.

[393] Jerry Moskal, Lansing *State Journal,* 12-9-76.

[394] Hugh Mc Diarmid, *Detroit Free Press,* Detroit Supplement, 1-23-77, p. 8-11.

[395] SCF Interview with Jerry Coomes, 8-17-01.

[396] SCF Interview with EL, 5-24-02.

[397] Robert H. Longstaff, et al, Booth Newspapers, 12-31-78, p. A4.

ENDNOTES: Part 5 (Chapters 25 – 28)

[398] MHF Interviews with EL, 6-20-01, and Anna Lockwood, 4-19-02, are the main sources for this boat trip.

[399] MHF Interview with EL, 9-13-01.

[400] MHF Interview with EL, 8-30-01.

[401] MHF Interviews with EL, 6-25-01, and Anna Lockwood, 7-23-01, are the primary sources for the WFFG story.

[402] WGOW News Radio noted Californian Gary Poole's hire at WFFG in the 1980s, per WGOW News Radio as accessed online on 9/4/01 at http://www.wgow.com/fm/bio_gary.htm

[403] MHF Interview with EL, 6-25-01.

[404] MHF Interviews with EL, 6-25-01, and Anna Lockwood, 7-23-01, are the primary sources for the Cuba incident.

[405] MHF Interview with Anna Lockwood, 7-23-01.

[406] MHF Interviews with EL, 6-25-01, and Anna Lockwood, 7-23-01, are the main sources on Marine Bank.

[407] MHF Interviews with EL and Anna Lockwood, 7-26-01.

[408] 1983 Marine Bank Annual Report.

[409] MHF Interview with EL, 6-25-01.

[410] MHF Interview with EL, 6-25-01.

[411] MHF Interview with Anna Lockwood, 7-23-01.

[412] MHF Interview with Freddy Van Gaever, 4-1-02.

[413] MHF Interview with Anna Lockwood, 9-13-01.

[414] MHF Interview with Franny Showerman, 10-10-01.

[415] MHF Interviews with EL, 7-26-01, and Anna Lockwood, 4-29-02 and 5-6-02, are the main sources on the Nairobi story.

[416] MHF Interview with Anna Lockwood, 7-23-01.

[417] MHF Interview with Harvey Hortman, 5-3-02.

[418] MHF Interview with EL, 9-13-01.

[419] MHF Interview with Steve Showerman, 4-8-02

[420] MHF Interview with Eric Lockwood, 3-16-02.

[421] MHF Interview with Freddy Van Gaever, 4-1-02.

[422] Partial lyrics from a traditional scouting campfire tune, author unknown.

[423] MHF Interview with Anna Lockwood, 8-9-01.

[424] MHF Interview with EL, 7-26-01.

[425] MHF Interviews with EL and Anna Lockwood, 6-20-01 and 4-19-02.

[426] MHF Interviews with EL, 6-20-01, and Anna Lockwood, 4-19-02 and 4-29-02, are the main sources for the East Coast Intercoastal adventure.

[427] MHF Interviews with EL and Anna Lockwood, 10-5-01.

[428] MHF Interviews with Anna Lockwood, 7-23-01; Bonnie Bender Hall, 9-20-01.

[429] MHF Interview with Bonnie Bender Hall, 9-20-01.

[430] MHF Interview with EL, 10-5-01.

[431] MHF Interview with Harvey Hoortman, 5-3-02.

[432] MHF Interview with Webb Gokey, 9-5-01.

[433] Susan McGarry, in "Lethal Yellowing of Palms," accessed 5-3-02 through the Univ. of Florida's Environment Horticulture Prog. at monroe.ifas.ufl.edu.

[434] MHF Interview with Webb Gokey, 9-5-01.

[435] MHF Interview with Webb Gokey, 9-5-01.

[436] MHF Interview with EL, 9-13-01.

[437] MHF Interview with Harvey Hortman, 5-3-02.

[438] MHF Interviews with EL, 7-26-01 and 9-13-01, are main sources for this incident.

[439] MHF Interview with Webb Gokey, 9-5-01.

[440] MHF Interview with EL, 9-13-01.

[441] MHF Interview with Harry Sawyer, 9-9-01.

[442] MHF Interview with Rick Roth, 9-6-01.

[443] MHF Interview with EL, 1-14-02.

[444] MHF Interview with EL, 6-22-01.

[445] MHF Interview with EL, 1-14-02.

ENDNOTES: Epilogue

[446] MHF Interview with Anna Lockwood, 8-19-02.

[447] MHF Interview with EL, 1-14-02.

[448] Gongwer News Service, 8-2-02.

[449] Alma *Morning Sun*, pages 1A and 6A, 8-4-02.

[450] *Lansing State Journal*, page 2B, 8-4-02.

[451] *The Detroit News and Free Press*, page 2B, 8-4-02.

[452] *Journal of the Senate*, No. 60, State of Michigan. Michigan Senate Resolution No. 247, adopted by the 91st Legislature on 9-17-02 and signed by Carol Morey Viventi, Secretary of the Senate. Offered by Senators DeGrow, Cherry, Young and Hoffman.

[453] "A Resolution adopted by The City Council of the City of Chicago, Illinois," presented by Alderman Edward M. Burke and signed by Mayor Richard M. Daley and City Clerk James J. Laski, 9-4-02.

[454] Copy furnished by Guy Vander Jagt, 9-12-02.

[455] Copy furnished by Richard Whitmer, 9-4-02.

[456] Copy furnished by Jerry Coomes, 8-14-02.

[457] Copy furnished by Bob Vander Laan, 8-14-02.

[458] Copy furnished by William G. McPherson, 8-14-02.

[459] Copy furnished by Eric A. Lockwood, 9-3-02.

[460] Excerpts from a poem entitled "The Forgetting," by Nancy Priff, quoted with permission of the author per email received 12-31-02. "The Forgetting" is published on pages 168-169 in *Love is Ageless: Stories About Alzheimer's Disease*, edited by Jessica Bryan (Lompico Creek Press: Felton, CA, 2002), as referenced by Franny Showerman in her eulogy.

[461] Copy furnished by Franny Showerman, 8-16-02 and email 9-17-02.

ACKNOWLEDGMENTS

Writing an official biography spanning a productive life of 82 years would have been unthinkable without the gracious and generous assistance of Emil and Anna Lockwood. Starting over a year prior to Emil's death in August 2002, he sat for long hours of detailed interviewing with each author, made crucial suggestions on other possible sources of information and insights, and threw open his cache of photos, newsclips, correspondence, and assorted memorabilia. Throughout the sometimes grueling hours of revisiting his past—with tape recorder running—Emil never lost his trademark sense of humor. Fittingly, he was able to read a polished draft of *MAN IN MOTION* before the final stages of his illness.

It is fair to say that this ambitious project would never have been realized without Anna's persevering presence in all aspects of the nearly two year long effort. In the process, she more than made good on her promise to Emil that she would help him in every way to fulfill his goal of chronicling his eventful life between the two covers of a book. Anna has helped carry out that dream with determination and equanimity since Emil's unexpected demise. For all that she has done to help us bring forth this book, we sincerely thank her.

Gratitude is due also to the Lockwood family—most particularly Eric Lockwood, Lori (Lockwood) Doles, and Fran Showerman—for their generous provision of essential photos, family background, their own memories, newsclips in certain instances, and memorabilia. They were also helpful in fact and name checking—indispensable to any writers.

To our main interviewees, apart from family members, who provided first hand insights and invaluable facts, we offer our special thanks as well. We especially single out: Emil's long-time business partner and dear friend, Jerry Coomes; Governor John Engler; Bill Ballenger, Editor, *Inside Michigan Politics*; as well as longtime friends and former associates Guy Vander Jagt, Bob Vander Laan, Rick Cole, Dick Whitmer, Freddy Van Gaever, and Bill "Mac" McPherson. Many thanks also to the "Duck Key Contingent": Sonny and Toni Appell, Webb Gokey, Ed and Bonnie Hall, Harvey Hortman, Harry Sawyer, and Sheriff Rick Roth.

Newspapers and news services with Capitol correspondents during the period covered by this book, along with Emil Lockwood's Senatorial district newspapers, contributed heavily to the sections on Emil's always eventful life in and around the State Capitol. Particular appreciation must be given to the Lansing *State Journal*, *Detroit Free Press*, *Detroit News*, Booth Newspapers, *St. Louis Leader-Press*, *Daily Record-Leader*, Associated Press, United Press International, Panax Corporation, and *Owosso Argus Press*. Their reporters' blow-by-blow accounts helped to cast a "You Are There" atmosphere that would be impossible to achieve without their insiders' expertise.

Thanks also to the staffs of the excellent State of Michigan Library, and the East Lansing Public Library for their unfailing cheerfulness in the face of incessant requests. Publisher Deborah Greenspan and the entire staff of Llumina Press deserve thanks for their professional assistance in matters of format, design, production, and marketing. Special thanks is also accorded to poet Nancy Priff for her permission to print excerpts from her poem "The Forgetting," in the Epilogue of this book, and to photographer Mike Quillinan for his fine work on many of the contemporary photos included. We also acknowledge the following institutions which granted permission to use their materials in this biography: the Bentley Historical Library of the University of Michigan, and the U. S. National Archives through the able services of Double Delta Industries, Inc.

The experience of researching and writing this book has been gratifying to both authors. In the process of winnowing a true representation of this engaging and multi-talented "man of action" from countless newspaper articles, photographs, pages of transcribed interviews, and family albums, we found ourselves in growing respect for the subject of our biography. Emil Lockwood's exemplary legacy lives on in the memories of the many family members, friends, and former associates whose lives he touched. To those who treasure those memories—and to those who will learn of Emil for the first time through reading this book—we invite you to share with us our portrait of a truly extraordinary man.

The Authors

ABOUT THE AUTHORS

Stan Fedewa's political background includes service as chief legislative director and lobbyist for the governor of Michigan, and top executive for two Speakers of the House of Representatives. He was vice president of a Los Angeles public relations and marketing firm, and holds degrees from Michigan State University and the University of Notre Dame.

Marilyn Fedewa served as vice president of Olivet College, overseeing public information, fundraising and alumni relations, and directed several national fundraising efforts and donor events for Michigan State University. She is writing a major work centered on a 17th century mystic, and holds a degree from Nazareth College in Rochester, New York.

Visit the authors at www.cambridgeconnections.net

Printed in the United States
16452LVS00005B/58-306